GOVERNMENT BY
COMMITTEE

GOVERNMENT BY COMMITTEE

AN ESSAY ON
THE BRITISH CONSTITUTION

BY

K. C. WHEARE, F.B.A.

GREENWOOD PRESS, PUBLISHERS
WESTPORT, CONNECTICUT

Library of Congress Cataloging in Publication Data

Wheare, Kenneth Clinton, Sir, 1907–
  Government by committee.

  Reprint of the ed. published by Clarendon Press,
Oxford.
  Includes index.
  1. Great Britain--Politics and government.
I. Title.
[JN318.W47 1979]   320.9'41   78-31211
ISBN 0-313-20955-3

Published in 1955, Oxford, at The Clarendon Press.

This reprint has been authorized by the Oxford University
Press.

Reprinted in 1979 by Greenwood Press, Inc.
51 Riverside Avenue, Westport, CT 06880

Printed in the United States of America

10 9 8 7 6 5 4 3 2 1

PREFACE

IN writing this book I am attempting to fly before I can walk.
I can explain and, I hope, justify the attempt. The student
of committees has to make a choice. Either he can try to
hack his way through the jungle on foot or he can try to get a
bird's eye view of the terrain from the air. If he chooses the first
alternative, the most he can hope for is to clear a portion of his
territory; if he chooses the second, the most he can hope for is
to produce a rough sketch-map of the whole area. Each course
has its advantages and its defects. The explorer on foot will know
a part, but he will not understand its relation to the whole; the
explorer from the air will see the whole but he is certain to miss
or to misread or to misunderstand some at least of the parts.
I have chosen to attempt a reconnaissance from the air, in spite
of its dangers, for it seems to me that when you are exploring a
jungle an aerial map is the first essential. I hope that others will
persevere with the exploration on foot and that, while they correct and amplify my map, they may testify that it had some
rough working value for them.

I have had a great deal of help in writing the book from my
friends, and I express my gratitude to them. The manuscript
was read in its entirety by Dr. A. L. Poole, President of St. John's
College, Oxford, and by Mr. D. N. Chester, Warden of Nuffield
College, Oxford. Parts of it were read by Mr. H. A. Clegg,
Fellow of Nuffield College, and by Mr. Graham Higgins. I must
acknowledge my debt, too, to the many colleagues with whom
I have sat upon committees and from whom I have learnt con-
tinuously. In particular may I refer to my fellow members of
the Oxford City Council with whom I have been associated
since 1940. I cannot refrain from recording also my debt
to two officials among many, Sir Douglas Veale, Registrar
of the University of Oxford, and Mr. Harry Plowman,
Town Clerk of Oxford, from whom I believe I have learnt
most, by precept and example, about government by committee.

My wife has not only read the manuscript of the book (I have made the indexes myself) but has endured with cheerfulness the experience of being married to an inveterate committee man.

K. C. W.

All Souls College, Oxford
St. Scholastica's Day, 1955

CONTENTS

CHAPTER I

The Scope and Method of the Essay

I

IN this book I try to examine quite a small part of what is really a large and important subject, namely, the conduct of business through groups of people acting collectively as distinct from its conduct by single individuals. Committees are probably the best known and they are certainly the most numerous examples of this way of behaving. They are to be found wherever people in Britain are working together for some common object—in trade unions, in churches, in musical and literary societies, in sports clubs, in business and professional organizations, in employers' associations, in schools and universities. They are in fact an important part of what is referred to with reasonable pride as 'the British way of life'. It is not surprising therefore to discover that they are no less prominent and significant in the working of modern British government. Indeed, in a moment of exasperation during the war, Mr. Churchill exclaimed: 'We are overrun by them, like the Australians were by the rabbits.'[1] Of the many phrases by which British government may be described shortly and with illumination, such as 'cabinet government' or 'parliamentary government' or 'party government' or 'constitutional monarchy', it seems justifiable to say that by no means the least accurate and significant is 'government by committee'.

From the vast field of study which collective group action provides not only for the political scientist but also for the economist, the sociologist, the social psychologist, even the anthropologist, I have selected for examination a few examples of certain types of committee. I have confined myself mainly to committees forming part of the machinery of government or closely attached to it, and even within this field I deal with a selection only of the many examples of the types of committee

[1] *The Second World War*, ii. 606.

involved. I have attempted to bring some order into my exposition by arranging committees into types, and the principle upon which the arrangement has been made is that of the function or process which the committee carries out rather than of the institution of which it forms a part or with which it is connected. Thus I speak of committees to advise, committees to inquire, committees to negotiate, committees to legislate, committees to administer, and committees to scrutinize and control. As examples of committees to advise I choose the elaborate and complicated structure of bodies operating under a variety of names—panels, councils, working parties, as well as committees —set up to advise the central government in this country. Of committees to inquire I consider again principally bodies acting on behalf of the central government—royal commissions, select committees of the House of Commons, departmental and interdepartmental committees. My examples of committees to negotiate are chosen principally from the bodies engaged in settling questions of hours of labour, rates of wages, and conditions of labour in central or local government service. Committees to legislate are illustrated by the standing committees of the House of Commons; committees to administer, by the committees used in their thousands by the local authorities of the country; and committees to scrutinize and control by three select committees of the House of Commons—of Public Accounts, on Estimates, and on Statutory Instruments. And in studying these examples of the six types of committee I try to make some comparison between them of their effectiveness and shortcomings.

There are certain obvious deficiencies and dangers in this way of proceeding. In the first place, to discuss committees in terms of their function lays one open to the risk of forgetting that how committees perform their function is governed a great deal by the nature of the institution of which they form a part. The legislative function of the standing committees of the House of Commons is performed in a different way from that of such committees in the American Congress or the French National Assembly, and the explanation of why these committees work as they do comes back quite soon to an explanation of the nature and status of the assemblies of which they are committees. The administrative function of committees in local government in Britain is not capable of being understood apart from the context of the nature and status of local authorities in the constitution of the country. The lesson we must learn from this is that in judging the work of committees, in explaining and discussing them in terms of their function, we must always take into account the institutional system to which they belong. If this is remembered, the method of exposition by function may escape some of the pitfalls to which it is admittedly prone.

Other difficulties suggest themselves when it is announced that comparisons are going to be attempted between the working of these six types of committee. Surely, it may be objected, if we are to have comparisons, we should compare like with like. Should not the standing committees of the House of Commons be compared with other legislative committees, such as those in the United States or France or Sweden? And if there is to be a comparison of committees to administer, ought it not to be made (if it must be confined to Britain) between committees in local government and, say, regional hospital boards or hospital executive committees or catchment boards or county agricultural executive committees or marketing boards or the area boards of such nationalized industries as gas and electricity? And should not some account be taken of committees to administer in central government, such as cabinet committees or committees of officials in departments or between departments—perhaps the most influential administrative committees in the country? And why not compare the committees to negotiate conditions of labour in the government service with those which operate in great numbers and with considerable success among employers and employees outside the government service? Are not these the lines upon which true and fruitful comparisons can be made?

There is no doubt that comparisons on these lines would be extremely valuable. It should not be assumed that they are free from difficulty and danger. Great care would have to be taken that the status and nature of each class of committee was fully appreciated so that true comparisons were made. The dangers, already referred to, that arise when committees are discussed according to function and not as part of the institutions to which they belong would still be present in a comparison of this kind. None the less such comparisons could and should be made. Indeed, it is my hope that one result of the somewhat restricted study which I have undertaken in this book may be that others will be encouraged to study the working of committees comparatively on the lines described above. The reasons why I have myself proceeded upon different lines may now be explained.

My first reason may be expressed in the words which Dr. Johnson addressed to a lady who inquired how he had come to make a certain mistake: 'Ignorance, madam, pure ignorance.' I have confined myself to a study of those committees about whose working I could obtain some knowledge either from printed sources or from personal experience. So far as committees of the House of Commons are concerned, we have fairly full accounts of their proceedings, and although it is not possible to attend the meetings of select committees, standing committees are open to the public and I have been able to watch them at work. To the published information which we have in large quantity of the work of committees to inquire, to advise, and to negotiate, I have been able to add some small personal experience. Very little has been written in any detail about the working of committees to administer in local government, and here I have relied very largely upon my own personal experience and discussions with others who have also had personal experience. Of most of the committees which I have excluded from my study it can be said that information about them is difficult to obtain because, like the committees in the nationalized industries or in the health service, they have not been in operation for long enough, or because, like cabinet committees or official committees, those who know most about their working are forbidden by the Official Secrets Act or by considerations of discretion from revealing what they know; or because, like marketing boards or county agricultural executive committees, although they have been working for a considerable time, nobody has yet made available to the outside student any detailed account of their working. Although there is this lack of knowledge about a great part of the field of committee work in Britain, it must be emphasized that the committees of which we do know a good deal are important and manifold. It seemed worth while, therefore, to make a study of this familiar though restricted field if only to prepare the way and to devise some methods for a wider investigation into the uncharted territory.

It is not enough, however, to explain why I have limited my study to the committees mentioned above; it is necessary also to explain how, within such limitations, some valid and useful comparisions can be made between the working of six different types of committee. Perhaps it is well to assert at the outset that there is more than one way of making a comparison. I have tried a method of comparison which has its obvious dangers but which I hope will have some value. Instead of putting examples of the same type of committee side by side and comparing their working, I choose instead to observe the working within different types of committee of certain 'characters' who find a place in all these types. In this way I believe we have certain fixed points of comparison which not only overcome the alleged incomparability of different types of committee, but also reveal and illuminate the working of these different types. I have chosen seven characters whose behaviour is to be followed—the chairman, the secretary, the official, the expert, the layman, the party man, and the interested party. Something will be said about each of these characters in the following chapter. For the present it is enough to say that if we compare the relative status and importance of each of these characters in the different types of committee we are able to make a judgement of the way in which these committees perform their function. While the comparison is primarily not a comparison of committees but of characters in committees, it is the sort of comparison which will provide criteria for judging whether each of the different types of committee in British government does its work well.

The use of this method of comparison justifies in my view the undertaking of a study of committees which is restricted in the ways in which this study is restricted. It becomes possible to compare like with like to as great a degree as that is usually possible in the study of political institutions.

2

It is important to have some idea of what is meant by a committee, if only because there are some bodies called committees which are not really such, and there are many committees called by other names. The essence of a committee is, surely, that it is a body to which some task has been referred or committed by some other person or body. It may be asked or required or permitted to carry out this task. But that is not all. The notion of a committee carries with it the idea of a body being in some manner or degree responsible or subordinate or answerable in the last resort to the body or person who set it up or committed a power or duty to it. It is difficult to state this position precisely. Suffice it to say that if a body or a person commits a power or duty completely to another body, and relinquishes this power entirely, surrendering full and final authority to this body, then this latter body is not a committee. There is inherent in the notion of a committee some idea of a derived or secondary or dependent status, in form at least; it lacks original jurisdiction. It acts on behalf of or with responsibility to another body. Any body which has a task committed to it in this way may be considered a committee, whether it calls itself a council, a commission or royal commission, a conference, a board, a bureau, a panel, or a working party. They are all committees and may be studied as such.

Too much must not be made of this distinction of status. Many committees act in practice in complete independence of the bodies which set them up and to which they are formally subordinate. Some business could not be transacted at all unless committees exercised exclusive jurisdiction. Their working in such circumstances is directly comparable with that of other groups conducting business collectively whose formal status is higher than theirs. At the same time too little must not be made of the question of status, for it often happens that the proper degree of responsibility or autonomy which a committee should enjoy in relation to its parent body is a question of the greatest importance in the working of a system of committees. Where committees differ from some other bodies engaged in the collective conduct of business is that the question of status *can* arise as a practical problem; it is potentially almost always a matter for argument.

But although our idea of a committee is governed partly by considerations of status—the notion of a body to which some other body has committed a task and to which it is in some sense subordinate—it is governed also by considerations of size. We have some ideas, even if only vague ideas, that if a body is smaller than a certain number or larger than a certain number

it can hardly be called a committee. Thus although people speak
sometimes of a committee of one, and although indeed the word
'committee' has had the connotation of one person to whom
functions were committed,[1] it carries with it today the notion of
at least two people acting together. Those who say that they
prefer a committee of one are usually taken to be expressing in
paradoxical form their disbelief in committees. In practice the
whole idea of a committee is that it should be a group and it is
seldom conceived of as less than three persons—the lowest number which permits of an exchange of views, of the election of a
chairman by majority decision, and of the conduct of business
without recourse to the exercise of a casting vote by the chairman. Although a committee of two permits of an exchange of
views, it contains the possibility of deadlock in the election of a
chairman, and, if that hurdle is surmounted, it permits all questions to be carried by the chairman's casting vote.

If a committee of one is thought of as a contradiction in terms,
so also is a committee of a thousand and one. Though, formally
speaking, a task may as easily be committed to a thousand and
one people as to one, and although those people may be entitled
to be called a committee, yet in practice we expect a committee
to be smaller than that. We cannot be precise about size, and
our ideas on size will certainly be affected by the function that
the committee is to perform, but we have certain upper limits
in our minds beyond which a body may be formally a committee but in practice is a public meeting. Yet it is well known that
one of the most famous committees in the world, the Committee of the Whole House of Commons, contains over 600
members. How are we to explain this anomaly?

The explanation is to be found in considerations of procedure,
which are worth describing because they cover many examples
of which the Committee of the Whole House of Commons is only
one. A first reason for a numerous assembly referring a matter to
a committee consisting of all its members is to ensure that there
will be a sufficient attendance at the deliberations. If it is feared
that many members will not attend or if it is known that some
can come at one time and others at another, it is a wise device
to make everybody members of the committee and thus have a

---

[1] It is still so used to describe an individual to whom the person or estate of a
lunatic is committed.

good chance that a sufficient number will be present. We are told that this was one of the reasons why bills came to be committed, in the seventeenth century, to committees of the whole House of Commons.[1] It will be apparent that committees of the whole House in these circumstances are really more like committees than their name suggests, for they would consist in practice of a smaller number of people than the whole House.

A second reason for referring matters to a committee of the whole is that in the consideration of some business by a numerous assembly some members are interested and competent in some matters and some in others. All desire the right to be able to intervene when their interest is aroused, though it is known that it will be seldom that the attendance is very large. In such cases it is wise to refer a matter to the committee of the whole, for it combines equality of opportunity for all the members with a virtual certainty of a smaller and more effective body considering the matter in practice. This is one justification—though not an explanation of the origin—of the practice of the House of Commons of dealing with its financial business in committees consisting of all the members of the House under the names of Committee of Supply, of Ways and Means, and of the Whole House, according to the stage which the business has reached.

When we come to consider the historical origins of this practice we reach a third reason for referring matters to a committee of the whole, and that is the advantage of a different procedure. There are stages in the discussion of a matter when, if it is referred to a committee, an advantageous change of procedure can be effected. Thus in the earlier history of the House of Commons the members wished, when they came to discuss finance and to decide how much money they should vote to the king, to keep their deliberations secret from the king. The Speaker of the House in those days was regarded by the House as the king's man and they feared that, if they deliberated in his presence, he would repeat what they said to the king. So they decided to discuss financial business in committee, which meant that the Speaker left the chair and a chairman took his place. Although nowadays the Speaker is no longer suspect, the procedure goes

[1] Ilbert and Carr, *Parliament*, p. 54.

on as before, with advantages quite unintended by those who devised it.

There are two procedural advantages which large bodies may obtain by going into committee of the whole. The first is privacy. Some public bodies—such as town and county councils, for example—are required to meet in public. If they wish to discuss something privately they may do so by referring the matter to themselves as a committee, and in this capacity they are not required to meet in public. They are not in practice a committee at all; their numbers are unchanged, but they can exclude the Press. A second advantage which may be gained by going into committee is that procedure is often more flexible and informal. Members are often permitted in committee to speak more than once, and if the meeting is also private, a freer discussion may occur. For both these reasons—privacy and freer discussion—many public bodies with large membership refer matters to themselves and thus formally constitute themselves as committees. But they are often committees in no more than name.

It would seem therefore that when a large body calls itself a committee it does so for certain procedural reasons which assist it to perform its work in a particular way, but that these ways of proceeding are not really what we mean by working through committees. There is fairly general agreement that committees are relatively small groups of people, and the exceptions found in the procedure of the House of Commons and of town and county councils are exceptions which prove the rule.

It may be worth while to add that, although committees are often composed of a selection from the members of a larger body, they need not be so composed. It is true that committees of the House of Commons do in fact consist only of members of that House; the same is true usually, but not always, of committees set up by town and county councils. But committees or commissions may be appointed by ministers, or, as in the case of royal commissions, by the sovereign on the advice of ministers, and in these cases their members may be chosen from a variety of places and their claim to the title of committee comes from the fact that a task has been committed to them by the minister. He appointed them; they report to or are responsible to him.

3

If we are to judge whether a committee is doing its work well, we must have in our minds certain criteria of success, which we must attempt to formulate in advance, however vaguely. In the first place it can be said that it is the job of a committee to come to a conclusion, to decide something. Its decision may be a finding of fact or a recommendation to its parent body or an administrative order or an appointment or a proposal to defer consideration. Whatever its function, however, it is its job to take a decision upon the matters before it. If it fails to do that, then it is not doing its work. It may seem absurd to assert so self-evident a proposition, but it has to be asserted because committees have been known to fail to perform this task.

But it is not enough to say that committees must come to a decision. They ought also to come to a good decision. If they are to do this certain conditions must be fulfilled. In the first place they ought not to be asked to decide a matter which is not proper for a committee's decision. In the second place, and the two points are connected, they must be so composed that they are fit to decide the matters referred to them. Stated in the abstract in this way, these propositions may command wide assent. In the pages that follow, however, we shall find many occasions when we have to ask of certain committees whether the task given to them was a proper task to give to a committee and whether, even if it was, the committee was properly composed to give a wise decision upon it.

Finally, we may ask of a committee not only: 'Is it doing its job and is it doing it well?' but also 'Is *it* doing the job?' The whole idea of using committees is that a group of people shall undertake a task collectively. If we find that in fact the committee is a mere screen behind which somebody else is performing its function, we must conclude that the committee is not doing its job. It may be that it should never have been asked to do it, or it may be that it could do it and do it well, if it were allowed to try. In all study of the working of committees an important question is whether the committee itself is actually operating or whether it is merely a formal façade for the action of others. This question will lead us often into the heart of the discussion of when and where committees may be wisely used or badly used. Though the answers to these questions will usually be matters of opinion upon which disagreement is possible, it cannot be doubted that these are the sort of questions to which an answer must be attempted if we are to judge the value of committee work.[1]

[1] Some stimulating suggestions about the study of committees are put forward by Professor W. J. M. Mackenzie in an article 'Committees in Administration', *Public Administration*, vol. xxxi, Autumn, 1953.

CHAPTER II

Seven Characters in Committee Work

I

BEFORE we look at the way in which the different types of committee do their work, it is important to have some ideas of what the seven characters in committee work are like. It should be explained at the outset that a member of a committee may well combine in himself more than one of these characters; they are by no means mutually exclusive. A chairman may well be an official and an expert; a layman may be also a party man and an interested party. It is necessary none the less to distinguish the capacities in which members of committees may be acting, if we are to understand clearly the influences at work in committees. It should be emphasized also that these characters, or people acting in one or more of these capacities, may have influence upon or take part in committee work without actually being members of the committees. Their influence must be studied whether it is exercised in or upon committees.

As we are studying committees which form part of the machinery of government in Britain, it is convenient to say a word first about the official. It is rare to find a committee in which the official is not concerned. He may be a member of a committee; he may be its secretary; he may be the servant through whom its decisions are executed; he may be a responsible officer of a department whose work a committee is to scrutinize and control; he may be the adviser of a minister in charge of a bill which a committee to legislate is considering; he may be a witness before a committee to inquire; he may be the means through which a department is seeking the assistance of a committee to advise. In any of these capacities we recognize the official who is a civil servant in central or local government. But officials are found outside the government service and these non-governmental officials take part also in committee work, whether as members or witnesses or chairmen or the like. Their status and responsibilities differ in some obvious ways from those of government officials, but they have also certain common characteristics which must be kept in mind. It is well to say a little about them at this point.

An official is, as a rule, an administrator, an organizer, a manager. He is engaged in running something. He is usually doing this as part of an organization, for, as his name implies, he is part of an 'office'; he is an office man. One characteristic of an office is hierarchy. It is an organization of people on the principle of superiors and subordinates, each with his allotted sphere of work, each reporting above and overseeing below. It involves the notion of a disciplined organization, with loyalties inside itself, between chiefs and subordinates and within one division or section as against another, and to the whole office as against the outside world. The official has a place in this hierarchy. He is responsible to his superiors and for his subordinates. He has his allotted area of responsibility and his loyalty to the office. He has prospects of promotion.

From this hierarchical nature of the office a second characteristic tends to show itself. The work of offices comes to be organized into certain prescribed procedures or modes of operation or routines. This is unavoidable if the proper duties are to be performed at each level, if those above are to be enabled to take decisions upon matters when they are ready for decision and not before, and if some relationship is to be kept between decisions. This predilection for working through prescribed procedures is a characteristic of any office where more than two or three people work. It often irritates those who have to do business with offices and more particularly with government offices. It is a feature of office work which can be carried to excess, so that the forms of work are placed before the work itself. An excessive devotion to prescribed forms and procedures is described as 'red tape' and it is an occupational disease to which officials are always liable.

A third characteristic of the office is that we think of officials as appointed and not as elected. This characteristic also is linked with the notion of hierarchy, for the principle of election would work against hierarchy. The whole idea of hierarchy depends upon superiors having the powers to appoint and promote their subordinates. If people held office by virtue of being chosen by some outside body to whom they were responsible and to whom they looked for reappointment, the relationship between people in an office would be changed fundamentally from what we understand by an office. When, as in this country and in others where representative or popular government operates, the heads of offices or departments are elected or are chosen from elected persons, they are always regarded as distinct from officials and their function is commonly supposed to be the control of the officials.

If officials are appointed and not elected, it is natural that their tenure should be conceived of as more secure than that of elected persons. A part of the idea of the official in Britain is that his tenure is determined by his capacity and industry and not by his party affiliations. This principle, already taken for granted in business and industry, is accepted in government service also. The official, whether civil servant or not, is a 'career man'. Being a career man and being engaged full-time upon his work, he is supposed also to have some skill and knowledge in his subject. He is indeed a professional in both senses of that word—he is in the work as a career, and he is also not an amateur.

Finally, the official has, as a rule, a characteristic which he shares with committees—they are both sedentary institutions. Committees sit to carry out their work; there is no clearer sign that a committee is out of order than that some of its members are standing up or wandering about. So also with the official. We picture him, rightly, as at work in his office chair. He works at his desk; he manages and administers from his bureau. Perhaps from their sharing this common characteristic of being sedentary workers, committees and officials find it natural to work together.

It is obvious that not all officials possess all these characteristics or exhibit them all to the same degree. But it may be said that what is likely to strike non-officials on a committee in their dealings with officials are characteristics of this kind—their sense of hierachy, of proper procedures and modes of doing business, their being appointed and not elected, their being permanent and not transient, their being professionals and not amateurs.

2

When Walter Bagehot came to consider the official in his *English Constitution* he made this observation. 'The truth is', he wrote, 'that a skilled bureaucracy is, though it boasts of an appearance of science, quite inconsistent with the true principles of the art of business. . . . One of the most sure principles is that success depends on a due mixture of special and non-special minds—of minds which attend to the means and of minds which attend to the end.'[1] For this man of non-special mind Jeremy Bentham had a name. He called him 'the lay-gent'.[2] The word 'gent' is nowadays become facetious and in the plural peculiarly specialized, but we may occasionally use Bentham's term, with its quaint charm, to describe what is normally called in modern times the layman. Good administration, in Bagehot's opinion, was the product of co-operation between laymen and experts. He considered officials to be experts in this context and he claimed therefore that if we were to get the best out of officials, we must associate laymen with our officials.

The terms 'layman' and 'expert' need some explanation at the outset. They are essentially relative terms. They are relative to a subject or a field or part of a field of knowledge and they are relative to persons. Most people are expert in a few things; everyone is a layman in regard to most things. The mere notion of an expert, implying a specialized knowledge or skill in a limited field, carries with it the implication of the non-special mind in relation to other fields. The status of layman or expert will be accorded to an individual in relation to a given subject in a given situation. Thus a committee of experts may appear, from one point of view, to be a committee of laymen, for though each member is an expert in his own field, he may be a layman in regard to the field of the men sitting next to him. It is proper to ask then: Who are the experts and where are they to be found? And we shall be interested particularly in those experts who find a place on or around committees in British government.

It is commonly assumed, as Bagehot evidently assumed, that the official is an expert. The assumption arises from the fact that the relation we think of most, in considering the role of

---

[1] p. 174 (World's Classics Ed.).
[2] *On Packing Juries* (1821). See *Collected Works of Bentham*, v. 159.

the official in committee work, is that between the ordinary elected person—the member of the House of Commons or of the local council—and the official. It is true that, as a rule, the elected person in this relation is usually a layman and that the official, considered in this relation, is not a layman. But must it follow that, if he is not a layman, he is necessarily an expert? An analogy from the terminology of the medical profession may help us here. Doctors are not all experts. Most of them are general practitioners, some only are specialists. Now it is true that, in relation to all doctors, be they general practitioners or specialists, most people are laymen; but we do not conclude from this that all doctors are experts.

When we look at the way in which offices are organized, both in the government and outside it, we find that, as a general rule, officials at the top or head of the office are not experts; they are usually general practitioners. This is in most cases a consequence of necessity, for those at the top must deal with a wider range of questions than those lower down and they are bound to be less expert. In British government and in a good part of British commercial and industrial organizations, it is indeed positively asserted that the officials at the top should be general practitioners and not experts. It is not thought odd or unusual to move the permanent head of the Ministry of Supply to be head of the Colonial Office or of the Ministry of Health. A high official of the Treasury is regarded as fit to be head of any department of government. It is general capacity—not specialized knowledge —which is encouraged by the recruitment and promotion policies of the British civil service. In local government, too, a town clerk, a chief education officer, or a treasurer are general practitioners. It is with officials at this sort of level that committees are usually associated and it will be common for them to find that they are dealing not with experts but with general practitioners.

If experts are rarely at the top of offices, they are rarely also at the bottom. Citizens who have been brought into contact with officials in the years since 1939, when so much of the economic life of the country has been subject to control by officials, have formed the firm opinion at certain times that they know a great deal more about these things than do the officials that deal with them. Even if officials higher up may have some technical knowledge of the subject under control, those lower down, dealing with the public at the office counter, are almost certain not to be expert. They are most likely to be laymen in relation to those with whom they have to deal. These subordinate officials usually concern committees only in so far as their work is carried out under the administration or the scrutiny and control of a committee, but it is none the less important to notice that they can usually lay no claim to the title of expert.

Which officials, then, are the experts? They fall into a number of groups. First of all there are those who may be called expert because they have committed to their charge a part of a department's work. Thus in a department like the Colonial Office there are officials who are experts in some part of the world, such as the West Indies, West Africa, the Pacific, or South-East Asia. A similar form of specialization is possible in the Foreign Office and the Commonwealth Relations Office also. Or in departments like the Ministry of Education or the Home Office or the Ministry of Food, officials may specialize in technical education or visual aids, aliens or police, licensing or fish or potatoes or livestock. The area of a department's activities is broken up on some principle of division, varying often with the nature of its work, and officials become experts through being concerned with one of these parts, branches, sections, or divisions.

But there is another group of experts which is of a rather different kind. They are expert in some skill or technique or branch of knowledge which may have a reference to more than one section of the department's work and may be needed anywhere. The legal adviser is the best example of this kind of expert. Most of the experts of this kind are advisers. The need for a legal adviser was early recognized, but with the increasing intervention of departments into many aspects of social life other expert advisers have been added. Economists, agricultural scientists, psychologists, anthropologists, medical men have all been enlisted to advise the official in his task of regulation and control. Some departments, like the Ministry of Agriculture, will have a lot of these specialists, particularly on the scientific side. The Colonial Office makes use of a whole range of experts including sociologists and anthropologists and every type of agricultural scientist.

The work of some departments requires that the scientific and technical experts should be more than advisers to officials and should actually undertake administration themselves. The service departments, for example, and the Ministry of Supply staff certain of their branches with experts in armaments, surveying, building and construction work, and engineering, to name only a few. Most of these administrators would be unable to perform their tasks unless they had a specialized knowledge of the fields with which they deal.

In the service departments and in certain other departments there are groups of officials engaged in inspectorial and supervisory work who have specialized scientific or technical qualifications. They hold positions at a variety of levels in a department's work, ranging from such officials as the senior chief inspector and the inspectors under him in the Ministry of Education, the factory inspectors and the inspectors of constabulary of the Home Office, or the veterinary inspectors of the Ministry of Agriculture down to the clerks of works, supervisors, and foremen on certain types of work done in and for government departments.

The location of the expert has been discussed so far almost entirely in terms of the central government department. Most of what has been said there is true also of the organization of local government departments. The chief officials tend to be general practitioners; the experts are found somewhat lower down. In some departments, like that of planning, say, most of the staff are experts with architectural or some other professional qualification; in the treasurer's department, similarly, most officials will specialize in some branch of the corporation's finance. In the organization of an education department there will be found specialists in areas of the department's work, such as primary schools or secondary schools, and also specialists of the other type—psychologists, advisers on music or physical education, school medical officers, and the like, whose expert knowledge is available throughout the whole range of the department's activities.

Most of the experts of whom we have been speaking so far are administrative officials. But it would be misleading to suggest that the experts in the civil service are always administrators. On the contrary many thousands of those employed in the civil service who could be classed as experts are not engaged in regulatory work at all. They may be engaged upon research or production in governmental employment under such departments as the Ministry of Supply, the Admiralty, the Air Ministry, the War Office, the Agricultural Research Council, or the Department of Scientific and Industrial Research. It is true that some of these scientific and technical officials have organizing work to do in connexion with research and production, but the great majority of them are not officials in the strict sense. They are in the civil service because the state has taken over direct responsibility for certain types of research and for the production of certain goods. The Atomic Energy Research Establishment at Harwell is a good example of this kind of organization. It is predominantly an organization of experts, some of whom are responsible for running it, but most of whom do not perform the administrative function. It is these scientific employees of the state who make up the greater part of the scientific civil service.[1] They far outnumber now the specialized inspectorial staffs or professionally qualified regulatory staffs which for a long time constituted the bulk of the technical experts in government service.

From the point of view of committee work it is apparent that these scientific experts who are not administrators are likely to be called upon for their services and should not therefore be disregarded in our analysis. They present special problems also, for in their contacts with laymen and with officials, more particularly with the general practitioners among officials, they find difficulty in presenting their views in sufficiently non-technical language or in the appropriate form to be effective. One of the problems in committee work is to make the best use of the expert and in particular of those experts in the scientific civil service.

But let us remember in conclusion that not all experts are in the civil service. Experts outside government service are to be found, for example, on the various committees to advise that are associated with British government. Scientists, economists, statisticians, philosophers and historians, antiquarians, educationists, lawyers, doctors, architects, chemists, sit along with experts in, say, the retail trade, in the affairs of some trade union, or in the problems of some industry or branch of agriculture. These latter types of expert belong also to the category of 'the interested party' of which more is to be said later in this chapter.

[1] See Cmd. 6679 of 1945, *The Scientific Civil Service*.

But it is worth while at this stage to notice that they have an expert status, though of a distinctive kind.

It will be found, too, that experts outside the government service, like experts within it, are sometimes officials, but sometimes not. In many cases they may advise officials both within and outside the government service. They illustrate once more the principle that to equate official and expert is misleading, and if the true function and importance of each is to be rightly understood in committee work the distinction must be kept clear. The principal purpose of the discussion of the expert which I have undertaken in these pages has been to emphasize this distinction.

3

What Lord Salisbury, as Secretary of State for India, wrote to Lord Lytton, the Viceroy, on 15 June 1877, still produces an echo of approval in the hearts of the British people: 'No lesson', he said, 'seems to be so deeply inculcated by the experience of life as that you never should trust experts. If you believe the doctors, nothing is wholesome; if you believe the theologians, nothing is innocent; if you believe the soldiers, nothing is safe. They all require to have their strong wine diluted by a very large admixture of insipid common sense.'[1] It is the function of Bentham's 'lay-gent' to dilute the experts' strong wine. And it was Bagehot's view, as we said earlier in this chapter,[2] that success in administration 'depends on a due mixture of special and non-special minds'. It will be our concern when we study the layman in committees to consider how far Bagehot's judgement is still true that the co-operation of laymen with experts is essential to successful administration.

The layman who sits upon committees concerned with British government is often an elected person, and the committees of the House of Commons and of local authorities contain laymen of this kind. But they may be appointed, like justices of the peace or certain lay members of committees to inquire or to advise; they may be co-opted, as certain members of local government committees are, or they may, like the laymen in the House of Lords, be partly elected (like the Scottish representative peers),

[1] Lady Gwendolen Cecil, *Life of Lord Salisbury*, ii. 153.
[2] See p. 15 above.

partly appointed (as are peers when first created), and partly hereditary. Again, the layman on committees is usually unpaid (though his out-of-pocket expenses may be met) but sometimes he is paid, as are, for example, members of the House of Commons. The layman usually, too, is a part-time worker. Though he may, like some members of Parliament or town councillors, spend all his time at committee work, he will be obliged to cover so wide a field that he will be able to devote only part of his time to any one. This is usually why he is or remains a layman.

It is worth while to have some ideas about what the qualities of a good layman in committee work may be. This is a subject about which something will be said later on when we consider the different types of committee work, for particular qualities will be needed of the layman in particular types of work. But there are some general observations which can be advanced at this stage which will be of value for our later study.

A first mark of the good layman is suggested by a use of the word 'layman' which is commonly encountered, namely, the contrast of 'layman' and 'clergyman'. Now this use goes back, of course, to the original distinction of the learned and unlearned in the days when the clergy were the educated people and the rest of the population were not. But nowadays the distinction between 'laity' and 'clergy' is not regarded as a distinction between the unlearned and the learned or even between the unholy and the holy. It is a distinction between those not in orders and those in orders. A layman might well be as versed in theology as a clergyman, and he might be as interested in religion or as religious as a clergyman. And, indeed, one mark of the good layman in church circles is that he is interested and concerned with church and religious matters. It is this characteristic which may first be mentioned as a mark of the good layman in committee work. A good layman on a committee is one who is, first of all, interested and concerned with the work of the committee. In this respect he must resemble the good layman in the church.

A second mark of the good layman has links with a second common use of 'layman'. This is not the ecclesiastical use of the term but the legal use. Just as there is a distinction between layman and clergyman, there is a distinction between laymen and lawyers, expressed in the House of Lords in the distinction between lay lords and law lords. But whereas the ecclesiastical distinction is not now based upon the distinction of learned and unlearned—though it was originally derived from it—the legal distinction is so based. It is the distinction between those who are unlearned in the law and those learned in the law. The layman is unlearned. But if that is all he is, he is not a good layman. He must be capable of understanding the issues put to him and of giving a judgement upon them. He may be ignorant but he must be educable. Lawyers do not expect justices of the peace to be experts in the law, but a good justice of the peace is one who can grasp the point of law which applies to the case before him and can apply it. It is recognized that he must be advised upon the law by one learned in the law—a legally qualified clerk—but to be a good lay justice he should be capable of understanding and following that advice. So also in committee work, the layman is not expected, by definition, to be the expert, but the good layman must be capable of grasping the issues as presented to him by the expert or the general practitioner. He must be capable of learning or of being taught.

A third mark of the good layman is suggested by experience in the world of business. It is the common practice for many undertakings in private enterprise and in public hands to associate lay directors with expert directors or administrators on the directing boards of these organizations. Not only banks and insurance and shipping companies but also a great technical undertaking like Imperial Chemical Industries Ltd.[1] find a place on their boards deliberately for lay directors. Men who have had distinguished careers in public life, in politics, in branches of business and commerce, in the army or civil service are sought after for the contribution they can make. If we look through the names of the directors on these boards we may find ex-Chancellors of the Exchequer, former Foreign Secretaries or ambassadors, colonial governors, or business executives still actively engaged in running a concern of their own but being associated also with the board of directors of a business in which they are not expert.

These lay directors, then, are often chosen because they have had experience and indeed are often experts in some other walk

[1] See *Large-Scale Organisation*, ed. by G. E. Milward, chapter by R. A. Lynex, Secretary of I.C.I., pp. 154–6.

of life, whether in politics or in some allied field of industry or commerce. In other words it is thought that a good layman ought to be an expert in something and preferably in something relevant. This mark of the good layman may be expressed by saying that he ought to be knowledgeable. By definition he is not expert or even knowledgeable on the matter concerning which he is a layman, but he should know something or even a good deal about other matters and preferably cognate or connected matters. So in committee work the layman who is used to doing something thoroughly, is a master of some trade or business or profession or subject, is usually qualified thereby to learn and make judgements about matters upon which he is a layman. A Jack of all trades seldom makes a good layman in committee work.

It is not so much knowledge, however, which a layman is expected to bring to his work in committees as sense, common sense. He is to check the excesses of bureaucratic and expert nonsense by the application of his own common sense. It is not enough for the layman to be interested, to be educable, or to be knowledgeable. He cannot make the best use of these qualities unless he has qualities of mind and temperament which mark him out as the sensible or reasonable man. The 'reasonable man' is a well-known figure in English law. What he considers to be excessive, negligent, slanderous, or dangerous is decisive. He is an equally important figure in British public administration. This man of good sense and moderate views is part of the idea of a good layman in committee work.

But though reasonable and moderate, he must not be passionless. He must provide some of that questioning temper of the outsider, some of that impatience of rigid procedure and accepted methods which is expected of the lay-director in private business. He must approach his committee work with an original and a critical mind. He must animate or galvanize. It is difficult to get one word to describe this quality of a good layman. It is rather like saying that he must have all the virtues of the reasonable man and also all the virtues of the unreasonable woman. Indeed, some of the best laymen are women and unreasonable women at that. It is the quality—often associated, by men at least, with women—of being unable to see the sense in what is being done, of questioning the whole basis of organization, of brushing difficulties aside, of ignoring logical argument, and of pressing a point beyond what most men consider a reasonable limit, which is required as part of the make-up of a good layman. It is against criticism of this kind that officials and experts should be required to justify their proposals and procedures in public administration. The reasonable man is not enough; we need the unreasonable woman also.

4

One of the principal reasons why laymen are found in British government, and particularly in the House of Commons and in local councils, is that British government is not only elective representative government but it is party government also. Such a system does not lead necessarily to the election of experts and is not intended to do so. It is fortunate that the layman is valuable in government; if he were not, he would none the less find his place in British government so long as it continued to be party government. It is important to say a word about the party man and his position in relation to the other six characters in committee work.

It may be well to emphasize at once that by 'party man' is intended something more than membership or adherence to a party. It means, in the context of the discussion of committee work, one whose position in or around a committee is that of speaking and acting as a member or supporter of a party. When a man acts in that capacity he is a party man for the purposes of our discussion. He may have other capacities; in other situations his character as party man may be irrelevant or unimportant. It is clear that a party man may be a layman; he may be an expert; he may be a chairman or he may be a partisan or interested party. In some situations one of these capacities of his may be of no less or of more significance than his capacity as a party man. In committee work the party man is not a separate and isolated character. He is often an aspect of the nature and function of a committee member, who may exhibit also other functions, as a layman or an expert or a chairman, and so on.

But it is necessary to pause for one moment and ask what is the relation of the party man to one other character in particular—the official. Here a more qualified answer must be given.

In the first place it may be said that an official in private employment may be a party man. Managers, trade union officials, and
the like take part in party politics and sit in Parliament or on
local councils as party men. Where there is any restriction upon
doing so, it is imposed not by the law but by the employer, who
for a variety of reasons may wish his managerial or controlling
staff to keep out of party politics. A bank may not wish its
manager to take a party line for fear that its customers may resent it; other employers may grudge the time spent by their
officials in party activity.

When we come to consider the officials in the government
service, more complicated considerations arise. Let us begin first
with those employed by the central government, the servants of
the Crown. Here the official is affected by a rule which applies
generally to all civil servants whether they are officials or not.
Civil servants are disqualified by statute from sitting in the
House of Commons.[1] They may be members of the House of
Lords, but, by a Treasury rule, though they may attend in their
place in the House of Lords when their official duties permit,
they may not take part in debate or vote until they have retired
or resigned.[2]

The statutory prohibition upon sitting in the House of Commons goes only a short way, however, towards regulating the
activities of an official who might want to behave as a party
man. Might he not stand for Parliament and resign if elected,
or might he not campaign for the election of others? Or might
he not take part in local elections? The proper behaviour of the
official in these matters is not regulated by statute but by rules
made by the Treasury or by departments. They have been the
subject of controversy and of a recent inquiry by a departmental committee.[3] It is not easy to summarize the position,[4] but
broadly speaking it may be said that certain officials—particularly those who work in the spheres where policy is determined
and those who work in local offices of central departments and
deal directly with the individual citizen in relation to his personal circumstances—are required in effect to abstain from poli-

[1] There are inconsistencies and obscurities in the law on this subject, but the
general principle is undeniable.   [2] Treasury Circular No. 11 of 1928.
[3] See *Report of the Committee on the Political Activities of Civil Servants* (Cmd. 7718
of 1949), presided over by Mr. J. C. Masterman.
[4] It is set out in detail in Cmd. 8783 of 1953. *Political Activities of Civil Servants.*

tical activities in the national field, though they are given permission where possible to take part in local government activities, subject to the exercise of discretion.[1] About 160,000 officials out of the 1,000,000 civil servants in Britain are restricted in this way. About another 220,000 obtain permission to take part in political activities local and national (short of standing for Parliament) subject to observing a code of discretionary behaviour.[2] These are mainly clerical officers. The remaining 620,000 are completely free, the great number of them belonging to industrial grades or to manipulative grades in the Post Office. They may stand for Parliament, though they must resign before nomination day, on the understanding that, if defeated, they are reinstated. The officials with whom the committees we study are concerned are for the most part within the category of those excluded from political activities in the national field but permitted, subject to discretion, to take part in local politics.

This prohibition of party political activities to certain officials in British central government is well known. Let us consider just what it means. It does not mean that the official is expected to have no personal preference between political parties. He has a vote and he is assumed to be able to express his preference with no less ease than other men. Nor should it be assumed to mean that in his work he will have nothing to do with party. In a narrow and personal sense that is true, of course. He must not be working for a political party on his own account. But let it always be remembered that the official in the higher ranges of the civil service is always working, professionally and in his official position, with a party, the party in power. Most of what he touches has party implications. He shares in the formulation of the policies of a party government. His Minister is a party man. The official in Whitehall is expected to do all he can to make his Minister's policy successful. His mistakes may lead to party troubles and even to the defeat of the party in power. He spends a great deal of time thinking of ways of answering the Opposition's criticisms, and many of these criticisms are party criticisms. He tries to protect his Minister, support him, and extricate him from difficulties. He is on the government side;

[1] The terms in which discretion is described are in Annex 2 of Cmd. 8783.
[2] See Annex 1 of Cmd. 8783. These were the figures for 1953.

he is out to help that side against the Opposition side. All this must be stressed when we say that the British civil service is outside party and that the official is not a party man.

What is really meant, perhaps, by saying that the official is not a party man is that he is not a one-party man. He is a government party man. He offers his best services to the party in power, to the government of any party. How far this is possible or desirable is a question often discussed. The record of the British civil service in this century shows that it has achieved this object to a very considerable degree. What is important here, however, is to stress that while the official in the civil service cannot be a party man, he works very closely with party men, and all that he touches is capable of party interpretation and party consequences. He is not above party. He is in the midst of parties and he is working in alliance, though only for the time being, with the party in power. The party man and the official are very closely associated and not least in committee work in modern British government.

What has been said so far about the circumstances in which the party man may not be an official has been concerned almost entirely with the central government. But the same principle substantially applies in local government. It is accepted that local officials will give loyal support to their councils, no matter which party has a majority on the council. If they have political party affiliations, they will not use their official position to promote their views against the views of the majority of the council. Normally, too, it is the rule that no official of a council may sit as a member of that council.[1] But there must be limits to this rule, of course. It need not be extended to all employees of a council any more than the rule against civil servants taking part in politics is extended to all employees of the state. Teachers in schools run by county and county borough councils, clerical and manual workers, who do not share in the framing of policy and in the making of decisions in association with committees, need not be excluded entirely from either taking part in politics or sitting on councils, other than that which employs them. The practice of councils differs in this matter, but the principle that the official must not be a party man is accepted.

[1] This rule is not found in any Act of Parliament and apparently is not formulated in writing. It is a convention of local government in Britain.

This is not the place to ask whether the doctrine of British government that the party man must not be an official in the central and local government service is good or even whether it is found to work in practice. It is proper to point out, however, one limitation upon its working. It works on the assumption that the divisions between party men are such that people of ability, of power, and influence, in the higher civil service, can feel no sense of impropriety, futility, dishonesty, or disloyalty either to the state or to their party (if they have one) or to their consciences by working as hard as they can to execute the policy of one party and defend it against the Opposition and then reverse the roles completely when the Opposition becomes the government. It means that they must believe that party differences, though important, are not as important as all that. They must hold the doctrine which makes democratic government possible, namely, that the party in power should be criticizable and that people should be allowed to work for its supersession by another party. They should not believe that one party has a monopoly of truth and is entitled to hold power and exclude its rivals from any part in the state. The British doctrine of the impartial civil servant is consonant, therefore, with the British idea of democratic government.

It follows then that what is said about the party man and the official cannot apply to, say, the party man in the Communist party. He cannot be expected to serve every party loyally. He believes in one party only and he looks forward to a time when that one party shall be left in the state. The official who is a Communist party man, therefore, does not fit into this picture of the official who supports the government, whatever its party complexion may be. He demonstrates that there are circumstances in which the relationship of the party man and the official which is accepted nowadays in British government could continue no longer.

5

To adopt the term 'interested party' to describe a wide and varied class of people has certain dangers. To begin with, it is a term which has a narrow and fairly well-defined connotation in the law, more particularly the law relating to local government, in the procedure of the courts, and in the procedure of Parliament. The rules of local councils provide, for example, that if a member is interested financially, directly or indirectly, in a matter before a council or its committees, he must declare that interest and take no part in the proceedings upon that matter. In the standing orders of the House of Commons on private bills a member whose constituency is locally interested or who is himself personally interested in a bill may not sit upon a committee dealing with that bill. So far as public bills are concerned, a member may not vote upon them if he has a direct personal pecuniary interest, but this is narrowly interpreted.[1] The existence of the interested party is thus recognized and in these particular cases certain steps are taken to see that his position as a member of a committee does not give rise to an abuse.

But although the idea of the interested party as embodied in the rules of local councils and of Parliament is fairly limited, it does not seem inappropriate to use it in an extended sense in this essay to cover all those who are closely identified with an organization or a point of view and who, in this capacity, take part in British administration. The whole category of interested party will range from the man who is concerned in a contract to supply meat to a civic restaurant to the woman who is secretary of the parish branch of a pacifist society. Their position as interested parties is, like that of the expert, a relative position. The meat contractor is an interested party when his contract is considered by the council or its appropriate committee, and if he is a councillor the rules about interested parties apply to him. The lady secretary is an interested party in relation, say, to a royal commission on the arms traffic, should she be appointed to membership of it or be called to give evidence before it. But the butcher before the royal commission on the arms traffic and the lady secretary before the town council when it considers the meat contract have no status of interested parties any more.

It may be thought that the term 'interested party' (less perhaps than the alternative 'partisan', which we shall employ occasionally) has the drawback that it suggests some notion of a sinister interest, a disqualifying interest. It is true that this suggestion is present and it is true also, surely, that the interest of an interested party is sometimes and rightly regarded as a

[1] See Erskine May, *Parliamentary Practice*, 15th ed., pp. 418 ff.

disqualifying, if not always in such cases a sinister, interest. It does not follow, however, that because an interested party is considered to be disqualified, for example, from taking part in the discussion or decision of a matter in which he is interested, that he is completely disabled from expressing his views. Nor should it be assumed that any disqualification or the same degree of disqualification should attach to an interested party in every sphere of administration or in relation to every kind of committee. What is certain, however, is that the interested party is in a category of persons whose position in relation to committees must always be considered. He raises special problems and questions. It would be foolish to act as if he did not exist. While it is not necessary to go to the length of regarding all interested parties as sinister, it is necessary to consider how best they can be made use of in public administration and what special opportunities or special obstacles should be placed in their way.

When we come to describe the nature of the interested party, we find that, like the expert, the members of this class fall into a number of groups. The first kind of interested party is one of whom something has been said already—the man with the financial interest in, say, a government contract. Often he does not represent any organization or association, though he may represent a firm. In many cases he is himself the interested party and his interest is clearly and demonstrably financial. There are, however, many cases of doubt in this relationship, where the interest is so indirect that it is not easy to say whether a man is an interested party or not. But the category itself is clear enough. To it may belong not only those who are involved in a matter through financial interest but also those who are, say, relations of persons concerned—parents of children to whom an education committee may make a grant, or brother of a sister who is an applicant for a post under a local authority.

From this relatively simple case of personal or financial interest, we can pass to that large collection of organizations whose sole or primary object is the economic welfare of their members, the trade unions and other associations of employees. With them may be considered the associations of employers who are concerned with them in discussions about economic and financial affairs. There are, as is well known, thousands of associations of employees in Britain, organized locally, regionally, and nationally, and they are to be found in every industry, profession, and calling. They may be well known to the general public like the National Union of Mineworkers, the National Union of Teachers, the Transport and General Workers' Union, or the Amalgamated Engineering Union. There are also the great associations on the employers' side comparable with the great trade unions—the Shipbuilding Employers' Federation, the Engineering and Allied Employers' National Federation, the British Trawlers' Federation Ltd., and the National Farmers' Union—while the British Employers' Confederation is a national body representative of a wide variety of employers. Or they may be known to a region or section of economic life which, though important, is not continually before a national public—such unions as the National Federation of Glass Workers or the Electrical Trades Union or the United Textile Factory Workers' Association or the National Union of Tailors and Garment Workers. All these and other such unions have their hundreds of constituent branches or even constituent unions and comprise a very large number of associations. But they do not begin to cover the enormous variety of even less well-known trade organizations, as a few examples may help to illustrate.

There are, for example, the United Chamois Leather Layers-out Society, the Amalgamated Society of Cane, Wicker, and Perambulator Operatives, the London Society of Tie Cutters, the Amalgamated Felt Hat Trimmers' and Wool Farmers' Association, the Progressive Society of French Polishers (London), the Book Edge Gilders' Trade Society, the National Plumbers' Society, the National Society of Brushmakers, the Pianoforte Tuners' Association, the Military and Orchestral Musical Instrument Makers' Trade Society, the Tugmen's Guild, the Institute of Linguists, the Bookmakers Employees' Association, the British Funeral Workers' Association, and the Welsh Union of Club Stewards.

On the employers' side there is no less a variety of associations. There are the Association of Animal Gut Cleaners Ltd., the Film Strippers' Association Ltd., the Refractory Users' Association, the Well Drillers' Association, the Tile Fireplace Makers' Association, the British Button Manufacturers' Association, the Coffin Furniture Manufacturers' Association, the Bradford, Leeds, Halifax, Keighley, and District Textile

Comb, Hackle, Gill, and Faller Makers' Association, the Buffalo Picker Manufacturers' Association, and the Hydraulic Mangle Finishers' Association.

It has seemed worth while to repeat the names of some of these bodies to illustrate the fact that the organized interest is a common everyday phenomenon in British society. It is expected that every man has his union; he can organize himself with his fellows to protect his interests. These organizations may concern themselves only with economic matters—rates of wages and hours and conditions of labour—or they may go further and attempt to protect the trade or profession by imposing standards of recruitment and insisting upon certain qualifications. Economic considerations are never absent entirely from these activities, but there is also some preoccupation with the raising or maintaining of professional standards and of rendering service to the public. Among such bodies are the National and Local Government Officers' Association, the various associations of teachers, inspectors, and administrators in the field of education, the Solicitors' Managing Clerks Association, the Sanitary Inspectors' Association, the District Auditors' Association, and the Association of H.M. Inspectors of Taxes.

These organized interests are accepted in Britain and recognized as part of the constitution. Their right to express their views and to speak on behalf of their members is freely admitted and what is more is made full use of by government departments. One of the best illustrations of this fact, perhaps, is that the Ministry of Labour publishes from time to time a *Directory of Employers' Associations, Trade Unions, Joint Organizations, &c.*, in which is to be found a list of all such bodies in so far as they are directly concerned with labour matters. It is accepted without question that the Ministry itself, other government departments, and private concerns would always consult these bodies when matters involving their interests are concerned. One of the ways in which they are associated with administration is through committees, either by membership or by presenting their views. It must be emphasized that this is only one of their ways of being used by the government whether central or local. There are formal consultations and informal day-to-day dealings which are even more important than what is done through committees. Yet their value in relation to committees is very great. There is hardly an occupation upon which a committee could deliberate in this country for which there could not be found some union or association to represent and advocate the interests of those engaged in it.

But the trade and professional associations, numerous and enormous as they are, by no means exhaust the list of organized interests which have a place in the British constitution. In addition to these organizations of private interests there are what might almost be called organizations of the public interest—though it should not be assumed that they will necessarily behave with more public spirit than the former. The various units of local government in the country organize themselves into associations to protect their interests which, formally at any rate, are the interests of the people of Britain demarcated or divided into local government areas. There is in England and Wales the County Councils' Association, the Association of Municipal Corporations, the Rural District Councils' Association, the Urban District Councils' Association, the Parish Councils' Association; Scotland has its Association of County Councils in Scotland, its Convention of Royal Burghs of Scotland, its Scottish Counties of Cities' Association; and Northern Ireland has its Ulster Association of County Councils and its Association of Municipal Authorities of Northern Ireland.

But that is not the end of it. Branches of local government activity organize themselves into associations, like the Association of Education Committees; groups of local authorities combine to protect their interests, like the Lancashire Association of Urban District Councils and the Metropolitan Boroughs' Standing Joint Committee. Local authorities join with other public bodies or with some department of the national government in forming an association to promote an interest, like the National Housing and Town Planning Council, or the National Committee for Visual Aids in Education, or the Association of British Market Authorities.

From organizations and associations of public bodies, presumably embodying the public interest, we pass to private organizations which advocate the public interest, voluntary associations of individuals and organizations which advocate or oppose some course of action in what they believe to be the public interest. There are such organizations as the Royal

Society for the Prevention of Cruelty to Animals and the National Society for the Prevention of Cruelty to Children; there is the Pedestrians' Association, the Howard League for Penal Reform, the Council for the Preservation of Rural England, the Roads Beautifying Association, the National Playing Fields Association, the National Smoke Abatement Society, the Libraries' Association, the Proportional Representation Society, the Royal Empire Society, the British Legion. The list of bodies of this kind, with their branches, would run into many thousands. Many of them would seldom, if ever, impinge upon the machinery of government, but there are many also, of which those mentioned by name above are good examples, which are often concerned with what the government is doing and which would be associated from time to time in the work of committees. They are to be added to the great number of organized interests whose position in certain circumstances could become that of an interested party in committee work.

One way of getting an impression of the number and range of persons and organizations which can be interested parties in modern British government is to turn to the pages of some such work of reference as, say, *The Municipal Year Book*, published annually in the United Kingdom. In this book is to be found a list of 'Associations, Societies and other bodies concerned with local government'. Although not all of the 900-odd organizations listed could qualify as potential interested parties, and although there would be of course many potential interested parties not included in the list, none the less there are to be found in it examples of most of the different types already discussed. There are the straightforward contracting interests like the Asphalt Roads Association Ltd., the Ballast, Sand, and Allied Trades' Association, the British Cast Concrete Federation, the Reinforced Concrete Association, the National Chamber of Trade, or the London Master Builders' Association. Then there are the associations of employees in local government who are concerned with rates of pay, hours and conditions of work, and, in some varying degree, professional standards. They include as well as the comprehensive National and Local Government Officers' Association and the National Union of Teachers, such bodies as the Association of Local Government Financial Officers, the Association of Education Officers, the Association of Borough Officials of Scotland, the Chief Constables' Association, the Society of Town Clerks, or the Society of Medical Officers of Health. Local authorities are not concerned only with trade and professional organizations confined to their own employees, and accordingly *The Municipal Year Book* lists such bodies as the Royal Institute of British Architects, the Institutions of Structural Engineers, of Sanitary Engineers, of Mechanical Engineers, of Highway Engineers, of Water Engineers, of Civil Engineers, of Chemical Engineers, and of Electrical Engineers, the British Medical Association, and the British Dental Association.

Needless to say, the various associations formed among local authorities themselves are listed, and there are to be noticed, finally, the organizations which advocate some belief or opinion or course of action in which local authorities are concerned, such as the Royal Society for the Prevention of Accidents, the Nursery Schools' Association of Great Britain, the National Playing Fields Association, the National Baby Welfare Council, and the Commons, Open Spaces, and Footpaths Preservation Society, in addition to those like the N.S.P.C.C. and the Pedestrians' Association already mentioned.

These different types of body are all concerned in some degree with local government. In appropriate circumstances they may become interested parties so far as the proceedings of some local or national committee is concerned. They are not regarded automatically as sinister pressure groups. Their names and addresses are published in a respectable reference book. Neither side wishes to excuse or hide or explain away their existence. This is not to say that their relations with local and national committees are entirely unregulated. There are legal rules and conventional rules which govern their activities, as we shall see in later chapters. But it is an accepted convention also that interested parties are recognized as part of the administrative structure in its broadest sense.

It is well to add, perhaps, that an interested party may be an expert in his own affairs or in the affairs of the organization he represents. There is nothing surprising in that, for almost by definition he cares very much about the matter in which he has an 'interest'. What is more significant, however, is that where organized interests are concerned, it is very common for them to be represented by officials, their own officials. In the trade unions and associations, both of employers and employees, in the professional associations and institutes, in the associations of local authorities with each other, in the voluntary bodies advocating some cause or opinion, there are officials as there are in the government. It is their job to maintain and strengthen the organization of the interest concerned, and they deal with governments, local and central, as one official with another.

6

No committee can do business without a chairman and a secretary. These two characters are its essential officers. The secretary, in the committees with which we deal, is usually also an official in the sense in which we are using this term. In committees to inquire, to advise, or to negotiate he is usually an official of the central government departments concerned; in committees to administer in local government he is the town or county clerk or some similar administrative official; in the committees of the House of Commons to legislate or to scrutinize and control he is an official of the House. In all these cases, however, he has a distinct function to perform as secretary of the committee and he must take care that his other loyalties and duties as an official do not overbear or distort his loyalty and duty to the committee. A secretary has indeed a distinctive and important position in relation to a committee. He is concerned to see that its business is transacted efficiently. He has a primary responsibility for preparing its agenda and for seeing that the material it needs for its deliberations is available to it at the right time and in the right form. He should be concerned to see that matters appear on its agenda when they are ready for consideration—not before and not after. He records and transmits a committee's decisions—a most important function. He is the channel through which people outside the committee deal with the committee. In all these functions he is the servant of the committee. He is not the servant or the subordinate of the chairman. The secretary and the chairman must work in co-operation, for there are many matters in which both are entitled to have a say, but they are co-ordinate officers of the committee. As a rule, in the committees with which we deal, while the chair-

man is a member of the committee, the secretary is not. Yet he
has his own peculiar function as guardian and adviser of the
committee, and on occasion indeed, as we shall see, he may be
called upon to assert the rights of the committee or some of its
members even against the chairman. That is why it is seldom
wise for the same person to hold the office of chairman and
secretary of a committee.

So far as the chairman is concerned he may well be one of the
remaining five characters in committee work—an official, a layman, an expert, a party man, or an interested party. And, of
course, he may be more than one for, as we have seen, they are
not all mutually exclusive capacities. As a rule there is some
reason in a particular type of committee why a chairman should
or should not belong to one of these other categories. It is seldom
a matter of complete indifference. If a committee is set up to
adjudicate, for example, it will usually be right that the chairman should not be an interested party.

The status and influence of the chairman varies greatly from
one type of committee to another and even within different
examples of the same type. His position will be affected by a
variety of factors—the function of the committee, the method of
the chairman's appointment, where the responsibility for the
leadership of the committee rests, and so on. Many illustrations
of these variations will be encountered in later chapters. At this
stage, however, it is interesting to see from what origins a chairman's authority comes.

The function of the office of chairman, put at its irreducible
minimum, is to promote and maintain order. To this end it is
agreed that, in a numerous body like a committee, the chaos
that would come if members addressed each other at will or at
random can be averted by providing that all remarks will be
addressed to one person. Simple and obvious as it appears, this
is the very foundation of order. The most elementary and ele-
mental form of being 'out of order' is to direct one's remarks to
someone other than the chairman. 'Please address the chair' is
the cry both of those who love freedom of speech and of those
who love order.

It is from this primary function of being responsible for order
and from this unique position of being the target of all remarks
in the course of a committee's work that a chairman's oppor-

tunities of leadership spring. To begin with, all questions are addressed to or through him. Soon he may find himself answering the questions, justifying the actions of the committee, perhaps justifying the actions of its officials, if it is an administrative committee. Soon the officials are supplying him with the answers to questions and criticisms and he may find himself acting almost like a minister defending actions which he comes to feel are his responsibility. Now it need not work in this way of course. A chairman can treat himself as no more than a channel through which questions pass to chief officials. But if he wishes to influence his committee, the opportunity often presents itself when questions are asked.

A chairman, too, is usually in a position to take the initiative. In a sense, and within very wide limits, he is never 'out of order'. A chairman thus has opportunities for intervention in a discussion which are denied to other members. He can always catch his own eye and he can choose his own moment for intervention. While the ordinary member of a committee may find it difficult to get an opportunity to speak more than once on a subject, a chairman, without actually making a set speech, may comment frequently as a discussion proceeds and in effect guide and influence the discussion. This influence flows naturally from the chairman's position as moderator or traffic policeman of the discussion, as its guardian of points of order.

A chairman's influence over discussions and decisions may be exerted also in his regulation of the proceedings. By his interpretation of what is in order and what is not, of what may be raised on a certain item of the agenda and what may not, of what line of argument is to be encouraged or discouraged, what questions pressed and what allowed to fade away, what motions and amendments accepted and what discouraged, deferred, or declined, a chairman can, within limits of course, influence the line of a committee's discussion. In the same way he has a certain discretion in calling upon other members of the committee to speak at an appropriate moment, and by allowing a member to open a discussion or to wind it up, or by calling upon a succession of speakers all of whom express the same views, he can influence the opinions of the committee as a whole. How often we hear the comment: 'Fortunately the chairman encouraged me', or 'Unfortunately the chairman gave me no help'—

illustrations of the fact that, quite legitimately, a chairman may by the use of his discretion assist or retard some particular course of action. And it is for reasons of this kind that members of committees who have something to say—and officials also—are keen 'to have a word with the chairman beforehand'. Needless to say, what a chairman can do in this respect depends in the last resort —as do most actions of a chairman—upon what a committee will stand. They can limit or nullify him at any time if they have the will to do so.

A chairman's actions in the sphere of order will be influenced, too, in many cases by the advice of the secretary. It is commonly a secretary's function to be something of an expert on points of order—in standing committees of the House of Commons or in local government committees—and since many chairmen are not expert in those matters, a secretary's advice may have great weight. In this respect sometimes a secretary is defending the rights of committee members or is intervening on the side of the efficient conduct of business, and may have to assert his opinion against the wishes of the chairman. But here again, the chairman gives the ruling but the last word will be with the committee.

A chairman has an opportunity to lead his committee also because of the desire, natural in a presiding officer, to bring a discussion to a close and get the question settled. This desire is often strong in members of a committee also, and chairmen are urged to get a decision and 'give a lead'. It is undoubtedly part of a chairman's function to bring a discussion to a conclusion and not merely to allow it to come to an end. But it happens often that after a discussion, and quite a valuable discussion, no decision can be taken unless someone can draw out some acceptable proposal from the course of the discussion and place it before the committee for acceptance or rejection. This is an opportunity which a chairman may and indeed very often should take. He can bring the issue to a point and suggest a line of action. In some cases where it is not clear what course of action will commend itself to a committee, almost any proposition from the chair is valuable because it will help to clarify issues and indicate where an acceptable solution may lie. Action of this kind is not and of course need not be confined to chairmen. In many cases an ordinary member of a committee may act even more effectively than a chairman, or a chairman may intervene with his proposal more effectively after other members have tried their proposals. What is apparent, however, is that from his function as the conductor of the discussion a chairman may suggest solutions and in this way affect the course of policy.

This influence which the chairman exercises may be seen round the other way when a chairman who wishes, for some reason and conceivably for some good reason, to avoid or postpone a decision is able to use all his powers and influence to prevent the discussion being brought to a conclusion and to achieve an adjournment or a stalemate or a truce. A chairman's opportunities for leadership may be used with equal effect both in construction and in obstruction.

A chairman's readiness to exploit his opportunities of bringing the committee to a decision is increased by certain other factors. A chairman tends to get himself identified with his committee not only in his own eyes but in the eyes of his colleagues and of the public. Advisory committees and royal commissions tend to be known by the name of their chairman and their report is spoken of almost as his report—the Haldane Report, the Simon Report. Their success or failure is his success or failure. If they are not doing their work well, people say: 'What is wrong with the chairman? He should not allow his committee to go on like that.' It is 'his' committee. He will be anxious, therefore, that what they do or decide or advise should be something which he can approve and support and defend. His influence in this direction is assisted, too, by the practice, common in committees or commissions which are set up to produce a report, of the chairman producing a draft report for discussion by his colleagues.

A chairman's tendency to regard a committee as 'his' committee is increased by the fact that he acts for the committee on various occasions. He represents them, if they need representation. He is speaker on their behalf, whether it be in words of congratulation or condolence or whether it be in negotiation or in opposition to the claims or demands of other committees. In times of emergency, too, he usually acts on their behalf, seeking their confirmation for his actions later, while in normal times it is common for them to authorize him to act for them upon routine or even upon exceptional matters. In these and in many other ways the one is made to speak or act for the many.

It may be suggested, finally, that a chairman has an opportunity of influence from the fact that he is entitled to have some say in the drawing up of the agenda for a committee meeting—usually an important matter. There is often some argument about who should determine what shall and what shall not go on the agenda. There can be no doubt surely that the last word on this question must rest with a committee. It must decide whether or not it will deal with a particular topic. This is not universally admitted by all secretaries. But what is more important in practice is not who has the last word upon the construction of the agenda but who has the first. The sound practice would seem to be that the secretary should prepare the agenda; but that he should consult the chairman at the earliest stages on all but routine items so that the chairman may have an opportunity of giving his views. If a chairman wishes to add an item to the agenda, that item should be inserted by the secretary. If the secretary objects strongly to the inclusion of the item, it will be the chairman's duty to see that the committee, having heard the facts of the case, decides whether to proceed with the item or not. The last word here should be with the committee. A similar procedure should be followed if a secretary desires to insert an item on the agenda and the chairman objects. The item should be inserted and the committee invited to express its views and to decide the point. Similarly, any question or dispute about the order in which the items of the agenda should be taken—a question, sometimes, of considerable practical importance—must be determined in the last resort by the committee. A secretary may give his advice, a chairman may give his ruling, but the committee has the last word.

In practice, disputes between secretaries and chairmen do not go to these extremes. Committees are seldom called on to determine such points. A chairman's ruling has considerable influence; his suggestions about the agenda have considerable weight both with the secretary and with the committee. A secretary is loath to resist a chairman on a point of this kind, for he relies upon him to get the business through, and he is often more likely to do this well if he does it in his own way. None the less the secretary exercises a very strong influence upon the drawing up of the agenda and upon the views of chairmen about it.

These general observations about the chairman and the secretary do not apply equally to all types of committee. The office of chairman is a post of potential leadership, but for a variety of reasons a chairman may not exercise leadership. The influence of a secretary and his importance in relation to the chairman will vary also, as we shall see. It seems worth while, however, to have in mind the basis of the influence of these two officers of a committee as a preliminary to observing in different committees the way in which their functions are performed.

CHAPTER III

Committees to Advise

I

THE category of committees to advise is so comprehensive that it is necessary to make some distinctions within it if our exposition of the use of committees is to be fruitful. There are two types of committee which may be distinguished at the outset. First, there is the committee which offers advice after undertaking an inquiry, and secondly there is the committee which offers advice after its members have negotiated with each other. Though these two types of committee are both in one sense and to some degree committees to advise, the processes which they follow before they offer advice are so significantly different that they deserve separate exposition and discussion. Moreover, although committees to inquire or to negotiate are usually charged also with the task of offering advice upon the basis of their inquiry or negotiation, there are cases where such committees are not required to offer advice but to determine issues for themselves. A committee to inquire may be asked to do no more than find the facts; a committee to negotiate may be authorized itself to make a decision or judgement. For reasons of this kind it seems best to consider committees to inquire and committees to negotiate—whether they also offer advice or not —in separate chapters, and to confine the discussion in this chapter to committees to advise in whose terms of reference or mode of working the conduct of an inquiry or of negotiation plays no significant or substantial part.

Put in a more positive way, the characteristic of committees to advise, in the narrower sense of the term, is that their members offer their advice from the resources of their own special knowledge and experience. They are chosen to sit upon committees of this kind because they are supposed to know about the subject-matter; they can speak with authority. They may, of course, have to undertake some inquiry or they may negotiate a little among themselves, but their predominant activity is to bring to the assistance of the government the knowledge of which they are repositories. Their terms of reference usually contain the words 'to consider'. Put rather crudely, whereas the members of a committee to inquire are looking for the answer, the members of a committee to advise, strictly so called, either know the answers or know where to find the answers.

The distinction between a committee to advise and a committee to inquire may be illustrated by looking at the way in which the Royal Commission on Population, appointed in 1944, organized its work. The Royal Commission itself was already an example of a committee to inquire. Its terms of reference required it 'to examine the facts relating to the present population trends in Great Britain; to investigate the causes of these trends and to consider their probable consequences . . .'. It is true that the Commission was also asked to give advice—'to consider what measures, if any, should be taken in the national interest to influence the future trend of population; and to make recommendations.' But that advice was clearly to be preceded by and based upon the findings of an inquiry. However, as the subject-matter of this inquiry raised technical problems of very great complication, it was considered wise that there should be attached to the Commission three expert committees which would advise the Commission on the statistical, economic, and biological and medical aspects of the problem. These three committees are examples of truly advisory committees. Their members were considered to have the knowledge or the skill to supply to the Commission the technical information needed for the inquiry.[1]

There are cases, of course, in which it is difficult to say whether a committee is a committee to advise or to inquire or to negotiate. Sometimes, as was the case with the Royal Commission on the Coal Industry presided over by Mr. Justice Sankey in 1919, representatives of interested parties—in this case the Miners' Union and the Mine-owners' Federation—are placed upon a committee to inquire, and this introduces the possibility, at any rate, of an element of negotiation. Or again, as in the case of the working parties set up by Sir Stafford Cripps in 1945 and 1946 in certain industries, committees may appear to combine

[1] See Cmd. 7695 (1949), particularly Appendix I.

the function of giving advice, the function of inquiry, and the function of negotiation. By inviting interested parties to meet each other and certain outside members Sir Stafford Cripps appeared to ask them not only to negotiate with each other, and to inquire, but also to make available their own specialist knowledge of the industry in which they worked either as employer or employee.[1] There are, as we shall see, many other such mixed or borderline cases. But the existence of borderline cases does not of itself invalidate a classification; it may indeed illuminate and confirm it.

2

Committees to advise may be consulted at any stage in the process of government—in the formulation of policy, in its application or administration, or in the review of policy and its application. In practice it is at the stage of application or administration that committees to advise are most widely used, while the committee to inquire is more usually found either at the stage of formulation or at the stage of the review of policy.

It would be difficult to say how many committees to advise exist in and around central and local government today. If we consider the central government alone, we have to remember that committees exist to advise the central departments not only at the centre, but in many cases in the localities also. The Lord Chancellor, in exercising his function of appointing justices of the peace, is advised by local committees—316 of them. The Post Office has an advisory council of twenty-two members in London, but it has advisory committees also in every important town in the country to a total of roughly 60; the Ministry of Fuel and Power in 1949 had nearly forty committees to advise it at the centre, but in addition it had 700 local fuel advisory committees.[2]

When the Prime Minister (Mr. Attlee) was asked in 1949 to

[1] That working parties are not ordinary committees to inquire seems to be indicated by this sentence from the *Report of the Working Party on Midwives*, 1949. 'A Working Party does not take formal evidence in the same way as a Royal Commission or Departmental Committee; it has to go and collect its own material', p. vi.

[2] It disbanded these 700 local fuel advisory committees in 1949, when the Electricity Act came into operation, but new committees were set up to take over their functions. 470 H.C. Deb., 5th ser., col. 190.

give a list of the bodies which existed at the centre and locally to advise government departments, he replied[1] that the task of compiling the list of committees at the centre had been quite arduous enough and that he did not think the labour of compiling a list from the localities was justified.[2] Mr. Attlee stated, however, that the total number of central or national committees to advise government departments was round about 700. These were distributed between the departments in varying numbers, of course. While the Lord President of the Council had nearly 100 committees to advise him,[3] excluding the fifty-five committees which advised the Department of Scientific and Industrial Research, for which the Lord President is responsible, the Treasury had thirty-one,[4] the Ministry of Supply twenty-nine,[5] the Ministry of Fuel and Power thirty-seven; the Ministry of Pensions was content with three, while the Commonwealth Relations Office appeared to admit to one only—the Society for the Overseas Settlement of British Women.[6]

Whether the total given in 1949 still stands today is a matter for conjecture. What we can be certain of, however, is that it would not be greatly different, for the use of committees to advise is an established practice by governments of all parties and has been so for many years.[7] Numbers may fluctuate, but they will never be small.[8] In general it may be said, perhaps, that those departments which are concerned with scientific

[1] 460 H.C. Deb., 5th ser., cols. 15–16. 18 Jan. 1949. The questioner excluded from his inquiry committees composed entirely of officials.

[2] The list of central committees was laid on the table of the House of Commons, but it was not printed as a parliamentary paper.

[3] The precise figure in the return was ninety-four.

[4] Including eleven regional boards for industry.

[5] Some of these on their own admission broke up into or had attached to themselves at least seventy-four boards, panels, committees, and sub-committees.

[6] The departments varied a great deal in the principles they adopted in making a return of their advisory committees. For example, some listed *ad hoc* royal commissions and departmental committees of inquiry and others did not. As a result the return does not provide an accurate basis for comparing departments in their use of advisory committees.

[7] For the use of committees to advise in the period before 1939 see the most interesting study edited by R. Vernon and N. Mansergh, *Advisory Bodies*. The subject is dealt with principally by departments.

[8] e.g., in evidence submitted to the Royal Commission on Scottish Affairs in 1953 the Department of Agriculture for Scotland listed 19 advisory bodies attached to it, the Department of Health listed 17, and the Home Department listed 29. See Vol. I of Memoranda submitted to Royal Commission, pp. 33–35, 60–61, 94–98.

matters—either like the Lord President's Office with a responsibility for science so far as it concerns the government, or like the Ministry of Supply as a user of scientific knowledge and scientists—are likely to have more advisory committees than others. Changes and developments of policy will often lead to the use of more advisory committees. Since 1940, when the policy of colonial development and welfare was inaugurated, the Colonial Office has set up a whole new series of advisory committees to assist it in formulating and applying policy in new spheres of activity. Whereas before 1940 there were only about half a dozen advisory bodies attached to the Colonial Office, there are now roughly twenty. But it is the change not so much in their numbers as in their subject-matter that is instructive. There is an Advisory Committee on Social Development in the Colonies, a Colonial Social Science Research Council, a Colonial Labour Advisory Committee, a Colonial University Grants Advisory Committee, a Colonial Research Council, a Colonial Economic Research Committee, a Colonial Medical Research Committee, and an Advisory Committee on Education in the Colonies, of which only the last named was in existence before 1940.[1]

Some advisory committees are distinguished by the fact that they have statutory authority; the department is obliged by Act of Parliament to set them up. Thus the Home Secretary must, under the Children Act of 1948,[2] appoint an Advisory Council on Child Care for England and Wales; the Minister of Education must, under the Education Act of 1944, appoint two Central Advisory Councils on Education, one for England and the other for Wales and Monmouthshire;[3] the National Insurance Act of 1946,[4] following the precedent of the Unemployment Insurance Act of 1934,[5] obliged the Minister of National Insurance to set up a National Insurance Advisory Committee. Statutory requirements to set up committees to advise are not confined to the national level. The National Assistance Act of

[1] It was set up in 1929.
[2] 11 & 12 Geo. VI c. 43, § 43. There is a separate Advisory Council for Scotland required by § 44 of the same Act.
[3] 7 & 8 Geo. VI, c. 31, § 4. The Education (Scotland) Act, 1946 (9 & 10 Geo. VI, c. 72, § 68), makes the setting up of an Advisory Council for Scotland permissive.
[4] 9 & 10 Geo. VI, c. 67, § 41 and Fifth Schedule.
[5] 24 & 25 Geo. V, c. 29, § 17.

1948 provided,[1] in terms adapted and expanded from the corresponding provisions of the Unemployment Assistance Act, 1934,[2] that the Assistance Board was to have associated with the local administration of its work Advisory Committees of persons having local knowledge and experience in matters affecting the Board's functions. As a result there are over eighty advisory committees,[3] working in close association with a similar set of committees established by the Ministry of National Insurance.[4] Although there are many such statutory bodies, they are nevertheless in the minority. The very great number of committees to advise are set up voluntarily by the departments and not in the execution of a duty imposed upon them by statute.

Central departments of government make most use of advisory bodies, but it is worth noting that where services are conducted either by central and local government in partnership or by local government alone, some advisory bodies have been established here also. The Central Advisory Council on Education for England and those for Wales and for Scotland are established to advise both the Ministry of Education (or the Scottish Office) and the local education authorities. In the field of further education, regional advisory councils have been established throughout England, composed of a group of local education authorities, together with universities in the region, and the task of these bodies is to advise the local education authorities and the universities in the region about further education. They have associated with them a number of specialized advisory committees upon different branches of further education which also offer advice to the local authorities and universities concerned.

3

When we come to look at the membership of committees to advise we notice that in most cases officials find a place upon

[1] 11 & 12 Geo. VI, c. 29, § 3.

[2] 24 & 25 Geo. V, c. 29, § 35 (3).

[3] In practice they work through sub-committees, so that the total is more like 330 than 80. For a list of the committees and sub-committees see *Report of the National Assistance Board for 1950*, Cmd. 8276, Appendix VIII.

[4] Ibid., p. 15. There is a good deal of common membership. There were 230 local advisory committees for the Ministry of National Insurance in 1951. See *Third Report of the Ministry of National Insurance*, 1951, p. 38.

them. The overwhelming majority of the 700 advisory bodies to which Mr. Attlee referred in 1949 contained officials of the central government among their members. In very few cases were the officials in a majority; in most cases they were a small minority; but almost always they were there. Sometimes departments do not have officials as full members of the committee; they have them there as assessors or observers. Thus the Ministry of Agriculture and Fisheries had two officials present as assessors to its Advisory Committee on the Provincial Agricultural Economic Service, and one official as assessor to its Advisory Board on the Licensing of Pest Control Articles. Sometimes a department has officials present as members and others present as assessors. The Ministry of Agriculture had one official as a member and one as an assessor on its Agricultural Statistics Advisory Committee. Not unlike the assessor is the observer, the official who attends to watch proceedings and who in practice tends to intervene or to guide discussion. The Air Ministry had two of its officials as members of its Air Training Corps Educational Advisory Committee and four as observers.

It is usual also for an official of the department concerned to act as secretary of an advisory committee, and his influence in this capacity will depend a good deal on his status in the department. In some cases an official acts as chairman of a committee to advise. This was the almost invariable practice in the series of advisory committees which were attached to the Ministry of Food at the height of its activities, but it was rare in the case of other departments.

This close association of officials of the departments with the committees set up to advise them is natural and necessary. The committees exist to place at the disposal of the departments the best advice they can offer on the matters which departments refer to them. The officials concerned in these matters must obviously be in close and direct touch with the committees, and a great deal of the advice they get can be best obtained by a process of discussion in which officials must take an active part. If officials were not present at the meetings of the committees and entitled to take a full part in the proceedings, the advice which the committees have to give might be general and vague and often irrelevant to the actual issues of administration with which officials are concerned. Officials should know the points upon which they need advice, and the best use can be made of a committee if it is enabled to direct its attention to the points about which officials of a department are concerned to receive guidance.

The official element upon committees to advise is not always confined to officials of the central government department concerned. Where a service is administered—like education—by central government and local authorities in partnership, it is usual to find local officials as well as central officials occupying places upon committees set up to advise the central government in these spheres. This is the case, for example, on the Central Advisory Councils for England and for Wales set up by the Ministry of Education and on the Central Advisory Council on Fire Brigades, which advises the Home Office. But the official element on many of these advisory committees is not drawn solely from central and local government; it comes also from organizations outside the government service. When an organization is invited to be represented on a committee to advise, it commonly chooses one of its officials or its chief official to represent it. The official element, whether drawn from within government or outside it, is strong upon and around committees to advise.

The presence of officials, particularly of government officials, upon a committee to advise can raise difficulties. If a committee's advice is to be published and if it concerns policy, an official may be reluctant or unable to concur in a report unless his department approves of it. As the greater part of the work of committees to advise, upon which officials sit as members, is done in private, and as their advice is offered in private, these difficulties seldom arise. In practice the non-departmental members of an advisory committee act almost like assessors to the officials. Where a committee to advise is expected or intends to publish its advice, it would usually be preferable for officials to attend its deliberations as assessors or observers or informants, rather than to be formally members of the committee.[1]

[1] The Working Party on the Recruitment and Training of Nurses (which reported in 1947) had attached to it a steering committee of officials from the departments concerned with whom it discussed its findings. But the Working Party alone was responsible for the report.

4

What place does the expert hold on these advisory bodies? It may be said at once that, from the nature of the function which advisory committees have to perform, it is inevitable that as a general rule experts will be needed among their membership. When the Minister of Works set up a committee in 1954 to advise him on policy and on special problems of felling and planting trees in the royal parks, it was natural that its members should have expert knowledge—the chairman was Sir William Taylor, a former Director-General of the Forestry Commission, and its members were Mr. R. C. B. Gardner, the Secretary of the Royal Forestry Society of England and Wales, Lord Hurcomb, a member of the Nature Conservancy and Chairman of the Advisory Committee on Bird Life in the Royal Parks, Mr. A. D. C. Le Sueur, a consultant in arboriculture, Mr. J. Macdonald, Director of Research and Education in the Forestry Commission, and Sir Edward Salisbury, the Director of the Royal Botanic Gardens at Kew.

When the Lord President of the Council sets up technical committees on hop research, on the control of weeds by chemical means, on bracken control, on the cultivation of maize and oil seed crops, on potato problems, on strawberry diseases, on sterility and infertility in cattle, or on pig diseases, he must include experts and technical specialists among the members of the committee. We should expect to find experts, too, as members of the Insecticide Standing Conference, the Medical Mycology Committee, the Dental Committee, the Vision Committee, and the Committee on Medical and Biological Applications of Nuclear Physics. On almost all the committees set up to advise the Department of Scientific and Industrial Research, too, experts are certain to find a place.

Even if we turn from these obviously highly technical matters associated with science, we find it essential to have experts on advisory committees in other spheres. The Advisory Committee on Buildings of Special Architectural and Historical Interest, set up by the Ministry of Town and Country Planning; the Board of Trade's Accountancy Committee, its Companies Act Consultative Committee, its Insurance Consultative Committee; the Ministry of Education's Advisory Councils for

England and Wales, its Handicapped Children Advisory Committee, its Commercial Education Committee, its Canteen Equipment Committee; or the Ministry of Labour's Engineering Advisory Panel, its Industrial Health Advisory Committee, or its National Advisory Council on Recruitment of Nurses and Midwives—to select a few examples from the 700 or so bodies existing in 1949—all required experts to be among their members, if they were to be effective in giving advice.

In legal matters, again, when advice is needed upon technical questions, the committees set up have necessarily been composed almost entirely of experts. Thus the Law Revision Committee set up by Lord Chancellor Sankey in 1934 with the duty 'to consider how far, having regard to the Statute Law and to judicial decisions, such legal maxims and doctrines as the Lord Chancellor may from time to time refer to the Committee require revision in modern conditions . . .' was composed of judges, practising lawyers, and academic experts on the law.[1] The same was true of such committees as those on the business of the courts,[2] the dispatch of business at common law,[3] the jurisdiction of quarter sessions,[4] and the circuit system.[5] These were not laymen's matters.

It must not be imagined, of course, that all the experts are to be found upon the committees. Far from it. Many more experts will be called in to give evidence or advice or information. The job of the experts on the committee is not only themselves to give expert advice, but both to know where other expert advice can be obtained and also to assist their colleagues on the committee in forming a judgement upon the advice tendered.

It should be remarked also that in some cases the experts will be drawn from government departments. In ministries where the scientific civil service plays a large part, its members may well sit upon advisory committees in association with ex-

[1] The Committee produced eight reports between 1934 and 1939, viz. Cmd. 4540 (1934), Cmd. 4546 (1934), Cmd. 4637 (1934), Cmd. 4770 (1934), Cmd. 5334 (1936), Cmd. 5449 (1937), Cmd. 6009 (1939), Cmd. 6032 (1939).
   A committee, similarly composed and known as the Law Reform Committee was set up by Lord Chancellor Simonds in 1952 'to consider, having regard especially to judicial decisions, what changes are desirable in such legal doctrines as the Lord Chancellor may from time to time refer to the Committee'. Its first report was Cmd. 8809 (1953).
[2] Cmd. 4265 (1933), Cmd. 4471 (1933), Cmd. 5066 (1936).
[3] Cmd. 5065 (1936).   [4] Cmd. 5252 (1936).   [5] Cmd. 5262 (1936).

perts from outside the service. Along with these expert scientists from the civil service there may be officials who are no more than general practitioners, responsible for the administration of scientific work or for work requiring scientific knowledge in the government service. Advisory committees have as one of their valuable functions the linking of the scientific expert inside the civil service with his colleagues outside the service and ensuring that the best advice is available to the government from both sides. This collaboration between experts is particularly valuable in the case of departments such as the Ministry of Supply, the Department of Scientific and Industrial Research, the Ministry of Health, and the Ministry of Agriculture.

5

It is difficult to proceed far in the discussion of the place of the expert upon committees to advise without considering another character in committee work who may often be himself an expert also—the interested party. For in seeking expert advice a government department often finds that it is the interested party to whom it must go. And it is sometimes the case that it is only after hearing the interested parties, and bringing them together to hear each other and perhaps to negotiate a little with each other, that a department can obtain the guidance it needs. With governments committed to planning and control of economic life, moreover, it is essential to obtain the co-operation of those affected by government policy. An official publication in 1948[1] asserted, for example, that 'Britain's economic planning must be on democratic lines. To secure this, the understanding and co-operation of those expected to carry it out must be sought from the beginning.' And there follows an account of the nature and functions of the more important advisory committees that exist in the economic field, on all of which interested parties had an acknowledged and important place. There was an Economic Planning Board, which was set up in July 1947 'to advise His Majesty's government on the best use of our economic resources, both for the realisation of a long-

[1] *Government and Industry: A Survey of Machinery for Consultation and Co-operation,* H.M.S.O. 1948. Reference Handbook No. 2 prepared by the Central Office of Information.

term plan and for remedial measures against our immediate difficulties'. Its chairman was an official, the chief planning officer of the government, and it was composed of three employers, three trade unionists, some government officials, and some economic experts. Interested parties, and in particular the representatives of employers and employees, were found also on such other advisory bodies as the National Production Advisory Council on Industry, and the National Joint Advisory Council (which was chiefly concerned with all matters affecting the relations between employers and workers),[1] as well as upon more specialized bodies associated with particular industries, such as the Building and Civil Engineering Joint Committee, the Shipbuilding Advisory Committee, the Engineering Industry Advisory Panel, or the National Brick Advisory Council.

Similar representation of interested parties is found on the committees to advise central departments at the regional and local levels. Employers and employees are all represented upon the bodies which advise the Ministry of Labour regionally and locally, such as its Local Employment Committees, its Juvenile Employment Committees, its Disablement Advisory Committees, its Building Training Advisory Committees, and its Agricultural Advisory Panels, to name only some of them.

The bodies so far discussed are standing or semi-permanent committees to advise. It is interesting to see how interested parties are associated in *ad hoc* committees. A good example is the setting up of the working parties for industry in 1945 and thereafter by Sir Stafford Cripps when he was President of the Board of Trade. These working parties were composed of representatives of the employers in an industry and of the employees of the industry in equal numbers, and to them was added a third element to represent the public interest, while an independent chairman presided over the whole party. As a rule there were four representatives each of the employers, employees, and of the public, making with the chairman a total of thirteen. Wages and conditions of labour were excluded from their terms of reference. They were invited 'to examine and inquire into the various schemes and suggestions put forward for improvements of organisation, production and distribution methods and processes in the industry, and to report as to the

[1] See *Annual Report of the Ministry of Labour for 1951*, pp. 148–9 and Appendix XI.

steps which should be taken in the national interest to strengthen the industry and render it more stable and more capable of meeting competition in the home and foreign markets'. Working parties composed on this model were set up for something like a score of industries. The government proposed to take action about these industries which had had a reprieve from nationalization. It believed that in the making of plans it was wise that the interested parties should be involved from the outset.

In still another kind of case an advisory committee representative of interested parties may work well. A department which is in the process of formulating or applying a policy may want to know, before it acts, what the interests feel. The series of committees attached to the Ministry of Food gives a good illustration of this case. The Ministry was advised by committees which included among others an Animal Feeding Stuffs Advisory Committee, a Bakery Advisory Panel, a Consultative Committee of the National Association of British and Irish Millers, a Flour Confectionery Panel, a Hay Advisory Committee, a Home-Grown Cereals Advisory Panel, a Bacon Industry Consultative Committee, a Kippering Advisory Committee, a National Jam Distribution Advisory Committee, a Consultative Conference on Rabbits and Poultry, a Domestic Salt Committee, and a Manufactured Pepper Consultative Committee. Now it is natural that on committees of this kind most of the members must be in the trade or business; they represent the producing or manufacturing or distributing interests. Sometimes there was one official only on the committee and he was the chairman; sometimes there was an official chairman and some other officials. The object of these committees was to discuss policy with the officials; they said what they wanted or what they could do or what they could stand; the officials endeavoured to discover from them what they needed to know in order to formulate or apply policy. The assessment of claims and the safeguarding of the public interest is usually in official hands. There is no reason to suppose that by this means valuable advice was not obtained from committees so constituted, although they contained no representatives of the consumers. Officials can often be good guardians of the public interest. And as the department had a policy to apply and intended to take action, the fact that the interests might not always agree did not lead to inaction.

6

But it is seldom that interested parties are left to themselves to provide advice to the government. It is usual to see to it that there is some other element on the committees to assist in the formulation of advice. The impartial expert or the layman or the party man, for example, may find a place alongside the interested parties, and in most cases the chairman will not himself be an interested party. The working parties set up by the Board of Trade provide good examples of the way in which other characters may be associated with interested parties.

It was an essential part of Sir Stafford Cripps's scheme of the working parties for industry that interested parties should be members of them. Indeed, it is suggested that at one stage in his consideration of the subject, he envisaged working parties consisting entirely of interested parties save for an independent chairman.[1] In the end, however, it was decided to include a group of members who were spoken of as representatives of the public interest in addition to the independent chairman. Thus the Cotton Working Party, the first to be set up, contained four representatives of the employers, four of the employees, and four other members, with a chairman in addition. Of the four other members one was an economist, one an engineer, one a scientist, and one an expert on factory organization.[2] The chairman was Sir George Schuster who had had wide administrative experience both in government service and in the world of commerce and public affairs. A similar plan was followed in the other working parties.[3] The independent members were scientists or economists or engineers—experts in some sphere relevant to the industry concerned—and one was usually specially qualified

[1] *The Economist*, 15 Sept. 1945, p. 362.
[2] 414 H.C. Deb., 5th ser., cols. 692–6.
[3] The names of the members of ten working parties appointed in March 1946 are printed in 420 H.C. Deb., 5th ser., cols. 779–82. The working parties concerned were those on carpets, domestic glassware, linoleum, lace, cutlery, and china clay. The members of the cotton, pottery, furniture, hosiery, and boots and shoes working parties are in 414 H.C. Deb., 5th ser., cols. 695–6.

in regard to the particular industry. In comparison with the interested parties, however, they were not narrow specialists, as a rule, but they had some specialized knowledge and were nearer general practitioners than laymen.

The working parties had a specific and limited task to perform. But the same principles which determined their composition are applied to standing or permanent advisory bodies. Here again the Board of Trade provides a very good example in the Cinematograph Films Council, a body set up to advise the President of the Board on matters concerning the production and distribution of British films. An element of negotiation entered into the functioning of the Council, for the majority of the membership of twenty-two people represented the interested parties—four represented the makers of British films, two the film renters, five the film exhibitors, and four the persons employed by makers, renters, or exhibitors of British films. The remaining seven members, including the chairman, were independent members. Among the seven have been included experts and laymen, the two categories being represented at the extreme in 1951, for example, in the person of two professors, one of whom, Sir Arnold Plant, was an outstanding expert, and the other[1] was very obviously a layman.[2]

The history of the working of the Council gives a good example of the strength and weakness of a body composed in this way. Sometimes the Council has made unanimous recommendations; sometimes, when the interests could not agree, the Council's recommendations were made by a majority consisting of some of the interests plus the independent members; sometimes no majority report was possible and the various groups expressed their own views to the President. The views of the independent members were always of importance, and were considered carefully by the representatives of the trade. Unanimity, and failing that the support of the independent members, was expected to be a valuable help to the trade in any recommendations that were put forward. The President would want to know what the independent members thought, and they

[1] Professor K. C. Wheare.

[2] It is interesting to notice that there were two Labour M.P.'s on the Council in the same year, one among the four representatives of persons employed in the industry, the other an independent member. It is an example of the party man being in one case also an interested party and in the other an independent.

were careful always to make their position known. The function of the independent members was to consider and judge the views of the various trade interests as against each other and in relation to the public interest. The influence of the chairman, the Earl of Drogheda, and of the very experienced expert independent member, Professor Sir Arnold Plant, in particular, had a great deal to do with the remarkable unanimity of the Council's recommendations.

It is interesting to notice how often unanimity is achieved upon committees to advise when interested parties are included in their membership. Here again the working parties set up by the Board of Trade give some examples. Out of seventeen working parties, thirteen presented unanimous reports,[1] two presented reports which were unanimous subject to one or two reservations,[2] while the remaining two were more seriously divided. The experience of most of the working parties led them to express a belief in the value of this form of advisory body and to suggest the setting up of some permanent machinery for each industry based upon the representation of interested parties supplemented by independent members and an independent chairman. One report at least made a specific reference to its confidence in this form of organization.[3] The two working parties which proved to be divided were those on the cotton industry, under the chairmanship of Sir George Schuster, and on the boot and shoe industry, under Sir Thomas Bennett, an architect. In no case did the division go so far as to lead to the presentation of a separate minority report, but in the report of the Cotton Working Party there was a lengthy memorandum of dissent by three of the four employers' representatives along with three of the independent members, a rejoinder to the dissenters by the four employees' representatives, a further note by one of the dissenting independent members, and a minute by the fourth of the employers' representatives. In the Boots and Shoes Working Party what division there was, again, showed itself in a dissenting memorandum by the five employers' representatives, and there were additional remarks by two independent

---

[1] Namely, the reports on the jute, china-clay, wool, pottery, linoleum, lace, jewellery, furniture, cutlery, rubber-proofed clothing, heavy clothing, light clothing, and carpet industries.

[2] Namely, the reports on the hosiery and glassware industries.

[3] *The Report of the Working Party on the Carpet Industry*, p. iv.

members. The slight difference in the Hosiery Working Party concerned the proposed council for the industry and here the employers' representatives dissented. On the other hand, the representatives of the employers and of the employees in the Scottish branch of the industry were unanimous in objecting to the proposed council so far as Scotland was concerned. Looked at as a whole, however, the degree of unanimity was remarkable.

7

The role of the chairman in the work of committees to advise is clearly important. Where the subject-matter upon which a committee is to advise is technical, should the chairman be an expert or not? In some cases the answer seems clear. It is not surprising to find that the chairman of the Advisory Committee on Sand and Gravel to the Ministry of Housing and Local Government had, after his name, the letters F.G.S., M.Inst.C.E., M.I.Mech.E., P.P.I.Struct.E., M.Inst.W.E., and M.Cons.E., among others.[1] It is natural that the chairman of the Scientific Advisory Committee of the Ministry of Defence should be a scientist and that of the National Advisory Council of the Ministry of Education an educationist. But it may be surmised that both will be general practitioners in relation to many of the other members of the committees over which they preside. In many technical subjects it is clear that either an expert, if the terms of reference of the committee are narrow enough, or a general practitioner, if they are wider, will make the best chairman, for no layman would find the discussion intelligible.

But if we leave narrowly technical spheres we find at once that there is scope for the lay chairman. And here again some examples may be taken from the working parties. Their chairmen in almost all cases were laymen, some more obviously so than others. Thus the chairman of the Linoleum Working Party, General Sir Ronald Adam, had just retired from the post of Adjutant-General to the Forces and might be thought, by the ignorant outsider, to be more likely to be familiar with carpets than linoleum, but his appointment was defended on the ground that he was 'a very able person who is not con-

[1] See *Consolidated List of Government Publications*, 1952, p. 388.

nected with the industry'.[1] The chairman of the Carpets Working Party, on the other hand, was Mr. Geoffrey Cunliffe, the managing director of the British Aluminium Co. Ltd., an official from outside the government service, but apparently a layman. Equally lay in status was the chairman of the Jute Working Party, Mr. S. J. L. Hardie, who was chairman of the British Oxygen Co.; the chairman of the Wool Working Party, Sir Richard Hopkins, who had been Permanent Secretary to the Treasury; the chairman of the Jewellery and Silverware Working Party, Mr. C. R. Morris, who was a headmaster, but had had experience first as a philosophy tutor at an Oxford college and later as a war-time civil servant; and the chairman of the Cutlery Working Party, Mr. J. L. Musgrave, who was managing director or director of a great number of engineering firms. Only the chairmen of the China Clay Working Party, Dr. W. R. Jones, and the Heavy Clothing Working Party, Sir Cecil Weir, could be described as experts in the field of their working party's activity, the former being a university professor with special knowledge of the subject, the latter, though a leading industrialist, having just concluded a period of war-time service as Director-General of Equipment and Stores in the Ministry of Supply. It might be concluded too, that as the chairman of the Lace Working Party was a woman, Miss Lucy Sutherland, Principal of Lady Margaret Hall, Oxford, and the chairman of the Hand-blown Domestic Glassware Working Party, Mr. Clough Williams-Ellis, was an architect and an artist, they brought some special knowledge and skill to their task. Generally speaking, however, it was clear that in choosing the chairmen of these and other working parties what was sought was independence and general experience, knowledge, and capacity.[2] They had almost all had administrative experience as officials, either in government service or outside, and they had all shown ability and experience as chairmen. Between them they provide as good a collection of examples of the lay chairman as could be found.

On the whole the layman is a comparatively rare bird on

[1] Sir Stafford Cripps, answering a supplementary question in the House of Commons on 11 Mar. 1946. 420 H.C. Deb., 5th ser., col. 784.

[2] The qualifications of these ten chairmen were set out in a written answer to a question by Sir Waldron Smithers on 18 Mar. 1946. 420 H.C. Deb., 5th ser., cols. 300–2.

committees to advise. This is not surprising. From the functions which these committees are expected to perform in advising central departments, it is almost inevitable that the expert and the interested party should play the biggest part. It is true that occasionally the interested party may be a layman also, but his presence upon the committee will be in his capacity as an interested party not as a layman. The layman's opportunties upon committees to advise will arise from one or two causes. He may be needed as chairman, as the examples just quoted will illustrate. Or he may be needed to dilute or modify the expert's strong wine upon committees where considerations of common sense or what is reasonable and practicable may be of importance. Or he may be needed as an independent member where it is thought that the interested parties should have their views submitted to the scrutiny and judgement of persons who are not themselves interested.

Upon some of the committees to advise which operate at the local or regional level of a department's activity, however, we find lay members playing a larger part, and performing the function of bringing the point of view of the ordinary citizen to bear upon official action. The best examples of this are perhaps the advisory committees attached to the offices of the National Assistance Board and the Ministry of National Insurance. It is interesting to notice that from the first the administration of assistance by the central government was associated with committees of local people who were invited to advise the officials upon the carrying out of their duties. Before the central government took over assistance, it had been administered by committees of local authorities, and it would seem that the central department did not wish to dispense entirely with the lay elements in administration. It was not possible, of course, to confide the actual administration of assistance to local committees, because the service was a central responsibility and administration had to be in the hands of the officials of the central government, but it was thought wise to provide officials with eyes and ears, and perhaps with a heart, so that their administration might be flexible and human. When the Unemployment Assistance Act was passed in 1934, therefore, advisory committees were established. The Unemployment Assistance Board came gradually to see that these committees were a most valuable help to it, and when the scope of assistance was widened in 1946 the use of advisory committees was continued. Although the National Assistance Act speaks of the members of these committees as having local knowledge and experience, it is not intended that they should be experts in the work of the Assistance Board. They are, at their best, interested and knowledgeable and intelligent laymen and one of their functions is to bring a questioning and critical and unofficial attitude to bear upon the work of official administration. Here is a sphere in which the layman can render valuable service upon the work of committees to advise.[1]

In choosing the members of these local advisory committees, however, the departments pay some attention to organized interests, which in some sense come near to being interested parties. Members of committees are chosen, in some measure, from panels of people nominated by employers' organizations, trade unions, local authorities, and certain social welfare organizations. The principal qualification is, however, that they are interested and knowledgeable persons; they do not sit on the advisory committees as representatives of the organizations which nominate them.

8

What judgement can we make upon the value of committees to advise? The range of their operation is so great that general conclusions can be attempted only with diffidence. What can be said at the outset with some confidence is that when departments bring an advisory committee into existence because they feel the need of obtaining knowledge either from experts or from interested parties, then it is almost certain that the committee will be of some use. The advisory committees attached to such departments as the Ministries of Supply, Food, Health, and Labour, or the Department of Scientific and Industrial Research, or to the Board of Trade, have been created usually because the officials in those departments felt the need of knowledge which was not available to them inside the department, or felt the need to discuss what they knew or proposed with people outside whose knowledge or opinion would be valuable

[1] An interesting account of the work of these local advisory committees is given by Miss Enid Harrison in *Public Administration*, vol. xxi, Spring 1953.

to them. It may be that some of these advisory committees meet seldom, but they are available for consultation when needed.

When, however, advisory committees are set up in order to placate public opinion or to give an impression that consultation is occurring or to keep the experts and interested parties employed and happy, their value is doubtful. It is difficult to escape the impression that at times motives of this kind have entered into the calculations of those who have set up committees to advise. There is nothing necessarily wicked about this. Political considerations sometimes require the setting up of committees of whose usefulness to the department in the way of advice officials, and ministers too, may well be sceptical. Sometimes the terms of reference of an advisory body are so wide and general that it is difficult to see what precise job it is to perform. It may survey the field and make recommendations from time to time, but unless it is asked to offer advice on a subject about which a department really needs its opinion and about which it intends to take some action, its usefulness is strictly limited. Such advisory bodies as the Council for Wales, for example, have such wide terms of reference that their advice can seldom be to the point. When such bodies exist, it often becomes the preoccupation of a department to think of something which can keep them busy. They may be intended to pacify or placate certain interests and in so doing they are not without value. But in comparison with advisory bodies dealing with topics closely related to the needs of departments, they are of relatively little value.

Size is important in determining the usefulness of a committee to advise. It may be said, with a little dogmatism perhaps, that if a committee to advise is so large that its members have to stand up to address each other, it is unlikely to be effective. Where an advisory body is large, it can be effective only if it breaks itself up into sub-committees, and meets as a full committee to discuss the reports of these sub-committees or to discuss certain questions of general principle. The work of such bodies as the Central Advisory Council on Education of twenty-one members for England and nineteen for Wales, of the Secondary Schools Examination Council of thirty or so, of the Central Housing Advisory Committee of thirty-one, of the main committee of women's organizations on Fuel Economy of sixty-four members, or of the Advisory Committee on Education in the Colonies of twenty-eight can hardly be effectively carried out otherwise. Occasionally—as with the National Production Advisory Council on Industry which consists of twenty-six members—the function of an advisory body may be that of general debate and discussion. But where it is expected to go beyond this either it must be small or if it is large it must work through sub-committees. When the National Joint Advisory Council was set up in October 1939, with its membership of thirty—fifteen nominated by the British Employers' Confederation and fifteen by the Trades Union Congress—it realized that, meeting quarterly and with so large a membership, it should establish a smaller body which could meet more frequently and could consider problems in greater detail. Therefore in May 1940 it established the Joint Consultative Committee, of seven representatives from each side, and thus the larger and the smaller body were enabled each to perform its appropriate advisory function. In fact most advisory committees are small, and where they are large they break up into panels or sub-committees. If they do not do so it is difficult to escape the conclusion either that they do not mean business or that they are not intended to do business.

It is wise to guard against advisory committees being too big; it is wise also to guard against the members themselves being too big. There is a tendency to appoint to some committees, particularly those at the national level, eminent and distinguished persons who are found in practice to be so eminent and so busy and so remote from the day to day work of the organizations they represent, that they are in fact not of much use as advisers. They circulate from one advisory body to another, seldom very well informed about the business of any one committee, and too much preoccupied with great matters to devote the necessary time to mastering a subject. It is true that upon some committees to advise, these great names are suitably placed, for they are often in the position of being able themselves to speak with authority on behalf of their organization or to commit it to some decision. Generally speaking, however, there is a class of eminent person—in the industrial, commercial, trade union, and scientific worlds particularly—whose presence is required upon so many bodies of importance and whose day is made up of attendance at so many committees, that his value upon committees to advise is not very great. The best advice is often to be obtained from persons of less eminence, still so little in demand that they are able to master fully one branch of knowledge or activity. It is upon advisory committees composed of people of this kind that valuable work can be done.

An important and perhaps unexpected result of the use of committees to advise is that they strengthen rather than weaken the hands of the government officials. And it is right to recognize that this may have its disadvantages. Through them officials have the opportunity to 'nobble' their most expert and influential potential critics. There is the risk that members of advisory committees may become a kind of private appendage of the department, bound to secrecy, giving advice but unable to say in public what that advice was or to carry criticism of the department into public. In some cases, it is true, the advice of a committee is published in a report. In some cases a minister is required to publish the advice he receives. The Minister of National Insurance, for example, is obliged to publish the report of his National Insurance Advisory Committee upon draft regulations submitted to them and to state how far he has accepted their recommendations and why he has rejected any of them.[1] Some committees to advise publish an annual report, though in few cases is it very informative. It is right to recognise, however, that it would be impracticable to expect the advice of committees to be published in very many cases, for it is offered at a stage when consultations are confidential and policy is under consideration.

Members of advisory committees, accordingly, cannot be completely free to say in public what the Minister or department is proposing to do. As they are involved in the machinery of government they must to some extent come under the influence if not the provisions of the Official Secrets Act. But in so doing they are prevented from criticizing government policy in public, or may do so only when it is too late. Once the department has placed them upon its advisory committee or council, their teeth are drawn. The ordinary citizen may be able to rely

[1] See Enid Harrison, 'The Work of the National Insurance Advisory Committee' in *Public Administration*, vol. xxx, Summer 1952.

upon them to give good advice in private, and to criticize the department in private, but he cannot hope to hear from them in public and he cannot know what they think. There is a risk in all this that all the best experts, all those who might influence or guide public opinion, may be captured by the departments, placed on their advisory committees, and so won over to the official side from the start.

And this leads to a further disadvantage. The drawing of the teeth of the experts may lead to the drawing of the teeth of Parliament and the public. An illustration of the way in which this works is sometimes found when, in the House of Commons, members attempt to criticize some part of the government's policy. They are assured by the Minister at once that what is being done has been done only after this or that advisory committee was consulted, that the policy has the support of all the interests concerned, and that it has been very carefully worked out with them. It is then indicated, perhaps explicitly, that as the scheme has been agreed to by all sides it must not be touched at all, otherwise it will fall to pieces and all the negotiations will have to start over again. Now it is right, of course, that this consultation and agreement should be obtained, but it must be stressed at the same time that it is open to abuse. It can mean that the House of Commons will find itself reduced to a body which must apply a rubber stamp to a policy or a decision which has been produced by the officials, the experts, and the interested parties not merely of Whitehall but also of Transport House, and of the headquarters of such other interests as are concerned in the matter. And it is often a danger that in these discussions, while the interests of the parties directly involved are represented, no one can be there to represent the public interest. Admittedly the official from Whitehall will have the public interest in mind, but why should not members of Parliament also be allowed to criticize the proposals effectively? Yet more and more they are liable to be confronted with a *fait accompli* as a result of the close co-operation of a department and its advisory committees.

While this danger should not be stated in extreme terms, it may be emphasized that members of committees to advise have a duty to consider whether they are not too much under the influence of a department, whether they are not serving an official interest rather than the public interest, whether they are not thinking of Whitehall and forgetting Westminster. If Whitehall can claim the monopoly of knowledge and the agreement of the interested parties, what can Westminster do? Has not the development of this whole elaborate and remarkably efficient machinery of committees to advise strengthened Whitehall at the expense of Westminster?

CHAPTER IV

Committees to Inquire

I

COMMITTEES to inquire are usually also committees to advise. It is seldom that a committee is asked to find out the facts of a situation without being asked also to suggest what should be done about it. Among the important exceptions are committees such as those set up under the Tribunals of Inquiry (Evidence) Act, 1921, of which that presided over by Mr. Justice Lynskey in 1948 is a well-known example,[1] whose task it is to investigate allegations of malpractice or mal-administration and to find the facts. Committees of inquiry into accidents and disasters are similarly often restricted in their terms of reference to the discovery of the cause of the occurrences. Generally speaking, however, the making of recommendations or the offering of advice forms a part, varying in importance from case to case, of the function of committees to inquire.

But although, from this point of view, committees to inquire may appear to form part of the wider class of committees to advise, and to fall to be considered under that head, they exhibit features which make it preferable to discuss them separately. The task which is committed to them and the way in which they set about it have certain characteristics which distinguish them from other types of committees to advise. In the first place their actual investigation of the situation or problem referred to them is regarded as of at least equal importance to the recommendations which they may make. Their report is looked to as an exposition of the situation or problem. They are expected to take evidence and in many cases this evidence is published, and is of interest and value equal to that of the committee's report —and sometimes of greater interest and value. Moreover, the

---

[1] Cmd. 7616 (1949) Another example was the committee presided over by Mr. Justice Porter (as he then was) to inquire whether any unauthorized disclosure was made of information relating to the Budget for 1936. Cmd. 5184.

report of the committee and its recommendations are expected to bear some relation to the evidence offered to them. Their verdict should not be contrary to the weight of the evidence. Their report should be something in the nature of a summing up and a judgement. It should constitute an authoritative contribution to the public discussion and consideration of the subject.

Not all committees to inquire exhibit these characteristics to the same degree. In some the recommendations may be of greater interest and importance than the exposition of the problem; in others it may be true to say that it does not matter what they recommend as long as they produce a full and fair and penetrating analysis of the situation. What is certain, how-ever, is that the investigation is an important part of the func-tion of a committee to inquire, and that this will influence both the choice of the persons to serve on such a committee and also the relative roles of the seven characters in committee work in whom we are interested. Its task is distinctive and it is proper therefore to consider separately the way in which it performs that task.

2

The commonest forms in which committees to inquire are met with nowadays in British government are the royal com-mission and the departmental or inter-departmental committee. The royal commission enjoys, in form at least, a higher status, for its members are appointed by the Queen whereas members of departmental and inter-departmental committees are ap-pointed by a minister or ministers. It is employed, therefore, for inquiries into matters which are considered to be of very great public interest and importance or which for some other reason appear to demand the dignity of a royal commission. Yet prac-tice is not rigid or uniform in these matters, and it would be possible to find matters of equal importance being investigated by a departmental committee and by a royal commission. What is certain is that royal commissions are comparatively rare;[1] the

[1] They were more common in the latter half of the nineteenth century. See H. McD. Clokie and J. W. Robinson, *Royal Commissions of Inquiry*. The authors seem, however, to attach too much importance to the difference between a royal commission and a departmental committee of inquiry, and as a result misinterpret the significance of the decline in the use of royal commissions.

greater part of the field of committees to inquire is occupied by departmental and inter-departmental committees.

One striking difference of practice between this century and the nineteenth century is the relative unimportance among committees to inquire of select committees of the House of Commons. They are still used, but their operation is almost entirely confined to inquiries into matters concerned with the working or privileges of the House of Commons itself. From time to time committees of the House investigate its procedure, or its control over delegated legislation or over the working of the nationalized industries; its committee of privileges inquires into any alleged breach of the privileges of the House. It is extremely rare, however, for a select committee of the House to be charged with the investigation of some public question or some problem of economic or social or political life.[1] In the nineteenth century select committees of inquiry were extensively used, sharing the field with royal commissions. Some of the great social reforms of the nineteenth century owed much to the investigations and reports of select committees of the House of Commons.[2]

3

Who are the people who sit on committees to inquire? The answer in respect of select committees of the House of Commons is simple and it is also significant, for it helps to explain why their use has declined. They are composed entirely of members of the House and in consequence entirely of party men. This means that most matters which involve policy cannot be confided to a select committee.[3] Select committees labour under the drawback, too, that since their membership is confined to members of the House, outside experts or laymen or interested parties are unable to take part in their deliberations. And finally,

[1] Among the few recent examples are the select committees on capital punishment of 1929 (H.C. 15 of 1930–1) and on shop assistants of 1930 (H.C. 148 of 1930–1), and on the Army Act and Air Force Act of 1953 (H.C. 223 of 1953–4).

[2] See *A People's Conscience*, by S. Gordon and T. G. B. Cocks, an account of the work of select committees in the early nineteenth century which investigated prison conditions, police, chimney boys, lunatic asylums, children in factories, and transportation to the colonies.

[3] The fact that, in practice, members of select committees of inquiry do not behave as party men is the result of confining their inquiries to matters in which party policy is not involved.

the number of inquiries now undertaken would be beyond the time and energies of members of Parliament. For reasons of this sort, the use of other kinds of committee to inquire has developed.

Upon these other kinds of committee to inquire, members of Parliament are found from time to time. The statutory commission on Indian Constitutional Reform (the Simon Commission) appointed in 1927 was composed entirely of members of the House of Commons and House of Lords and was representative of all three parties.[1] More usually one or two members of the House of Commons are included on committees. Occasionally they may occupy a seat because they represent interested parties, such as trade unions, or because they have some special knowledge or experience of the matter under inquiry, but more often they are there as politicians providing the party element in inquiries into matters of public importance. Thus members of the House of Commons were included on the Ullswater Committee of inquiry into the B.B.C. in 1935–6[2] and on the Beveridge Committee on the same subject in 1949–50.[3] It is usual in cases of this kind to see to it that the two major parties, at least, are represented. One valuable result of this practice has been pointed out by Mr. Herbert Morrison: 'It is wise', he wrote, 'in the appointment of all committees to consider the inclusion of M.P.s, for this gives them valuable experience and ensures well-informed contributions to parliamentary debate.'[4]

4

It may be useful to consider next the role of the official and in particular of the government official. And here it should be noticed that the influence of officials can be exercised in ways quite distinct from their being members of the committees. When ministers appoint committees to inquire, and determine their terms of reference and select their members, they are advised by officials. Some ministers of course will have more say than others in these matters, and some committees will owe more

---

[1] Cmd. 3568 and 3569 (1930). Sir John Simon, the chairman, was a Liberal, Mr. Attlee and Mr. Vernon Hartshorn were Labour, and Lord Burnham, Lord Strathcona, the Hon. Edward Cadogan, and Col. Lane Fox were Conservatives. The report was unanimous.   [2] Cmd. 5091 (1936).
[3] Cmd. 8116 (1951).   [4] *Government and Parliament*, p. 275.

to a minister's personal views and selection than others. But generally speaking a minister has little time for the detailed consideration of suitable names, and officials must be largely concerned in the process of selection. Where terms of reference are concerned, in some cases a minister or the Cabinet will have a large say in determining their scope, but even here officials will have advised and drafted and will have suggested pitfalls from which it is desirable to be protected. There can be no doubt that by the time a committee to inquire has been appointed, generally speaking, the officials will have exercised a considerable influence upon the work it will be likely to do.

When the extent of official influence upon committees to inquire is being considered it is important to remember also that a committee's secretary or secretaries are usually officials and are usually officials of the department or departments which have set up the committees. It would be foolish to conclude from this that the department runs the committee. A great deal will depend upon the secretary's influence upon his committee and the department's influence upon the secretary. The influence of a secretary will depend upon his seniority and experience, upon the nature of the committee's inquiry, and upon the status and capacities of the chairman and the other members of the committee. Any secretary has scope for influence. He prepares the agenda, in consultation with the chairman; he has a large hand in organizing the committee's work and particularly in arranging for witnesses; he must advise the chairman and the committee from time to time upon their terms of reference and the fruitfulness or otherwise of proposed lines of inquiry. In some cases he has a large hand in preparing the first draft of the committee's report.

But, while he is the committee's servant, he is at the same time an official of a government department, and it is in no way improper for him to attempt to see that the views of his department—if it has any—receive favourable consideration from the committee. At times he may think, as an official in a departmental hierarchy, that it is in no way inconsistent with his duty as a servant of the committee to discuss with his colleagues and superiors in the department the lines along which the committee's recommendations appear to be going, so that action may be taken, if it is thought fit, to encourage the committee to form different conclusions. The extent to which such action by a secretary is wise or likely to succeed will vary a great deal. Considerable discretion and tact will be called for, if a committee is not to resent departmental nursing and guidance. None the less, it is clear that through the secretary there is an opportunity for official influence, difficult as it is to judge how great that influence may be.

In some cases we find officials from the departments concerned being appointed to membership of committees to inquire. This is by no means the invariable practice—unlike the committees to advise, where as explained in the last chapter, it is a common thing for officials to be members of the committees. But examples can easily be found. A most striking example was the Committee on Ministers' Powers appointed by the Lord Chancellor in 1929.[1] Upon it there sat no less than three heads of important departments—the head of the Lord Chancellor's department itself, Sir Claud Schuster, the Permanent Secretary to the Treasury, Sir Warren Fisher, and the Permanent Under-Secretary of State at the Home Office, Sir John Anderson. The Royal Commission on Licensing in England and Wales, of 1929, included a high official of the Home Office, Sir John Pedder.[2] The Inter-Departmental Committee on Children and the Cinema which reported in 1950[3] included among its members an official from each of the three departments which jointly established the Committee—the Home Office, the Ministry of Education, and the Scottish Office.

Sometimes an official is actually chairman of a committee to inquire. Sir Godfrey Ince, of the Ministry of Labour, was chairman of the Committee on the Juvenile Employment Service of 1945. The chairman of the committee set up in 1943 to consider the position of scientists in government departments[4] was Sir Alan Barlow, a high Treasury official, and one of the other three members was the chief official of the Department of Scientific and Industrial Research.

Officials who are members of committees to inquire or are chairmen of them will naturally act to some extent as channels or instruments of departmental influence upon a committee's deliberations and decisions, and their influence will usually be

---

[1] Its report is Cmd. 4060 (1932).   [2] Cmd. 3988 (1932).
[3] Cmd. 7945 (1950).   [4] Cmd. 6679 (1945).

greater than that of officials who act as secretaries of such committees. They will feel completely free, unembarrassed by any possible conflict of loyalties, to consult their colleagues in the department on the course of the committee's deliberations and they may receive instructions about the line which they should take. They are in a position, too, to exercise influence by showing reluctance to sign any report which conflicts with their department's policies or which appears to criticize what their department has done. They are likely also to claim some share in the drafting of a report, for this is the kind of task with which they are accustomed to deal and which forms a regular and normal part of their day's work. They are skilled, too, in placing their views and proposals before a committee in written form— a talent which may place them at some advantage over their non-official colleagues who are not so apt in expressing themselves convincingly in writing. In expressing their views they have behind them also all the resources of their department.

A role which officials might play on committees to inquire is well illustrated by the experience of the Inter-Departmental Committee on Social Insurance and Allied Services, set up in 1941 under the chairmanship of Sir William Beveridge. This Committee consisted, apart from its chairman, entirely of officials, each of them the expert representative of one of the departments concerned in the inquiry. The justification for this official nature of the Committee was that the government conceived the work of the Committee to consist in the consideration of administrative issues rather than issues of policy, and who would be better fitted to deal with these than a committee of the officials concerned, presided over by a clear-headed, experienced chairman? But quite soon the chairman made it clear that he conceived the Committee's function to go far beyond administrative arrangements, and he raised big issues of policy. The Treasury

realized that the Committee were going to deal not with administrative detail, but with fundamental problems, and that the members of the Committee, being Civil Servants, could not, without consulting their ministers, sign a Report answering the questions that would be asked of them. If they signed after consulting their Ministers, they would thereby commit the Ministers individually and the government, before the Report had been seen as a whole.[1]

[1] See Lord Beveridge's autobiography, *Power and Influence*, p. 298.

It was decided, therefore, that the officials on the Committee must act as advisers or assessors only and that they would not sign the report. In the result, although the officials remained members of the Committee and took a full part in all its work, including the examination of witnesses and the discussion of the report, Sir William Beveridge alone signed the report.[1]

It is difficult to avoid the conclusion that if officials are members of committees to inquire, and if issues of policy are involved in the committee's terms of reference, they must, as a rule, either attempt to convert the committee to their department's view or, if they fail to do so, decline to sign the report. In either case they are likely to cause embarrassment to the non-official members of the committee. The view of the Treasury, in the case of the Beveridge Committee, that officials should be advisers or assessors was surely right, and it would seem to be applicable to most committees to inquire. Once it became clear that policy and not merely administrative arrangement was to be discussed by the Committee, it was proper for the Chancellor of the Exchequer to say that the Committee needed reconstruction. Indeed it is clear that the Chancellor realized that the wrong type of committee had been chosen when he suggested to Sir William Beveridge 'that it might be advisable to add to the Committee two or three non-departmental representatives who would make and sign the Report with me [i.e. Beveridge]'.[2]

On committees to inquire, where policy arises, the place for officials then is as assessors or as witnesses; it is seldom upon the committee itself. With committees to advise the situation is different. There, as a rule, it is the non-departmental members, the experts or interested parties for example, who are there to advise officials; their function is largely consultative. Issues of policy are clearly the officials' responsibility and they make what use they think fit of the advice of their fellow members of a committee. Even here, however, it may sometimes be wiser for officials not to be members of the committee.

In considering the official element in committees to inquire, it is proper to mention also that it is common to find among the

---

[1] Ibid., p. 300 and pp. 303 ff. The Report is Cmd. 6404 (1942) and the position of the officials is explained in para. 40.

[2] Ibid., p. 299. Sir William Beveridge comments: 'I did not welcome this suggestion, but could hardly reject it myself.' In the outcome it was not proceeded with.

members of such committees officials who have retired from the civil service. Indeed, a retired senior official is often in great demand for committee work as a member or as chairman. Thus Sir Maurice Holmes, Permanent Secretary of the Ministry of Education from 1937 to 1945, was chairman of the East African Salaries Commission in 1947 and of the Caribbean Public Services Unification Commission in 1948, two committees of inquiry set up by the Colonial Office. Sir Thomas Gardiner, who was Permanent Secretary of the Post Office from 1936 to 1945, is greatly in demand by committees to inquire. He was chairman, for example, of the Committee on the Organization, Structure, and Remuneration of the Professional Accountant Class in the Civil Service in 1951, and a member of the Royal Commission on Scottish Affairs of 1952. Sir Ernest Gowers, formerly chairman of the Board of Inland Revenue, has a long record as a chairman or member of committees to inquire. He was chairman, for example, of the committee to inquire into the admission of women to the foreign service in 1945; of the committee of inquiry into the closing hours of shops in 1946;[1] of the Committee on the Preservation of Historic Houses in 1949;[2] of the Committee on Health, Welfare, and Safety in Non-Industrial Employment in 1949;[3] of the Royal Commission on Capital Punishment of 1949–53,[4] of the Committee on Foot and Mouth Disease of 1952–4.[5] The Committee on the Political Activities of Civil Servants, appointed by the Treasury in 1949, included among its members a former Permanent Secretary to the Treasury, Sir Richard Hopkins.

While these retired officials are in many cases sitting upon committees whose work is not connected with their former departments, and while it should not be assumed that even if their former departments were concerned, they would necessarily agree with the policies these departments now pursue, it is proper to remark that retired officials are likely to have sympathy for official methods and points of view, and that their influence upon committees is likely to be upon the official side. This must not be exaggerated nor wholeheartedly condemned, but at the same time it should not be ignored.

[1] Cmd. 7105 (1947).   [2] 63–116 (1950).
[3] Cmd. 7664 (1949).   [4] Cmd. 8932 (1953).
[5] Cmd. 9214 (1954).

5

It is difficult to decide in what circumstances interested parties should sit upon committees to inquire. One recalls the opinion of the Departmental Committee on the Procedure of Royal Commissions, which reported in 1910: 'A Commission selected on the principle of representing various interests starts with a serious handicap against the probability of harmony in its work, and perhaps even of a practical result from its labours.' The Committee remarked that 'appointments have sometimes been made to Commissions of individuals whose proper place would rather have been in the witness box than on the tribunal'.[1] The classic cases that are usually quoted in this connexion are the Sankey and the Samuel Commissions on the Coal Industry. The Sankey Commission of 1919 contained representatives of the interested parties—three mine-owners nominated by the Mining Association, three union officials nominated by the Miners' Federation, three economists nominated by the same body, and three representatives of the main industries dependent on coal, nominated by the government. First of all, at the interim stage, the Commission produced three reports, one signed by the chairman and the three representatives of industries dependent on coal, another signed by the three union officials and the three economists, and a third signed by the three mine-owners.[2] At the next stage of the inquiry, the Commission presented four reports, one by the chairman alone, another, as before, by the three union officials and the three economists, a third by the three mine-owners and two of the representatives of the industries dependent on coal, and a fourth by one of these latter representatives.[3]

Contrast with this, it is suggested, the composition and outcome of the Samuel Commission of 1925. Its members were not interested parties but independent persons—one, Sir Herbert Lawrence, a banker and industrialist who had also been a distinguished soldier, another, Sir William Beveridge, an economist with civil service experience, another, Mr. Kenneth Lee, a leading cotton manufacturer. The result was a unanimous report.[4] And the conclusion we are asked to draw from this is that it is

[1] Cd. 5235 (1910), p. 6.
[2] Cmd. 359 (1919).
[3] Cmd. 360 (1919).
[4] Cmd. 2600 (1926).

inadvisable to have interested parties upon committees to inquire. The matter is not as simple as that, however, and it needs some more careful examination.

It is possible to state with fair confidence that there are certain circumstances in which interested parties ought not to be placed upon committees to inquire. To begin with, the old rule that a man should not be judge in his own cause should apply. If a committee has been set up to inquire into the truth or validity of some charges or allegations or opinions that have been put forward, or into the advisability or practicability of some proposals that have been advocated, it would seldom be right that those who make the charges or advocate the proposals or opinions under inquiry should themselves be represented upon the committee to inquire. This is abundantly clear in the case of a tribunal of inquiry, such as those presided over by Mr. Justice Porter or Mr. Justice Lynskey, and it would apply in most cases to committees whose terms of reference required them to behave judicially, or to adjudicate rather like a tribunal. The Monopolies Commission, a permanent committee of inquiry, whose function it is to investigate the extent to which monopolistic tendencies and practices exist in trades or businesses referred to their attention by the Board of Trade, clearly must be composed of impartial members, free from association with interested parties. When a royal commission was set up in 1947, under the chairmanship of Sir David Ross,[1] 'to inquire into the control, management and ownership of the newspaper and periodical press and the news agencies, including the financial structure and the monopolistic tendencies in control', it was clearly proper that there should not be found among its members representatives of the newspaper proprietors or of their employees or of any other interested parties. Their views should be given from the witness box. The inter-departmental committee appointed in 1947 to inquire into the effect upon children under 16 of attendance at the cinema and in particular into the working of children's cinema clubs did not include among its members anyone engaged in the film industry whether as producer or renter or manager. Those whose activities are under investigation must not be judges in their own cause.

There was an interesting exchange of opinions in the House

[1] Cmd. 7700 (1949).

of Commons upon the advisability of having interested parties on a committee of inquiry when the Minister of Health (Mr. Iain Macleod) was asked, on 7 May 1953, whether he did not think it a bad thing that the committee he had set up to inquire into the cost of the National Health Service contained no members who knew anything about the work and management of hospitals. He replied: 'The inquiry is to be independent and objective: the members appointed have, therefore, no direct connection with any part of the Health Service. . . . If we once start having representatives of hospitals in any sense of the term, I should have to have representatives of doctors, consultants, dentists, local authorities, opticians and the rest. I wanted this problem to be examined by a committee of five wise men, or four wise men and one wise woman—whatever we like to call it. I think we shall get the best result from that.' It was for this reason, he said, that he had not referred the question to the Central Health Services Council—an advisory body, representative of all the interests in the health service. 'For that reason, in my view, it is the wrong body for this kind of inquiry.'

It is apparent, then, that if the function of a committee is to undertake an impartial and judicial inquiry, the case for excluding interested parties from its membership is almost always overwhelming. If the results of the inquiry are to have some chance of commanding public confidence, that is essential. But it must be emphasized that not all committees to inquire are charged with investigations where the impartiality of the members is a prime consideration. There are cases where it is possible to say that the presence of interested parties upon a committee to inquire does good and their lack of impartiality does little or no harm. For one thing the interested parties themselves may feel more confidence in the work and findings of a committee if their representatives have been associated with it. They may feel that there has been someone there to see that they get fair play and that their interests have not been overlooked. For another it may be valuable for interested parties to hear each other's arguments and to attempt to persuade each other of the rightness of their views. There may be an aducational value to members of the committee, and perhaps to the public also, in the expression of views which are conflicting upon a controversial or complicated subject.

But, it may be said, is it not likely that the presence of interested parties, as the departmental committee said in 1910, will make it less likely that a committee will submit a unanimous report? In some controversial cases this is obvious. A teetotaller and a brewer on a royal commission on the licensing laws are unlikely to agree on much. But to this two things may be said in reply. First of all most issues are not as clear cut as that between the teetotaller and the brewer. On most matters referred to committees of inquiry there is a considerable measure of common ground, and antagonists so extreme as the teetotaller and the brewer do not have to be brought into the discussion. The second thing is that unanimity is not necessarily the best result of a committee's labours. It is often good that a government and the public should have before it the conflicting views of interested parties, with their case stated as they wish it to be stated, and with the considered judgement upon it of the rest of the members of a committee of inquiry. When a government has to decide its policy upon a difficult problem, it does not necessarily suffer from the fact that the interested parties, after inquiry, have failed to agree. On the contrary its own views may seem the more reasonable or acceptable or practicable on that account.

It is in the light of considerations such as these that the experience of the Sankey and the Samuel Commissions should be judged. Though the Sankey Commission was divided and the Samuel Commission unanimous, it would be a bold man who would say that the Samuel Commission was more successful than the Sankey. In both cases the wide division of the miners and the mine-owners was apparent—in the case of the Sankey Commission it was displayed on the Commission, in the case of the Samuel Commission it was revealed by the general strike in 1926, the year of the Commission's report. There was a good case for proceeding either way, and no great hope anyhow that the miners and the mine-owners would be able to accept the report that resulted.

The presence of interested parties on the Sankey Commission has another aspect, however, which should be mentioned here, if only briefly. The Commission was dealing with the field of industrial relations where interested parties are organized and negotiate with each other. It was proper to consider that to place interested parties on the Commission might give them an opportunity not merely to state their own case and assert their own rights and perhaps to appreciate each other's point of view better, but actually also to undertake some degree of negotiation. While the primary purpose of the Commission was to inquire, it was expected also to make recommendations and in this sphere there was room, if need be, for negotiation. We stand here on the border-line between committees to inquire and committees to negotiate, and there are cases in which it is not always easy to say upon which side of the line a given committee falls. What is certain, however, is that there is an element or possibility of negotiation within the terms of reference of most committees to inquire, particularly perhaps when the framing of recommendations comes under discussion. The presence of interested parties—along with other types of member of course—may be valuable upon committees to inquire where this element of negotiation is concerned. That was one of the reasons which justified their presence upon the Sankey Commission. Whether it was wise to have them or not is difficult to judge. It will usually be difficult, indeed, to decide this question where committees to inquire are concerned, but it is important to emphasize that there are circumstances where the presence of interested parties not only does no harm but even has a positive value.

6

What is the proper place for the expert and the layman in relation to committees to inquire? It is apparent that experts can place their views before a committee by appearing as witnesses. On many subjects, too, the number of experts is so large, each being a specialist in some part of it, that it would be impossible to place them all or a representative selection of them upon the committee itself. In many cases, moreover, experts differ and it would be difficult to select them in such a way that the committee could command the confidence of expert opinion. For reasons of this kind it is often thought best to keep experts off committees to inquire and to arrange for them to express their views as witnesses.

But although this course has much to commend it in inquiries into some matters, it can be seen that difficulties will arise in relation to others. For it is not enough to say that experts may put their views forward as witnesses. The question arises: Who, on the committee, will be capable of understanding these views, of forming some judgement of their value, or of expressing an opinion where a conflict of expert opinion occurs? While it should not be assumed without question that a layman is unable to understand and judge the value of expert evidence, there are subjects where some knowledge of a specialist kind is needed if expert evidence is to be grasped at all. Thus when a royal commission is set up to study the working of the income-tax legislation, it is surely essential that upon the commission there should be some members with knowledge of economics or of public finance or of litigation in the taxation field. None of these members need be an actual expert, though it would be an advantage if one or two experts were there, but they should be at least general practitioners. They should know enough to be able to grasp what the experts say, or to ask the proper questions of the expert, or to appreciate whether the expert is putting forward a coherent or convincing opinion, in the light of knowledge in cognate fields of study. It is not suggested, of course, that all the members of a commission on income-tax or some similar complex subject should be general practitioners or experts. There is a place, even here, in most cases for the layman, as we shall see. But there is an important function for general practitioners and even for experts to perform in making the best of what the expert witnesses have to offer in evidence.

From this point of view the procedure adopted by the Royal Commission on Population may be referred to once more. It was asked, it will be remembered, 'to examine the facts relating to the present population trends in Great Britain; to investigate the causes of these trends and to consider their probable consequences; to consider what measures, if any, should be taken in the national interest to influence the future trend of population; and to make recommendations'. It was clear that, so far as the first part of the Commission's terms of reference was concerned, expert evidence, from statisticians, economists, biologists, and doctors, would be required, while as to the second part there would be room for the views of laymen. In order that the expert's contribution should be related closely to the work of the Commission and also that it should be appreciated fully, two steps were taken. In the first place some experts were placed upon the Commission itself—in particular there was a statistician familiar with population questions, Sir Alexander Carr-Saunders, an economist, Sir Hubert Henderson, and a doctor, Professor A. W. M. Ellis, Regius Professor of Medicine at Oxford. The second step was unusual. There were set up three committees of experts to advise the Commission upon the statistical, the economic, and the biological and medical aspects of the problem respectively, and so that the work of these committees should be related to that of the main Commission Sir Alexander Carr-Saunders, Sir Hubert Henderson, and Professor Ellis were appointed to be chairmen of each of these three committees.

The organization set up is of interest to the student of committees because it shows the way in which committees to advise can be related to the work of committees to inquire. The Royal Commission had the task of inquiry and the formulation of recommendations; the expert committees had as their terms of reference to formulate, for the assistance of the Royal Commission, the statistical particulars or the economic factors or the biological and medical factors relevant to the Commission's inquiry and generally to advise the Commission on the statistical or economic or biological and medical aspects of their inquiry. The advisory committees were entirely composed of experts as was proper; the Royal Commission needed some experts and it linked them with the advisory committees by making three of them chairmen of these committees. We have an illustration here of the greater role which the expert can and should play upon committees to advise than upon committees to inquire— a point which emerged in the discussion in our last chapter.

It should not be supposed that the Royal Commission on Population relied upon its expert committees alone for its expert evidence. On the contrary it followed the usual course of receiving evidence from a variety of expert sources. But its use of the expert advisory committees was unusual and represented an attempt to organize and master the intricate problem which it was called upon to investigate. It may be doubted whether so elaborate an organization can often be justified in the work of committees to inquire. There is such a thing as having too much expert knowledge. It may be wondered whether the members of the Royal Commission found themselves overwhelmed by the information supplied by their expert advisory committees.

The layman's function, in relation to expert evidence, is by no means negligible even when he has the assistance upon a committee of expert colleagues. There are at least two tasks he can perform. Though he may defer a good deal to expert witnesses and to the opinion of his expert colleagues, he is entitled to express his own view, the view of common sense upon expert sense. He may perform the function of which Lord Salisbury spoke of diluting the strong wine of the expert. He is there to say whether he thinks what the expert says makes sense or not. It must be admitted that truth does not always make sense to the layman, but there are many cases where what the expert says does not contain the whole truth, and the wisdom of the layman may help to emphasize this point. Even where the weighing of expert evidence is concerned, then, there is often room for a layman's opinion upon committees to inquire. His second task will arise when the committee comes to consider its recommendations. Here, while the findings of expert opinion will have their place, there is a great deal of room for discussion about what is best to do, and in this sphere the layman is recognised to be important. It is not surprising to find, therefore, that upon the Royal Commission on Population, where the need of expert members was recognized, there were to be found also members who were not expert—though they were experienced and included people who were familiar with the problems of the family. They exhibited that quality of being knowledgeable which we suggested earlier to be a mark of the good lay member.

7

The place of the lay and the expert member of a committee to inquire cannot be discussed for long without raising the question of the chairman. To which category should he belong? The test to apply perhaps comes down to this. It is a great drawback to the work of a committee of inquiry to have a chairman who is unable to grasp the essential issues under inquiry. Sometimes, when the subject-matter is technical, only an expert chairman could cope with the evidence and the discussion. But provided that the chairman can pass the test of being able to understand the issues before the committee, it is not necessary that he should be an expert. It is sometimes forgotten by technical experts that in many fields it is possible for a lay chairman to learn quickly the essentials of the subject-matter, 'to get up the brief'. And this phrase reminds us that lawyers are often chosen as chairmen of committees of inquiry, for it is their profession to master the essentials of a problem, to know what use expert opinions can be, and to know how to extract what is relevant and needful from witnesses. Lawyers and, even more so, judges are skilled also in summing up the arguments upon different sides and they may be expected therefore to be of value in the drafting of a report. Judges bring to an inquiry also an independence and impartiality which is essential in inquiries where allegations are being investigated, but is valuable also in any inquiry where opinions differ and interests conflict. Chairmen with legal training and experience are therefore commonly employed in committees to inquire, and yet they are laymen as a rule in relation to the experts who sit with them or come before them as witnesses. Yet though laymen in relation to the subject-matter of the inquiry, they come near to being experts in the art of chairmanship.

It is this combination of impartiality and skill in dealing with a variety of technical matters which makes lawyers and especially judges good chairmen of committees to inquire. It was for reasons of this kind no doubt that Mr. Justice Sankey (as he then was) was chosen to be chairman of the Royal Commission on the Coal Industry of 1919. It is interesting to notice over what a wide range of inquiries lawyers and judges have presided. Thus Judge Holman Gregory was chairman of the Royal Commission on Unemployment Insurance of 1930;[1] Lord Justice Scott of the Committee on Land Utilization in Rural Areas;[2] Mr. Justice Uthwatt (as he then was) of the Expert Committee on Compensation and Betterment;[3] Lord Fleming (of the Scottish Court of Session) of the Committee on the Public Schools and the General Educational System;[4] Lord Alness (also of the Court of Session) of the Committees on Night Baking,[5] on

[1] Cmd. 3872 (1931) and Cmd. 4185 (1932).
[2] Cmd. 6378 (1942).
[3] Cmd. 6380 (1942).
[4] Its report was published by the Board of Education in 1944, but it has no reference number.   [5] Cmd. 5525 (1937).

Nursing in Scotland,[1] and on Grants to Scottish Universities;[2] Lord Dunedin of the Royal Commission on Honours[3] and of the Committee on Local Taxation in Scotland;[4] Lord Tomlin of the Royal Commission on the Civil Service;[5] Lord Macmillan of the Committee on Finance and Industry;[6] and Lord Justice Cohen of the Royal Commission on the Taxation of Profits and Income.[7] When Lord Justice Cohen resigned the chairmanship in 1952, and the government proposed to appoint Lord Waverley as his successor, there was some criticism of the proposal on the ground that Lord Waverley had expressed decided views on taxation and would not therefore be an impartial chairman. As a consequence Lord Waverley declined to accept the appointment, and another judge, Lord Radcliffe, succeeded Lord Justice Cohen as chairman. The versatility of a law lord as chairman may be illustrated by the fact that Lord Oaksey presided over the Committee on Police Conditions of Service in 1948[8] and over the Committee on the Export and Import of Cattle Semen in 1952.[9] A good example of the use of a judge as chairman of a commission of inquiry where the subject-matter was bound to be technical and where also impartiality and independence were essential was the Royal Commission on Awards to Inventors set up in 1919, which sat for over fifteen years and over which first Lord Justice Sargent and thereafter Lord Tomlin presided. A similar commission set up after the war of 1939–45 was presided over by Lord Justice Cohen.

The committees which have been mentioned above have been chosen from outside the field of legal administration. Within that field, needless to say, it is usual for judges and lawyers to be chosen as chairmen of the committees appointed to inquire into the administration of the law and its amendment. In these fields judges and lawyers are experts and most of the members of the committees too are legal experts. Their

[1] Cmd. 5866 (1938).   [2] Cmd. 5735 (1938).
[3] Cmd. 1789 (1923).   [4] Cmd. 1674 (1922).
[5] Cmd. 3909 (1931).
[6] Cmd. 3897 (1931). Lord Macmillan spent so much of his life as a chairman that he felt justified in devoting one chapter in his autobiography to the subject, under the title 'In the Chair'.
[7] Cmd. 8761 (1953). The second report of the Royal Commission is Cmd. 9105 (1954) under Lord Radcliffe's chairmanship.
[8] Cmd. 7674 and 7831 (1949).
[9] 518 H. C. Deb., 5th. rev., col. 552.

position and function is different from that which they hold in non-legal inquiries, where they are usually laymen, if well-informed and intelligent and educable laymen.

A valuable source of lay chairmen is the House of Lords. It gives dignity to a committee to be presided over by a lord; but in many cases lords bring also to the task experience in public affairs and public service, both at Westminster and in the provinces, which make them good lay chairmen. Some lords indeed are almost professional laymen, either as members or as chairmen of advisory committees. Among committees over which a peer has presided as a lay chairman may be mentioned the Royal Commissions on Cross-River Traffic in London, 1926 (Lord Lee of Fareham),[1] on London Squares, 1927 (Lord Londonderry),[2] on Local Government of Greater London, 1921 (Lord Ullswater),[3] on Local Government, 1923 (Lord Onslow),[4] on Decimal Coinage, 1918 (Lord Emmott);[5] the Committees on Gold Production, 1918 (Lord Inchcape),[6] on Slow-burning Films, 1938 (Lord Stonehaven),[7] on the Cinematograph Films Act, 1927, 1936 (Lord Moyne),[8] on the Production of Fuel Oil from Home Sources, 1917 (Lord Crewe),[9] on the Miners' Welfare Fund, 1931 (Lord Chelmsford),[10] on Broadcasting, 1925 (Lord Crawford),[11] 1935 (Lord Ullswater),[12] and 1949 (Lord Beveridge),[13] and on Television, 1934 (Lord Selsdon).[14]

But although lay chairmen are commonly used, whether recruited from the House of Lords or not, it would be a mistake to conclude that chairmen must be either lay or expert. Just as officials cannot be classified exhaustively into lay or expert, but include a class of general practitioners, so also there exists a class of general practitioners among chairmen. These are people with a general knowledge of a particular field and perhaps an expert knowledge of part of it, sufficient knowledge at any rate to make them familiar and at home in the subject-matter of the committee's concern. Chairmen of this kind are usually

[1] Cmd. 2772 (1926). [2] Cmd. 3196 (1928).
[3] Cmd. 1830 (1923).
[4] Cmd. 2506 (1925), Cmd. 3213 (1928), and Cmd. 3436 (1929).
[5] Cmd. 628 and Cmd. 719 (1920). [6] Cmd. 11 (1918).
[7] Report published in 1939 as a Home Office non-parliamentary paper.
[8] Cmd. 5320 (1936). [9] Cd. 9128 (1918).
[10] Cmd. 4236 (1933). [11] Cmd. 2599 (1926).
[12] Cmd. 5091 (1936). [13] Cmd. 8116 (1951).
[14] Cmd. 4793 (1935).

sought when a committee is to deal with such fields as economic and financial affairs, agriculture, or education. Perhaps the classic example of a chairman of this kind was Lord Colwyn, the banker, who presided over the Treasury Committee on Bank Amalgamations in 1918,[1] over the Royal Commission on the Income Tax of 1919,[2] and over the Committee on National Debt and Taxation of 1924.[3] Lord Colwyn was much in demand as a chairman, and presided also over committees dealing with the supply of flax,[4] the construction of merchant ships in admiralty dockyards,[5] railway agreements,[6] and building construction contracts,[7] where his position was more that of a layman than a general practitioner. Then there was Lord Cunliffe, who presided over the Committee on Currency and Foreign Exchanges in 1918;[8] Lord Linlithgow, who presided over the Committee on the Distribution and Prices of Agricultural Produce in 1922;[9] Lord Astor, who presided over the Committee on the Production and Distribution of Milk in 1917;[10] Lord Bledisloe, an agriculturalist, who presided over the Royal Commission on Land Drainage in England and Wales in 1927;[11] Lord Balfour of Burleigh, who presided over the Committee on Commercial and Industrial Policy appointed in 1916;[12] and Sir Arthur M. Balfour (later Lord Riverdale), an industrialist, who presided over the Committee on Industry and Trade, which was appointed in 1924 and, sitting for four and a half years, produced six interim reports and a final report.

8

When we come to consider in a general way the value of committees to inquire we find that, in the first place, their usefulness depends upon a consideration similar to that which we found to apply to committees to advise. If a department

[1] Cd. 9052 (1918).
[2] Cmd. 615 (1920).
[3] Cmd. 2800 (1927).
[4] Cmd. 281 (1919).
[5] Cmd. 581 (1920).
[6] Cmd. 1132 (1921).
[7] Cd. 9179 (1918).
[8] Cd. 9182 (1918).
[9] Cmd. 1854 (1923), Cmd. 1892 (1923), Cmd. 1927 (1923), Cmd. 1971 (1923), Cmd. 2008 (1924).
[10] Cd. 8608 and Cd. 8886 (1917), Cd. 9095 (1918), Cmd. 315 (1919), Cmd. 483 (1919).
[11] Cmd. 2993 (1927).
[12] Cd. 9032, Cd. 9033, Cd. 9034, Cd. 9035 (1918).

means business, if it is really anxious to determine some issue of policy or to undertake some reform of administration, then the setting up of a committee to inquire may well have some value. Sometimes, of course, a committee to inquire is asked to do no more than find the facts of a problem or situation and no question of action by a department may be involved. As a rule, however, even where a committee of inquiry is not asked to make recommendations, some action is involved as a result of their report. If their work is not to be wasted, it is usually essential that departments setting up committees of inquiry should have some intention of acting, not necessarily of course in accordance with the committee's report or recommendations, but as a result of it.

But the value of the work of a committee to inquire goes beyond this. It is intended to do something to educate opinion. Its report, and often the evidence submitted to it, are a contribution to the study of the subject and the basis of discussions about it both in the department and outside. Even, therefore, when a department has no very strong intention of acting upon a committee's report, it by no means follows that the committee's work is wasted. It may perform an educative function, which in the end, perhaps, may lead to some action.

We may bear these two criteria in mind when we consider the use of committees to inquire and particularly when we consider some of the motives which lead departments to set them up.

There is, first of all, the committee to pacify. 'A committee keeps a cabinet quiet', wrote Mr. Gladstone in 1869.[1] If a government is faced with a demand or agitation for some inquiry into policy or administration in which it is either not interested or not prepared to contemplate any change, it may find it worth while to set up a committee to inquire into the matter, and in that way pacify those who are concerned and secure a respite for itself. It should feel fairly certain that nothing surprising or calling for action will come out of the inquiry before it sets it up. Governments may find that committees set up to pacify may not produce the desired result. They may add fuel to the fire and force governmental action. These are risks which must be taken.

It is a matter of conjecture, of course, as to what the motives

---

[1] Morley, *Life of Gladstone*, i. 691.

of departments were in setting up particular committees, but it may be suggested that in all probability the principal object before the government in setting up, say, the Royal Commission on the Private Manufacture of and Trading in Arms, in 1935, under Sir Eldon Bankes, a former Lord Justice of Appeal,[1] was to pacify the critics, to pacify the pacifists. It may well be that the same motive was present, among others, in the setting up of, say, the Royal Commission on the Press, under Sir David Ross, in 1947,[2] the Royal Commission on Equal Pay for Men and Women in 1948,[3] and the Committee on Scottish Financial and Trade Statistics in 1949 followed by the Royal Commission on Scottish Affairs in 1952 in response to the Scottish demand for more home rule.[4] It probably was present in large degree to explain the setting up of the Royal Commissions on Gambling under Sir Sidney Rowlatt in 1932[5] and under Mr. H. U. Willink in 1949.[6]

Then there is the committee to delay or postpone. This is distinct from the committee to pacify. The government may want delay until action is possible or until action is unnecessary. This is not necessarily wicked. Indeed in the period of delay, the public may be given an opportunity to educate itself and form its opinions on the subject, more particularly from the evidence given before the committee. But the use of committees of inquiry in order to delay can be bad, for delay sometimes makes things worse. Examples of committees to inquire which have been set up by the government primarily to buy time are perhaps the Royal Commission on Marriage and Divorce in 1951, where the government appreciated that something might have to be done but wished to postpone it for as long as possible, and the Royal Commission on Capital Punishment of 1949, where the division of opinion within the parties meant that delay would be appreciated by both sides if it could be obtained. In both these cases the government was referring to a commission a subject upon which in the end the public and members of Parliament must be the judges; there was little upon which

[1] Cmd. 5292 (1936).   [2] Cmd. 7700 (1949).
[3] Cmd. 7079.
[4] Cmd. 8609 (1952) and Cmd. 9212 (1954). Lord Catto and the Earl of Balfour where the respective chairmen.
[5] Cmd. 4234 (1933) and Cmd. 4341 (1933).
[6] Cmd. 8190 (1951).

advice could be obtained from a commission whether of experts or of ordinary people, but there was an opportunity for the formulation and education of public opinion by the consideration of evidence offered and by the reports of the commissions themselves. Delay had its uses.

In the third place there are committees set up with the object of killing a proposal either by reporting against it; or by revealing so great a divergence of opinion that no action is possible; or by keeping it out of sight so that public interest ceases to be concerned with it. By smothering, strangling, drowning, or tearing to pieces, the proposal is killed. In order to make sure that this result is achieved departments are tempted to choose the members of the committee with that end in view. This can be done either by securing members whose views are known to be satisfactory or by choosing representatives of interests who are certain to conflict and so produce chaos or nullity. It was alleged that the Palestine Partition Committee under Sir John Woodhead of 1938,[1] which was charged with the duty of showing how the plan of partition proposed by the Peel Commission of 1936 could be put into practice, was intended to prove the impossibility of the plan. Be that as it may, it certainly helped to kill it. Perhaps a similar object lay behind the government's setting up in 1929 of a committee to examine and report on the economic aspects of proposals for a channel tunnel.[2] At any rate the government endorsed the minority report of one of the members who regarded the scheme as producing greater disadvantages than advantages.[3] And may it be that the government hoped not merely to pacify but also to put to sleep advocates of decimal coinage and of proportional representation by the appointment of royal commissions to deal with those subjects in 1918[4] and 1908[5] respectively?

Finally, there is the committee for form's sake. The government has decided on its policy, or is fairly certain what it will be. It sets up a committee to secure approbation for its policy or perhaps to demonstrate the futility of the conflicting interests or to show that it has done its best. But it uses the committee as

---

[1] Cmd. 5854 (1938). The report of the Peel Commission is Cmd. 5479 (1937).
[2] Cmd. 3513 (1930).   [3] Cmd. 3591 (1930).
[4] Cmd. 628 and Cmd. 719 (1920). There were two minority reports.
[5] Cd. 5163 (1910).

no more at best than an instrument to prepare or educate the public on its policy and at worst as a screen, a dressing of the shop window, a façade, or a camouflage. Needless to say, a committee which is intended to perform this function must be carefully selected. An example of this use of a committee of inquiry may be found on the occasions when a government has decided to make cuts in expenditure and has appointed a committee to advise upon it. This was the function of the Geddes Committee of 1921[1] and the May Committee of 1931.[2] In the field of expenditure by local authorities, a similar task was performed in 1932 by the Ray Committee for England and by the Lovat Committee for Scotland and in these cases the committees were composed of representatives of the local authorities.[3] No doubt the Treasury would have been quite competent to advise the government on the cuts needed, but it looked better that they should be considered and recommended by a body of eminent men in the world of business, finance, and industry or, as in the case of local authorities, of the interested parties themselves.

Although these four ways of using committees of inquiry—to pacify, to delay, to nullify, and to camouflage—may be capable of abuse, it must be admitted that these abuses are neither flagrant nor frequent. After all, the responsibility for formulating and applying policy must rest with departments of government; it cannot be assumed by committees. If governments seek to pacify people, if they seek to buy time, if they wish to put a project to sleep, or if they wish to seek support for their policies, that is often a legitimate activity. It is seldom that the public is intentionally deceived. No doubt the qualities of caution, timidity, procrastination, and conservatism can be bad at times, and if governments use committees of inquiry for these reasons they run the risk of providing bad government. But it is not always foolish or wicked. The worst abuse that can with certainty be charged to committees under this head is that often a great deal of time of experts, officials, and public-spirited laymen is consumed, and a good deal of public money is expended, upon inquiries and reports which were not always really and entirely necessary. Sometimes, too, a surfeit of knowledge and

---

[1] Cmd. 1581 (1922).   [2] Cmd. 3920 (1931).
[3] Cmd. 4200 (1932) and Cmd. 4201 (1932) respectively.

a desire for more advice and information produces, or is produced by, an inability of a government to take a decision and give a lead in policy. These are ways in which committees to inquire may give rise to abuse. They may postpone action and produce a paralysis in departments where decision and action are needed.

9

It remains to mention in conclusion certain other features of the working of committees to inquire which may occasionally cause disquiet and are capable of constituting abuse. The first is over-indulgence in compromise. It should not be assumed always by the chairman or the members of a committee of inquiry that the supreme test of whether they have been successful or not is whether they have produced a unanimous report. Sometimes, it is true, a unanimous report may be more readily accepted by the government. But unanimity has its dangers as well as its virtues. It may often be the case that it is better to be divided and state the issues involved strongly, than to give way too much and produce a lukewarm document. The public is entitled to hear divided views strongly and ably argued, and the government may find itself pushed to adopt a more drastic policy, in response to public opinion, than it would have followed had a mild compromise scheme been recommended. And we may ask ourselves once more, which was the more influential, the divided Sankey Commission or the unanimous Samuel Commission?

Members, and especially chairmen, of committees must be on their guard also against conceding point after point to a persistent minority, only to find in the end that it is of no avail and the minority still proceeds to publish its own report or reports. It is a nice question of judgement how far unanimity should be sought. A great deal will depend upon the way in which the committee has been selected. If conflicting vested interests are there, it is apparent that the attempt to reconcile them should not be prolonged. It may well be that they intend to be a minority. If they do not, nothing will bring them round so quickly as the sight of the majority getting ahead with the draft of its report. Sometimes, of course, there are several minorities. If compromise is impossible, or if it is possible only at the price of producing recommendations of little value, it is clearly best that the department should be made aware (if it is not aware already) and the public convinced of the irreconcilability of the interests concerned. Division in such a case is often more valuable than unanimity.

In selecting members to sit on a committee of inquiry a department may have chosen people of conflicting views in the hope that some moderate and innocuous compromise may be unanimously recommended. A committee must ask whether it is consistent with its duty to the public to produce a report of this kind or whether it should educate the public and throw responsibility back upon the department by bringing into the open the conflicting issues in the case. No hard and fast rule can be laid down about this. What it illustrates however is that the selection of members of a committee is a matter of great influence in the determination of its proceedings and, secondly, that the belief that unanimity in a committee is the sole criterion of success is not always valid.

A second question is how far the reports which committees give to departments and ministers should be published. In the case of committees to advise we saw that publication of advice was not invariable, nor was it necessary that it should be so. Committees to inquire, however, are in a different category. We normally expect that the report of any committee of inquiry whose appointment has been announced publicly and which has been receiving evidence from the public will itself be published. Sometimes there is a delay in publication, often because the government wishes to announce at the same time its attitude to the report. But unless considerations of security arise, a report is expected to be published, since the use of committees to inquire, from the public's point of view, lies in the educative value of their reports. Evidence submitted to a committee, on the other hand, is not always published, sometimes for perfectly justifiable reasons of expense, sometimes because it has been decided that if the inquiry is to be successful it is best to assure witnesses that what they say will be treated as confidential. The evidence upon which the Report of the Committee on Intermediaries of 1950[1] was based, for example, could not be published in its entirety. In many cases, however, where the public is unable to see the

[1] Cmd. 7904.

evidence upon which the report is based, it would be better that it should. The justification for the committee's recommendations could be examined and discussed. It is fair to add, however, that evidence is usually lengthy and a great deal of it repetitious and dull. It may be noted that in many inquiries in which considerable public interest was aroused, such as the Royal Commissions on the Press and on Capital Punishment, and the Committee on Ministers' Powers, the evidence was published, and played a valuable part in the education of public opinion.

CHAPTER V

Committees to Negotiate

I

IN the working of committees to advise and of committees to inquire an element of negotiation is often found. Sometimes it is present in so great a degree that, as in the case of the Working Parties for Industry set up by Sir Stafford Cripps at the Board of Trade, it is difficult to say whether they should be classed as committees to advise or to negotiate. A similar difficulty arises in classifying such bodies as the Local Government Manpower Committees, set up for England and Scotland in 1949 to review and co-ordinate the existing arrangements for ensuring economy in the use of manpower by local authorities and by those government departments which are concerned with local government matters, and to examine in particular the distribution of functions between central and local government and the possibility of relaxing departmental supervision of local authority activities and delegating more responsibility to local authorities. These committees were composed of representatives of local authorities and of the central government departments concerned with them.[1] They, and the various sub-committees and panels which they associated with them, clearly possessed considerable knowledge and experience of the problems committed to them and could offer advice upon them. Clearly also they undertook some inquiry into the working of the system. In some degree they were committees both to advise and to inquire. But it is certain also that when they came to consider the relations of central departments and local authorities some element of negotiation came in as they discussed their recommendations. They were, indeed, composed of interested parties in the belief that only by some process of negotiation between

---

[1] See, for example, *First Report of the Local Government Manpower Committee*, Cmd. 7870 (1950), and *First Report of the Scottish Local Government Manpower Committee*, Cmd. 7951 (1950).

those who were at once experts and interested parties could any useful result be expected from their deliberations.

Further examples in the same field were the committees appointed to investigate the operation of the exchequer equalization grants in England and Wales and in Scotland, which reported in 1953.[1] These committees were composed of representatives of the central government departments and of the associations of local authorities, and, in the case of the London County Council and the City of London, for example, of representatives of these authorities. Their chairman was a senior official of the central government department concerned —the Ministry of Housing and Local Government so far as England and Wales were concerned, and of the Scottish Home Department in the case of Scotland. Although they were described as committees to investigate, and although in fact a large part of their work was inquiry and investigation, it is clear that, as they were invited also to make recommendations both to the ministries concerned and to the associations or the local authorities represented upon the committees, some measure of discussion and negotiation was bound to be involved in their work. The extent to which they could negotiate with central government representatives was limited by their terms of reference in that it was laid down that the government could not contemplate changing the system in any way which would increase the burden of grants on the Exchequer. The element of negotiation was further reduced by the understanding that none of the parties represented on the committee was committed by the fact that its representatives signed the recommendations contained in the report. There was no authorization to the various sides on the committee to negotiate a settlement.

It is difficult, therefore, to say in what category the committees fall. They were clearly in some important measure committees to inquire. By their composition and terms of reference they were also in some measure committees to negotiate. What is more, in that they were composed almost entirely of experts— treasurers of local authorities and finance officers of the central government departments—they performed the function of committees to advise, offering from the wealth of their knowledge

---

[1] Published by the Ministry of Housing and Local Government and by the Scottish Home Department, respectively. There is no reference number.

and experience a judgement upon how the equalization grant was working and what might be done to improve its working. What can be said with some confidence, however, is that the aspect of negotiation in the committees' working was not subordinate to their task of inquiry and advice and that their composition was deliberately intended to give scope to the element of negotiation.

From these borderline cases it is possible to pass to examples of committees where the process of negotiation is predominant. One clear example is the Rail and Road Transport Conference set up in 1932 under the chairmanship of Sir Arthur Salter to attempt to reconcile some of the conflicting interests of road haulage and rail haulage. The Minister of Transport decided that the Conference should consist of four representatives of the railway companies and four representatives of the road haulage interests, with an independent chairman. To the surprise of most people, the Conference produced a unanimous report. Committees to negotiate are set up from time to time in the political sphere also. The Bryce Conference on the Reform of the Second Chamber in 1918,[1] the Party Conference on the Second Chamber in 1948,[2] the Conference on Devolution in 1919 under the chairmanship of the Speaker of the House of Commons,[3] are examples of this kind, being composed in each case of members of all parties and from both Houses of Parliament.

But it is in the field of relations between employer and employee, in the consideration of their rates of pay and conditions of labour, that the greatest development of committees to negotiate can be encountered in Britain. It is clearly outside the scope of this essay to consider committees to negotiate over the whole of this wide field. Our examination must be confined to them in so far as they affect central and local government. Two broad classes of committee to negotiate fall within this field. There are those committees whose task it is, after negotiation, to advise the government upon labour questions in particular branches of industry, and there are, secondly, those committees set up to conduct negotiations where the employees of central and local government are themselves involved, where, that is

[1] Cd. 9038 (1918).   [2] Cmd. 7380 (1948).
[3] Cmd. 692 (1920).

to say, negotiations are going on between the government and its servants. Something may be said now of the machinery which exists to undertake negotiations in these two spheres.[1]

2

The greater part of the field of labour relations in Britain is regulated by voluntary agreements arrived at as a result of the work of committees to negotiate. It is in a small part of the field only that state intervention is provided for, and here as a rule the procedure is for negotiating committees to offer advice to the government. One example of this procedure is the system of Wages Councils, established under the provisions of the Wages Councils Acts, 1945 and 1948. Wages councils are established by the Minister of Labour, either on his own initiative, or as the result of the report of a commission of inquiry. About sixty wages councils existed in Great Britain in 1953, the greater number of them (52) having had a previous existence as trade boards and being converted into wages councils by the Minister under the powers given him in the Wages Councils Act of 1945. They are empowered to submit proposals to the Minister for fixing remuneration to be paid to the workers in the industries with which they deal and for requiring employers to allow their workers holidays with pay. When the Minister receives the proposals of a wages council, he may either make an order to give effect to them or refer them back to the council for reconsideration and the council may resubmit them to the Minister with or without amendment as it thinks fit.[2]

The composition of wages councils accepts the principle, which prevails in the voluntary negotiating machinery, that the interested parties will be represented on the councils. The Minister appoints members representing employers or workers in equal numbers. They are chosen with a view to giving representation as far as possible to all the main types of establishments and classes of workers affected and the principal districts

[1] The factual information given in the following pages is derived principally from the *Industrial Relations Handbook*, published by the Ministry of Labour in 1953.

[2] In 1948 and again in 1953 the Minister referred back proposals from wages councils. They were resubmitted to him substantially unchanged and he then approved them. (In one case in 1948 he referred proposals back once more, but approved them on the second resubmission.)

or centres in which the workers are employed. Before the Minister appoints the members representing interested parties, he is required to consult organizations representing the employers and workers concerned, and as a rule he appoints the candidates whom they suggest.

But the interested parties are not left to themselves. The Minister is empowered to appoint to a wages council not more than three independent members. One of the three independent members must be appointed by the Minister as chairman—a wages council does not appoint its own chairman—and another may be appointed by the Minister to act as deputy chairman in the absence of the chairman. These independent members have a number of functions. In the first place their independence has a certain value. They may assist the negotiations between the interested parties and they may mediate on occasions. They represent some wider interests also and may on occasions put the point of view of the public interest. They may be expected to consider the wider repercussions of the proposals or decisions of the interested parties. They are either lawyers or university teachers or social workers. In some cases they have an expert knowledge of the trade with which the wages council deals; in some cases they may be good general practitioners, like economists; more often they are intelligent, experienced, and knowledgeable laymen.

The votes of the independent members can clearly be decisive. No meeting of a wages council is duly constituted unless at least one independent member is present, together with a third at least of the whole number of members representing the interested parties. Although every member of a wages council has a vote, there are occasions when voting is carried out by sides. The chairman may, if he thinks fit, and must if requested by more than half of either side, take a vote by sides and in such a case the vote of the majority of the members on either side present and voting is the vote of that side. In a division of this kind the independent members do not vote, so that a decision of the council could be reached without their participation. If, however, the two sides disagree in a division of this kind, the question may be decided by the majority vote of the independent members or, if only one is present, by his vote.[1]

[1] When the proposals of certain wages councils were resubmitted to the Minister

Another example of committees to negotiate in the industrial field, whose duty it is to offer recommendations to the government, is the system of Catering Wages Boards set up under the provisions of the Catering Wages Act, 1943. Here again the Minister of Labour may set up wages boards for branches of the catering industry after an inquiry has been conducted and recommendations made by a permanent commission, the Catering Wages Commission. Five catering wages boards have been set up by the Minister as a result of the Commission's recommendations. They are empowered, like wages councils, to submit proposals for remuneration and for holidays with pay to the Minister, but in addition they may make proposals for fixing intervals for meals and rest for workers in their branches of the catering industry. Catering wages boards are constituted on the same principles as wages councils, with equal representation to both sides of the industry, and with independent members playing the same role and recruited on the same principles. Between them, wages councils and catering wages boards in 1953 were responsible for something between two and a quarter and two and a half million workers.

3

When we look at central and local government we find that almost all their employees are regulated, so far as remuneration and conditions of service are concerned, as a result of the proceedings of committees to negotiate. The powers and composition of these committees vary from case to case, but a common principle throughout is the representation of the interested parties. It is worth while to look at some examples.

For the non-industrial civil servants in the central government there is a National Whitley Council, Departmental Councils, and in some departments also Office Whitley Committees. Each of the councils or committees has an official side and a staff side, usually equal or roughly equal in numbers. The National Whitley Council, for example, has twenty-six members on each side. The members of the official side are appointed

of Labour in 1953, after having been referred back by him, a number of them came forward with the support of the employees' side and of the independent members only.

by the government and, according to the Constitution of the Council, 'shall be persons of standing (who may or may not be civil servants) and shall include at least one representative of the Treasury and one representative of the Ministry of Labour'.[1] In practice[2] members of the official side are appointed yearly by the Permanent Secretary of the Treasury, and they are in the main heads, deputy heads, or principal establishment officers of large or important departments, including the Ministry of Labour and, of course, the Treasury. Thus, in November 1953, the official side consisted of the heads of the Treasury, the Board of Inland Revenue, the Post Office, the Board of Customs and Excise, the Ministry of Works, the Ministry of Food, the Ministry of Supply, the Ministry of Labour, the Ministry of Transport, the Admiralty, the Board of Trade, the Department of Scientific and Industrial Research, the Ministry of Fuel and Power, the Scottish Office, the Ministry of Defence, and the Ministry of Housing and Local Government, together with the First Civil Service Commissioner, a second high official from the Ministry of Housing and Local Government, and six other high officials from the Treasury.

The twenty-six places on the staff side are divided between certain groups of staff associations. In November 1953, for example, there were seven such groups. There was the Post Office group, with six members from the Union of Post Office Workers, two from the Post Office Engineering Union, one from the association of Post Office Controlling Officers and one representing the Society of Telecommunication Engineers, the Federation of Sub-Postmasters, the Postmasters' Association, the Telephone Contract Officers' Association, and the Telecommunications Traffic Association. The Civil Service Alliance had six members, three from the Civil Service Clerical Association, two from the Inland Revenue Staff Federation, and one from the Ministry of Labour Staff Association. The Executive Group had five members, two from the Society of Civil Servants and one each from the Customs and Excise Federation, the Association of Officers of the Ministry of Labour, and the Association of H.M. Inspectors of Taxes. The remaining four

---

[1] See E. N. Gladden, *Civil Service Staff Relationships*, Appendix I.
[2] See paper by A. J. T. Day (chairman of staff side) and A. J. D. Winnifrith in *Whitley Bulletin*, July, 1953.

groups were the Association of First Division Civil Servants with one member, the Institution of Professional Civil Servants with two members, the Federation of Civil Service Professional and Technical Staffs with one member, and the Civil Service Union with one member.

The Constitution of the National Council provides that the chairman shall be chosen from the official side and the vice-chairman from the staff side, and in 1954 the chairman was the Permanent Secretary of the Treasury—though this had not always been the practice.[1] The terms of reference of the Council are wide, and it is 'empowered to deal with all matters affecting the conditions of service of the staff, and in particular to determine the general principles governing such conditions as recruitment, hours, promotion, discipline, tenure, remuneration and superannuation'.[2] Most striking of all perhaps is the provision that the Council has the power to reach operative decisions. 'The decisions of the Council', says the Constitution, 'shall be arrived at by agreement between the two sides, shall be signed by the Chairman and Vice-Chairman, shall be reported to the Cabinet, and thereupon shall become operative.' Needless to say, the government's control over the decisions taken is increased by the fact that the members of the official side would not be likely to agree to a decision without authority from ministers, but none the less the conceding of the power to the Council to take operative decisions makes its proceedings a reality.

In the ninety or so departmental Whitley Councils similar principles are enshrined. They, too, have the power to make operative decisions; they are composed of members representing the official and staff sides according to the numbers they determine—and they need not be equal. Departmental councils are autonomous; their powers in relation to the National Council are limited only by the provision that they cannot adopt decisions or principles inconsistent with those of the National Council. But there is no appeal from departmental councils to the National Council. The Office Whitley Committees are found

[1] The Chairman from 1919 (when the Council was first set up) to 1932 was Sir R. Russell Scott, Controller of Establishments at the Treasury, and from 1932 to 1942 Sir Horace Wilson, Chief Industrial Adviser to the Government until 1939 and thereafter Head of the Treasury until 1942.

[2] A. J. T. Day, loc. cit.

usually in those departments with staffs scattered in offices over the country such as the Post Office, the Ministry of Labour, and the Inland Revenue Department. These are small committees, with three or four members on the official side drawn from the management of the office, and about the same number on the staff side drawn from the branches of the staff associations. Thus throughout the non-industrial civil service in the central government committees to negotiate, consisting in practice of interested parties only, are empowered to discuss almost all matters of common concern and to take decisions, where appropriate, upon all the most important matters that affect their conditions of service. It may be added that if they fail to agree on certain matters affecting emoluments provision exists for reference to arbitration by a specially constituted Civil Service Arbitration Tribunal.

For the industrial civil servants there are two types of committee to negotiate. There are joint councils for a particular department which deal with matters other than wages and trade questions, as for example the interpretation of departmental regulations on questions of welfare. Then there are Trade Joint Councils which deal with wages and trade questions which are often common to a number of departments. There are Departmental Joint Councils in, for example, the Admiralty, the Air Ministry, the Ministry of Supply, the Ministry of Works, H.M. Stationery Office, the War Department, and the Royal Mint, while there is an Engineering Trades Joint Council, a Miscellaneous Trades Joint Council, and a Shipbuilding Trade Joint Council. The last named deals with wages of the various classes of industrial employees in the Admiralty, whereas the Engineering and the Miscellaneous Trades Joint Councils deal with wages matters in such departments as the Ministry of Supply, the War Office, the Air Ministry, and the Ministry of Works.

It is interesting to notice how these joint councils are appointed. The trade unions having members employed in the department or departments concerned appoint the representatives of the employees' side. On the official side, the members of a departmental joint council are appointed by the department concerned, except that one member is appointed by the Minister of Labour; while the official members of a trade joint council are appointed by the departments concerned and include a representative from the Treasury and from the Ministry of Labour. The chairman of a departmental or of a trade joint council must be chosen from the official side, while the vice-chairman is chosen from the trade-union side.

There is, in addition to departmental and trade joint councils, a joint co-ordinating committee for government industrial establishments, which undertakes for industrial civil servants the same sort of functions as the National Whitley Council performs for the non-industrial civil servants. Its task is to consider general service questions affecting government industrial employees generally. The official side of this co-ordinating committee is composed of representatives of the employing departments, and, as usual, of the Treasury and of the Ministry of Labour, while on the trade-union side it is composed of representatives of the Engineering, Shipbuilding, and Miscellaneous Trades Joint Councils, thus providing, on this side, an organic link between the joint co-ordinating committee and the trade (not the departmental) joint councils.

4

In local government in Britain, committees to negotiate in the sphere of wages and conditions of service cover almost the whole field of employment, and in their composition the principle of representing the interested parties is firmly accepted. Over 900,000 people, in 1954, had their wages and working conditions determined by such bodies. Some examples will illustrate their structure and functions.

There is, for example, the National Joint Council for Manual Workers in Local Authorities' Services, which was first instituted in 1919 but was reconstituted in 1951. It consists of thirty-two members on the employers' side and sixteen on the employees' side. On the employers' side there are two representatives from the Association of Municipal Corporations, two from the County Councils' Association, two from the Urban District Councils' Association, one from the Rural District Councils' Association, one from the London County Council, twenty-two representing the employers' side of the Provincial Joint Councils which also operate throughout the country, and two from the employers' side of the National Joint Council for County Council Roadmen. On the employees' side there are seven representatives of the National Union of General and Municipal Workers, three from the National Union of Public Employees, and six from the Transport and General Workers' Union. The function of the National Council is to secure the largest possible measure of joint consideration and determination of the wages, hours, and working conditions of all manual workers employed by local authorities, other than those whose wages and working conditions are regulated by other recognized joint negotiating machinery. There are in addition sixteen Provincial or District Councils covering practically the whole of England and Wales, similarly composed of representatives of the constituent local authorities in the area and the trade unions concerned. Until 1947 the provincial councils settled wages and working conditions in their areas, subject to a veto by the National Council, but in that year the National Council took over the jurisdiction of the provincial councils in regard to wages. Generally speaking the functions of the provincial councils are now to take executive action within their area in connexion with decisions arrived at by the National Council; to act as Conciliation Boards at the request of parties to a dispute in their area, referring the dispute to the National Council when agreement is not achieved.

In other branches of local government employment similar negotiating bodies exist. There is a National Joint Council for Local Authorities' Administrative, Professional, Technical, and Clerical Services; a National Joint Council for County Council Roadmen; and a National Joint Council for Local Authorities' Fire Brigades in Great Britain. This last, it will be noted, includes Scotland along with England and Wales. In other services Scotland is usually organized separately. There is, for example, a National Joint Industrial Council for Manual Workers in Local Authorities in Scotland, and a National Joint Industrial Council for Administrative, Technical, and Clerical Staffs in Local Authority Services in Scotland. There are at present no provincial or district councils in Scotland, though the constitutions of the national joint councils provide for them. The provincial councils in the administrative, professional, technical, and clerical services in England and Wales do not determine salary scales, but they exercise appellate jurisdiction in disputes between a local authority and its officers, with a further appeal to the National Council. There lies an appeal to the National Council also where there is a difference of opinion between the employers' side and the staffs' side of a provincial council. It should be noted also that the National Joint Council for Local Authorities' Fire Brigades in Great Britain differs from the other negotiating bodies so far dealt with in that their recommendations are not addressed to their constituent bodies but to the Home Secretary and the Secretary of State for Scotland, and if approved by them become mandatory on the local fire authorities.

Chief officers and some of the higher-paid officers of local authorities are dealt with by separate machinery, though it is constructed in a similar manner. There is the Joint Negotiating Committee for chief officers of local authorities, composed on the employers' side of four representatives of the Association of Municipal Corporations, four of the County Councils' Association, two each of the Urban District and of the Rural District Councils' Associations, one of the Metropolitan Boroughs Standing Joint Committee, and two of the Association of Education Committees, and composed on the employees' side of three representatives of the Association of Local Government Financial Officers, three of the Institute of Local Government Engineers and Surveyors, two of the Association of Education Officers, two of the County Architects' Society and Society of City and Borough Architects, two of the National and Local Association of Government Officers, and one of the Deputy Clerks of Borough and County District Councils, making a total of fifteen on the employers' side and thirteen on the employees' side. The salaries of town clerks and clerks of district councils (but not of the clerks of county councils and clerks of the peace) are negotiated in a separate committee composed of ten members on the employers' side—three each from the Association of Municipal Corporations, the Urban District Councils' Association, and the Rural District Councils' Association, and one of the Metropolitan Boroughs Standing Joint Committee—and nine from the employees' side—three each from the Society of Town Clerks, the Society of Clerks of Urban District Councils, and the Local Government Clerks' Association.

Education is the most expensive service in the hands of local authorities in Britain today. How are the salaries of teachers determined? Here again a system of committees to negotiate covers almost the whole of the field. So far as teachers in primary and secondary schools and in technical colleges and schools are concerned two Burnham committees operate. Their constitution is decided by the Minister of Education;[1] they deal only with the remuneration of teachers; and their recommendations, if put forward in agreed form, must be either accepted by the Minister—in which case they are mandatory on all local education authorities in the country—or rejected; they cannot be amended. If the two sides of a Burnham committee do not agree, the Minister is unable to fix scales of remuneration. One Burnham committee—known as the Main Committee—deals with salaries of teachers in primary and secondary schools, and is composed on the employers' side of six representatives of the Association of Municipal Corporations, nine of the County Councils' Association, six of the Association of Education Committees, three of the London County Council, and two of the Welsh Joint Education Committee, and on the employees' side by sixteen representatives of the National Union of Teachers, four of the Association of Teachers in Technical Institutions, two each of the Incorporated Associations of Assistant Masters and of Assistant Mistresses, and one each of the Incorporated Associations of Headmasters and of Headmistresses. The other Burnham committee[2] is called the Technical Committee and is composed on the employers' side of representatives of the same bodies as the Main Committee (though in smaller numbers) and on the employees' side of six representatives of the Association of Teachers in Technical Institutions, two of the Association of Principals in Technical Institutions, two of the National Society of Art Masters, one of the National Federation of Continuative Teachers, and two of the National Union of Teachers.

Associated with the work of the Burnham committees are two committees to negotiate which deal with those classes of employees in the service of local education authorities who, not being teachers, do not come within the ambit of the statutory provisions under which the Burnham committees are set up by

[1] Education Act, 1944, § 89.
[2] There is a third Burnham committee dealing with teachers in farm institutes.

the Minister of Education—educational psychologists, school meals organizers, inspectors of schools (appointed by the local education authorities), and teaching staffs of training colleges. These two committees deal not only with salaries but also with conditions of service, but their recommendations are not submitted to the Minister of Education for implementation. The negotiating committee for the staffs of training colleges is composed on the employees' side of twelve representatives of the Association of Teachers in Colleges and Departments of Education, while on the employers' side there are found, in addition to the representatives of the principal local authority associations already encountered, three representatives of the Council for Church Training Colleges, two of the Methodist Education Committee, two of the Catholic Education Council, and two of the British and Foreign School Society. Similarly, in the case of the negotiating committee for inspectors and organizers, while the employers' side is composed of representatives of the usual associations, on the employees' side there are representatives not only of the National Union of Teachers but also four representatives of the Association of Inspectors and Organizers, two of the Association of Organizers of Physical Education, two of the British Psychological Society, one of the National Association of Local Education Authority Youth Service Officers, and one of the Institutional Management Association.

One or two points may be noted at this stage about the Burnham committees—Main, Technical, and Farm Institutes. They are composed of equal numbers on each side—twenty-six on each side in the Main Committee, thirteen in the Technical Committee, and eight in the Farm Institutes Committee. Secondly, their chairman is an independent person appointed from outside. Almost all the other committees to negotiate in the local government service choose their chairmen from among the interested parties represented on the committee.[1] Thirdly, it will be noted that the Burnham committees, unlike the two negotiating committees associated with them, deal with salaries only. When other questions arise, however, it is usual for them to be dealt with by negotiating committees, constituted *ad hoc,*

---

[1] The National Joint Council for Local Authorities Administrative, &c., Staff and that for Manual Workers also have independent chairmen, but at the provincial and local levels they do not.

but agreements arising from such negotiations to be effective require the confirmation not of the Minister but of the bodies represented in the negotiations. Finally, it will be noticed that the carrying into effect of the agreements of the Burnham committees, like those arrived at by the two National Joint Councils for Local Authority Fire Brigades in Britain, requires the assent of the central government. For the education service, like the fire service, is carried on by local and central government in partnership.

Whereas in the fire and education services the central government is content to exercise its share of responsibility by accepting or rejecting the recommendations of committees to negotiate, in other cases it claims representation on the committee itself. Thus the Home Office has two representatives on the employers' side of the Joint Negotiating Committee for Probation Officers, sitting along with four representatives of the Association of Municipal Corporations, four of the County Councils' Association, and three of the Magistrates' Association.

It is in the police service, however, that we see an interesting development of the idea of a committee to negotiate in which central and local governments are associated. From 1919 to 1953 there existed a Police Council upon which all the interested parties were represented. The Home Secretary (or the Secretary of State for Scotland in the case of the corresponding Scottish council) was required, before making regulations regarding police pay, allowances, and conditions of service, to submit a draft thereof to the Police Council. But it was maintained that the function of the Council was consultative and advisory; it was not empowered to negotiate. Out of its membership of forty-eight, there were fourteen representatives of the Home Office, one of the Scottish Office, six of the Association of Municipal Corporations, and six of the County Councils' Association, together with representatives of the Police Federation and of chief officers of police. Members were appointed by the Secretary of State after consultation with the local authority associations. So composed, there can be no doubt that some element of negotiation entered into the Council's proceedings but the consequences of its negotiations clearly fell far short in authority of that accorded to other employees of local and central government.

In 1953 the Police Council was reconstituted with the function of discussing and negotiating on matters affecting the general conditions of service of all ranks in the police forces in Great Britain. Its composition was accordingly altered. It was organized now in two sides, on the Whitley Council model. There was an official side of twenty-six members, drawn from the Home Office, the Scottish Home Department (for the one Council now deals with Great Britain, instead of there being separate councils for England and Wales and for Scotland), and the local police authorities of the country. There was a staff side of twenty-seven members, drawn from the police associations and representative of all ranks of the force. It was provided also that a woman representative should be included on the staff side. Then, like the Burnham committees and unlike the Whitley councils in the Civil Service, the Police Council has an independent chairman. He is appointed by the Prime Minister —the first choice fell, in 1953, on Sir John Howard, a lawyer who had had experience as Chief Justice of Ceylon. The powers of the Council were to negotiate upon pay, hours, and other conditions of service (breaking up into three panels for the purpose), and to make recommendations to the Secretaries of State concerned, who were empowered either to accept or reject or refer back (but not to amend) the agreements put forward by the Council—another point of similarity with the Burnham committees. If the two sides do not agree, however, provision is made for reference of the dispute to three arbitrators, who also are appointed by the Prime Minister. The reconstituted Police Council is already now a committee to negotiate, with powers to make agreements very much like those enjoyed by wages councils or by the Burnham committees, though with certain reservations upon matters of discipline and promotion which one would expect in the case of a service of this kind.

5

To discuss the working of these committees to negotiate in any detail falls far outside the scope of this essay and the competence of its author. Our interest lies particularly in their working as committees with reference especially to the part played by our seven characters in committee work. In this context a first broad distinction which may be drawn is between those committees to negotiate whose membership is confined entirely to representatives of the interested parties and those which include among their members some 'outsiders'. We may consider the latter class first. It includes, as will be remembered, all the wages councils, the catering wages boards, the Burnham committees, and the Police Council as reconstituted in 1953. But whereas the Burnham committees and the Police Council confine their outside membership to having an independent chairman, the wages councils and catering wages boards have in addition certain other independent or outside members, though their number, including the chairman, must not exceed three.

So far as chairmen are concerned, the Burnham committees have aimed at having a man of public standing, with an interest in education but not an expert, and of independent position. From their first chairman, Lord Burnham, they have evidently developed a preference for a peer, and thus the chairmanship has been held by Lord Soulbury and Lord Percy (both of whom had been in the past Ministers of Education)—but a distinguished exception was Sir Malcolm Trustram Eve. In the case of the Police Council, the choice by the Prime Minister of Sir John Howard, a lawyer and former Chief Justice of Ceylon, illustrated the emphasis placed upon impartiality and, at the same time, provided another example of the practice noticed in committees to inquire, namely, the choice of lawyers or judges to preside over discussions which involve complicated and technical subject-matter.

The same preference for lawyers is shown in the choice of chairmen for wages councils and catering wages boards. The chairmen (and deputy chairmen) of those bodies are chosen, it will be recalled, from the independent members of the councils and boards, and they are usually lawyers. Where conflicting claims and representations are put forward, the lawyer's training and detachment are needed. The chairmen are not experts, although with experience they are bound to pick up a good deal of knowledge of the industries with which they are concerned. In many cases they preside over a number of councils and other committees to negotiate. The width of their experience may be illustrated perhaps by the case of Mr. G. G. Honeyman who, in 1954, was chairman of several wages councils, chairman of the Civil Service Arbitration Tribunal (to which disputes unsolved in the National Whitley Council go), and chairman of the Agricultural Wages Board.

So far as other independent or outside members are concerned, it is the practice to include certain experts, particularly academic experts, on the wages councils and catering wages boards, and also persons who, through social work for example, have an interest in the conditions obtaining in the trades or industries.

It is to be noticed that the party man, as such, is not included. An interesting exception was the practice adopted in regard to the National Whitley Council for the Civil Service from 1922 to 1930 of including three members of the government party in the House of Commons among the official side. The idea behind it, perhaps, was to associate some of the government's supporters with the negotiations and perhaps to make them better informed about civil service problems. On the recommendation of the Royal Commission on the Civil Service under Lord Tomlin in 1931, the practice was discontinued.[1] If members of Parliament appear now on the committees to negotiate which we are discussing they are there in some other capacity. Thus Mr. Douglas Houghton, M.P., finds a place on the staff side of the National Whitley Council as a representative of the Inland Revenue Staff Federation. He is there, that is to say, as a representative of interested parties, not as a party man.

This is not to say that the deliberations of these committees proceed without reference to party considerations. Inasmuch as the recommendations of wages councils, catering wages boards, Burnham committees, local authorities' fire brigades councils, and the Police Council require the approval of a minister of the central government before they come into effect, it is clear that government policy must play some part in the carrying out of their decisions. So far as the National Whitley Council for the Civil Service is concerned, inasmuch as the official side will take care not to commit the government without ministerial approval, political considerations are bound to enter into its deliberations, though no party man as such sits on the Council. The same will be true of the proceedings of departmental and

---

[1] Cmd. 3909 (1931), para. 496.

of government trade joint councils. On the joint councils concerned with the various classes of employees of local authorities not only will the employers' side be bound to take account of what local authorities will approve, but as a general rule elected councillors or aldermen find a place among the representatives of the official side and the party man as such thus sits upon the negotiating bodies. The local authorities' negotiating bodies in this respect differ from most of those which operate in the field of central government.

It is worth remarking perhaps that the committees to negotiate which we are considering differ from almost the whole of the rest of the negotiating bodies in Britain in associating their proceedings with government or party policy. Over the great part of trade and industry, terms and conditions of employment are settled by collective agreements arrived at by negotiation through voluntary machinery without state intervention. It may seem odd that a matter of such importance to the economic life of a country is decided without the consent of the government in these days of economic planning, but it is so. Where the government's own employees are concerned, of course, it is natural that it should take part in the negotiations and decisions. It is just like any other employer in that respect. The negotiating bodies for central and local government employees are not really an exception therefore to the general rule of collective bargaining in the country. It is only in the wages councils and the catering wages boards that a real exception is found, and their adoption has been justified on the ground that machinery for regulating remuneration in the trades to which they apply either did not exist or is not and cannot be made adequate for the purpose.[1]

It is appropriate to say a little more about the interested parties who occupy most or all of the seats upon the committees to negotiate with which we are concerned. In those concerned with local authority services, as has just been mentioned, they include on the employers' side, among the representatives of the associations of local authorities, some councillors or aldermen. For the most part, however, they are officials, and officials of two kinds. Where negotiations concern local and central government it is natural that on both the employers' and em-

[1] *Industrial Relations Handbook*, 1953 (Ministry of Labour), p. 144.

ployees' sides people employed in government service, namely, officials, will find a place on the committees. The employers, whether on the National Whitley Council, on departmental or government trade councils, or on the negotiating bodies for local government services, will rely greatly on their chief or senior officials to take part in the negotiations. They will be confronted by other officials, also employed by central or local government. But there is another type of official concerned with this sort of work, namely, the union official, whether the union be an association of employers or employees. Where negotiations of this kind occur it is usual for the discussions to take place between organizations, not between individuals. On the official side in central government this hardly happens, of course, because there is only one central government. But where local authorities are concerned it is their associations which meet the associations of their employees, and in wages councils and catering wages boards again, associations of employers and employees meet each other. In work of this kind the officials of the associations play an important and often a predominant part. On the Burnham committees, for example, it is the Secretary of the Association of Education Committees on the official side and the General Secretary of the National Union of Teachers on the staff side who take a leading share in the negotiations. On the National Whitley Council for the Civil Service, too, although some members of the staff side of twenty-six are serving civil servants, the majority are officials of the associations of civil servants, engaged full-time upon union work. And the same is true on wages councils and catering wages boards, especially where the representatives of the employees are concerned.

The reason for this is fairly plain. Negotiations of this kind are technical matters; they can be best handled by experts with a detailed knowledge of the whole subject. Their preparation and conduct takes time and only the full-time officials of an association can hope to cope with them. Other representatives have a part to play, but they would be lost without their officials. Among the interested parties who form so large a part of the membership of committees to negotiate, therefore, union officials occupy a large and influential place, and they may be counted also as experts. The function of these negotiating bodies, indeed, is very largely to bring together expert knowledge in an industry or employment, and for the two sides to explain to each other just what is involved in a discussion or dispute. On each side will be people who know a great deal about some aspect of the question, but they will be less well informed on other aspects. The point was well made, in connexion with Whitley councils in the Civil Service, by a Treasury official who sits on the official side when he said:

In the Civil Service—it may be different in other occupations—the management consists largely of amateurs. In the ordinary way a senior civil servant will spend only a part of his career on staff administration. Quite frankly, I am ready to admit that the management, if only because of its amateur status, does not always know what is best. It is therefore of the utmost value to the management side to have the benefit of informed staff opinion before introducing any changes in conditions of service.[1]

What is true of the civil service is true also, in large measure, of the local government service, and in other occupations as well.

In the outcome, employees and employers, ministers, members of Parliament and local councillors, and the electors they represent must rely predominantly upon the official, whether government official or union official, to conduct the proceedings of these committees to negotiate through the complicated and technical labyrinths of industrial relations.

6

One criticism which is offered about the workings of committees to negotiate is that they become too remote from and independent of the people or organizations upon whose behalf they act. This criticism deserves some consideration, for it is a judgement upon the record of these committees as committees. So far as the employers' or official side of the committees is concerned, the criticism would not apply with much force to the Whitley councils concerned with the central government, for there the departments are directly represented and are in close touch with their ministers. But where local government is concerned, the employers' side is composed of representatives of associations of local authorities and their actions are in practice

[1] Mr. A. J. D. Winnifrith in *Whitley Bulletin*, July, 1953, p. 104.

scarcely controlled at all by the individual local authorities upon whose behalf they act. Of course, they will always wish to act in such a way as to command the approval of their constituents, but in fact they have very great independence. Their negotiations with the staff or employees' side are carried on in private and it is not until an agreement has been reached that local authorities know just what has been decided on their behalf. It is difficult then to protest.

On the staff or employees' side the practice of leaving decisions almost entirely to the representatives of organizations is, of course, completely established. It is the consequence of trade unionism. The individual member cannot expect to be consulted on proposed salary and wage scales. He leaves that to the central organization. It is difficult to see how, in negotiations at the national level, anything else could be done. Confronted by such centralized organization on the employees' side, employers, whether they be local authorities or private employers, must also organize themselves and carry out negotiations through representatives who are left free to make the best bargain they can. Committees to negotiate come in effect to exercise delegated powers, acting on behalf of their members' constituents who cannot act for themselves. They provide a good example of committees acting in almost complete independence of those who set them up. They may, at times, be responsive, but they are not responsible to their constituents.

The effect of this situation upon the working of local government in Britain must be noticed. Individual local authorities have, in effect, no say in deciding the rates of pay and the conditions of service of their employees. These are determined for them and they must accept them. Since wages and salaries are a large part of local expenditure, the level of rates is determined to an important extent not in town and county hall, but in the sittings of national joint councils and Burnham committees. No doubt the councils' side in negotiating committees does its best to keep salaries and wages down, and it may be conceded that it does better than most councils could do if they acted individually. But the fact remains that these matters are now settled for local authorities and not by them. It is not surprising, therefore, that individual local authorities protest to their associations from time to time about the remoteness of their representatives in these national negotiations and the lack of consultation with local authorities or with provincial councils prior to the taking of decisions in these matters.

It should be emphasized that what is said above applies to committees to negotiate operating on the national level. On provincial joint councils and still more on local Whitley councils or committees, both individual local authorities and their staffs obtain direct representation in the discussions. Representatives of both sides are in closer contact with those they represent and are more effectively responsible to them. But it will be remembered that, important as these contacts are, the determination of wages and conditions of service are outside the scope of local and most provincial councils; it is handled by the national negotiating bodies.

What is true of the committees to negotiate in local authorities' services is true also, though in varying degrees, in wages councils and catering wages boards, not to mention also the vast range of negotiating bodies whose agreements do not require the approval of a minister before they become effective. It is difficult to see how this can be avoided, once it is agreed that collective negotiation shall be undertaken. No doubt where the number of employers in an industry is small, their control over their representatives on the employers' side in a committee to negotiate can be more effective than where, as in local government, their number is large. But collective negotiation means negotiations between organizations, and if these negotiations are to be effective the representatives of the organizations must have authority not merely to discuss but also to agree or to decide. Ratification by individual employers seldom fails to introduce uncertainty, delay, and ineffectiveness into the machinery. The conclusion is difficult to escape that committees to negotiate must, if they are to work at all, enjoy a degree of independence or autonomy in relation to their parent bodies which gives them a unique position in the sphere of committee work.

CHAPTER VI

Committees to Legislate

I

THE use of committees may be demonstrated by two arguments, each of which might appear at first sight to contradict the other. It can be said that a committee should be used because it enables more people to be associated with a particular governmental process. It can be said, on the other hand, that a committee should be used because it enables fewer people to be associated with a process. There is, of course, no necessary contradiction between these two statements. A glance at the reasons which justify the use of committees by town and county councils illustrates the point. A council sets up committees because, on the one hand, it believes that the conduct of administration should not be confided to so numerous a body as a whole council, and because, on the other hand, it believes that the conduct of administration should not be confided to a single person or to a few isolated individuals. In the case of council committees few people could be found to argue that the whole council should control administration; where room for difference of opinion arises is upon the question whether it is wise to confide administration to a plural rather than to a unitary institution—a question which will be discussed in the next chapter. In other spheres of government, however, an argument arises not upon the merits of the committee as against the single individual, but as between the committee and the larger body of which it is a part and from which it obtains its commission. This is the case in particular with those standing committees of the House of Commons which are set up by the House to take a share in the legislative process.

Few, if any, would argue that the House should delegate its entire legislative function to ministers, although a considerable measure of such delegation exists. But there is room for discussion of the extent to which the House as a whole should undertake the legislative process or should confide it or some stage of it to committees of itself. As the standing orders of the House of Commons now read, it is the accepted policy of the House to send bills (with certain exceptions) after their second reading for consideration by standing committees. 'When a public bill (other than a bill for imposing taxes or a Consolidated Fund or an Appropriation Bill, or a bill for confirming a provisional order) has been read a second time, it shall stand committed to a standing committee unless the House otherwise order', runs Standing Order 38 (1).[1] And it is provided that there shall be as many standing committees as are necessary to cope with the business.[2]

The House goes still farther in the case of bills relating exclusively to Scotland. Not only does it provide that such bills may be dealt with by a standing committee after second reading, but it provides also that a bill relating exclusively to Scotland may be referred to a standing committee for what is in effect its second reading unless ten or more members of the House object.[3] It is provided similarly that the Scottish estimates may be considered in standing committee,[4] whereas other estimates are taken in the Committee of Supply, a committee, it will be recalled, of the whole House. The full significance of this special treatment of Scottish bills and Scottish estimates, however, will be appreciated when it is mentioned that the standing committee to which these matters are referred is a committee composed of all the members representing Scottish constituencies together with not less than ten nor more than fifteen members nominated in respect of the particular business under discussion.[5] As there are 71 members representing Scottish constituencies, it is clear that purely Scottish business is largely in the hands of Scottish members.[6] It may be added that the provision that second readings and estimates may be taken in standing

---

[1] References are to the 1953 edition of the Standing Orders of the House of Commons.

[2] Standing Order 57 (1). Before 1947 a maximum number of standing committees was fixed in standing orders, but the limit was removed by sessional order from 1945 and the change was made part of standing orders in 1947.

[3] S.O. 60.   [4] S.O. 61.

[5] S.O. 59.

[6] The arrangements for second readings and estimates provided in S.O. 60 and 61 were introduced in 1948 as part of the government's plan to meet Scottish demands for greater control over Scottish affairs. See Cmd. 7308 (1948), *Scottish Affairs*.

committee is a privilege confined to Scottish business only. Although there is a provision that public bills relating exclusively to Wales and Monmouthshire may be referred to a standing committee after second reading and that, in such a case, the committee must be so constituted as to comprise all members sitting for constituencies in Wales and Monmouthshire,[1] no such arrangement is provided for second readings of such bills or for estimates.

It is clearly an accepted principle in the House of Commons that some share in the process of legislation shall be confided to committees of the House, and in the case of Scottish bills that this share shall cover almost the entire process in the House. For other bills, however, the share is confined to a particular stage in the process—what is called the 'committee stage'. This means in fact that the standing committees do not receive a bill until the House has decided in favour of its principles by giving it a second reading. The committee is limited in its consideration, therefore, to matters within the principles already decided upon by the House. It is important to bear this restriction in mind. It distinguishes the function of standing committees of the House of Commons in the legislative process in Britain from that permitted to committees in other parliaments, such for example as the American Congress or the French Parliament or indeed of most parliaments on the Continent of Europe. In the United States—both in the Congress at Washington and in the Congresses of the forty-eight separate States—and in continental legislatures on the French model, a bill is submitted to a committee of the Parliament for consideration before it has been considered, much less approved of, by the Parliament as a whole. As a result the committee may consider everything in the bill and may propose amendments of principle as well as of detail. Whether this is a good thing or not is a matter for discussion when later we come to ask of what use the British standing committees are, and whether they are given enough scope to be of use. For the moment the important thing to notice is that, with the exception of the Scottish Standing Committee—and that is not a substantial exception, for as few as ten members can prevent the bill going to the Scottish Committee at the second-reading stage—the share of committees in the legislative

[1] S.O. 58. There is no record of this Welsh Standing Committee having met.

process of the House of Commons is confined to that stage in the
process where the principles of the bill have been determined
and lie outside the ambit of the committee.

2

Before considering in any detail the nature and value of the
work which standing committees do in legislation, it will be
well to consider how our seven characters are related both to
the committees and to each other.

The first important fact about the members of the standing
committees is that they are all, with scarcely an exception, party
men. There are a few independent, non-party members of the
House of Commons, and they find a place from time to time on
a standing committee, but the great majority of the members
are party men and for practical purposes we may regard the
standing committees as composed of party men. Moreover it is
accepted and expected that the members will vote on party lines.
There is nothing very surprising in this. The standing committees are dealing with legislation, and legislation is a step and
often the last step in the process of the formulation of policy.
They are therefore in the area where party differences are
expected to show themselves. They reflect, indeed, the party
division which is to be found in the House as a whole; they are
really each of them little Houses of Commons. That is the position, at any rate, where government bills are concerned. Where
a standing committee is considering a private member's bill,
opinion may cut across party lines, though even there if the
government leader or the Opposition leader should express an
official opinion upon a clause or a proposed amendment and
should advise the committee to take a certain course, voting
tends to follow party lines.

The fact that the members of standing committees are party
men and are expected to behave as such is reflected in the rules
which govern the appointment of members to the committees.
Appointments are made by the Committee of Selection, a body
of eleven members, composed in accordance with the strengths
of the parties in the House. The Committee of Selection first
appoints a nucleus of twenty members for each standing committee and in doing so is obliged to have regard to the composi-

tion of the House. It is empowered thereafter to add to this nucleus not more than thirty members, in respect of any bill referred to a particular standing committee, to serve on the committee during the consideration of that bill, and in doing this it is obliged to have regard to the qualifications of the members.[1] On the face of it, then, it is possible that a standing committee could be set up with a majority of Opposition members on it, for if the first twenty only are to be appointed with regard to the composition of the House, would it not be possible that enough of the next thirty, appointed with regard to qualifications, might be appointed from the Opposition party to give that party a majority on the committee? This could happen but it does not. And it is not surprising, perhaps, that it should not when we remember that the government party is bound to have a majority on the committee of selection. In fact, it is understood that the composition of the standing committees will reflect the composition of the House, although the standing order lays down this principle only so far as the nucleus of twenty members is concerned.[2]

Members of standing committees face each other across the floor of the committee room, with government members sitting on the chairman's right and Opposition members sitting on his left, just as in the chamber of the House of Commons.[3] Instead of informal conversation and discussion between members sitting around a table, each member of a standing committee rises in his place and addresses the committee. Divisions are on party lines. The Whips are in charge of committees[4] and they must see to it that a quorum is kept and that a majority is at call.

[1] S.O. 58.

[2] When the government's majority in the House is small, its representation on standing committees must be exaggerated if the system is to work. When the Labour Government was returned in 1950 with a small majority, a literal following of the principle of proportional representation resulted in the Labour Party receiving twenty-five members on standing committees, the Conservatives twenty-four, and the Liberals one. When the government got into difficulties, it was decided that it must be given a majority on the standing committees. The Speaker ruled that it was proper for the selection committee to reconstruct standing committees to ensure this. 485 H.C. Deb., 5th ser., cols. 668–75 (8 Mar. 1951).

[3] It may be added that the public is admitted to debates in standing committees unless the committees order otherwise. S.O. 57 (1).

[4] Though this has been the regular practice since 1947 only.

3

The fact that party is predominant in the standing committees affects the position of the chairman. In standing committees
leadership is in the hands of a minister; the chairman is concerned only with questions of order and the conduct of business. He is a reflection in the committee of Mr. Speaker or the
Chairman of Committees in the House as a whole. This is a
consequence or illustration of the British system of cabinet
government, in the development of which the chair has declined
in importance politically[1] but has increased in power and prestige as an institution of order in the conduct of business. It
should not be assumed that this must be so. Ministers could be
chairmen of committees, and chairmen of committees could be
forceful and influential party leaders. On the British model of
cabinet government this has not happened, and there are good
reasons for saying that the way in which the system has
developed exhibits certain advantages. Chief among them is the
separation from party control of important questions of order
and fairness in debate which are of fundamental concern.

For it must not be assumed that the chairman, since he lacks
the power to lead the standing committee, is without importance. On the contrary he has an important role, though it is
not the role of leadership. Put quite shortly and in general terms,
it is the chairman's duty to see to it that, on the one hand, the
minority on the committee is given a fair hearing and that, on
the other, the majority is not obstructed in the carrying through
of its business. An example of the chairman's power to protect
the minority is the authority conferred upon him to exercise his
discretion in accepting a motion to bring debate to an end by
proceeding to a vote. If a member claims to move 'That the
question be now put', the chairman is entitled to consider
whether such a motion 'is an abuse of the rules of the House or
an infringement of the rights of the minority', and if he thinks
that it is, he may refuse to accept the motion.[2] On the other
hand, the chairman will consider whether in fact there has been

---

[1] There was a time when the Speaker of the House of Commons was not only
a party man but also a party leader (see Campion *et al.*, *Parliament: a Survey*, pp.
150–1), the position now held by the Speaker of the House of Representatives in
the United States.
[2] S.O. 57 (5).

a full enough debate, bearing in mind that the majority is entitled, after full discussion, to have its way. The chairman is given powers, too, to select from the numerous amendments put down by the Opposition to the clauses of a bill those which he thinks merit discussion, and he can in this way shorten the debate and assist in the expedition of government business.[1] This is a very great power to give to a presiding officer and it is clear that it could only be exercised by one whose impartiality was above all question. It was first conferred upon the Speaker alone and it was not until 1934 that it was extended to chairmen of standing committees. In matters of this kind the chairman has come to acquire the status and powers of the Speaker— he can check members for irrelevance and repetition and he can refuse motions which in his opinion are dilatory, just as the Speaker can. In these ways he is given powers which, in the hands of a firm and respected chairman, can have an important influence on the conduct of proceedings. He is, like the Speaker, something much more than a mere presiding officer, putting motions to the vote and calling upon members to address the committee. He has his own distinct and important role to play, but he is the guide and guardian of the committee rather than its leader.

The chairman's impartiality is reflected in the way he is appointed. He is not, like the chairmen of select committees in the House of Commons, or of committees in town and county halls, elected by the members of the committee. He is appointed by Mr. Speaker. He is chosen, however, not from among the members of the committee itself but from a special panel of members of the House, the Chairmen's Panel, consisting of the chairman of Ways and Means, the deputy chairman, and other members appointed by the Speaker to act as temporary chairmen of committees of the whole House. These men are all back-benchers; they have usually had experience of the work of chairmen and they have an interest in this kind of work.[2] They are chosen from all parties, though the chairman of Ways and Means usually belongs to the government party. It falls out

[1] S.O. 57 (5).
[2] The Chairmen's Panel is indeed a recognized institution in the House. It holds meetings and makes reports and recommendations to the House from time to time on procedural questions, and particularly upon the working of standing committees.

therefore that an Opposition member may preside over a standing committee, or a member of the government party may do
so. The Speaker will select the chairman and the choice will
be made on grounds of ability and convenience and not on
grounds of party.[1]

With the chairman performing this special and important role,
the main share in leading the committee falls to the Minister.
His business is to steer the bill through the committee. It is
axiomatic that he will be a member of the committee, as also
will his parliamentary secretary or under-secretary—provided
of course that they are members of the House of Commons. If
a minister is in the House of Lords, it will be the task of his
assistant to steer the bill through the standing committee of
the House of Commons. As a general rule it is the Minister who
does most of the talking on the government side of the committee; he replies to Opposition amendments and indicates
whether they are acceptable to the government or not, and
whether he is prepared to make concessions along the lines advocated by the Opposition. It is only when a bill contains proposals
to which government supporters are opposed, or about which
they are uneasy, that they feel obliged to enter into the debate.
For the rest they are content to leave it to the Minister to deal
with the Opposition. Members on the government side are not
expected to keep the debate going as they are in the House as a
whole, or to defend government policy against the Opposition.

4

It should not be concluded that, in performing their respective roles, the chairman and the Minister act single-handed.
Both are assisted by officials, who advise them upon the course
they should pursue. The chairman has on his left a senior clerk
of the House of Commons who is, in effect, the secretary of the
committee. He advises him on questions of procedure, and
keeps the formal records of the committee. On the chairman's
right is an official of the parliamentary counsel's department to

---

[1] It is interesting to mention, perhaps, that members of a standing committee
address the chairman by name, not as 'Mr. Chairman'; a practice which obtains
also in addressing the chairman or deputy chairman of committees in committee
of the whole House.

advise him upon amendments. Before the sittings of a committee, the chairman will have consulted these advisers upon questions of selection of amendments and of what amendments are in order and what are not, and throughout the sittings he is able to ask for further advice from them. In some cases a chairman is an expert himself in these matters, but even so he will welcome the assistance which his expert advisers give him, for rulings on points of order can often involve intricate questions and the consultation of precedents. Generally speaking the best qualification for a chairman, in addition to impartiality, is not so much expert knowledge of procedure as a capacity to act firmly and wisely upon advice given to him by the experts, a capacity which comes partly from the ability to grasp and understand points of order quickly, partly from good sense and good temper, partly from experience with such matters in the chair. As a general rule, no doubt, members of the Chairmen's Panel know more about parliamentary procedure than the average member of the House, but they need not be experts. The expert advice is there for them if and when they need it.

The Minister is in a similar position. He must rely upon his advisers. And they are present in the committee room for all to see. On the right of the chairman, beyond the officer of the parliamentary counsel's department, sit the officials of the Minister's department, and he is in constant consultation with them as the debate proceeds. His seat is near them and he does not hesitate to get up and consult them when necessary. As it is known before each day's sitting of a standing committee what clauses of a bill and what amendments are to be taken, there is an opportunity, of course, for a minister to consult his advisers about the line he should take in dealing with them and what answers he should give. He cannot be certain, however, what the Opposition will say in proposing amendments, and he must expect to consult his advisers a good deal during the course of the debate. A minister, in charge of a complicated bill, cannot be expected to be an expert on the whole of it or even perhaps on a large part of it. After all few officials, if any, in his department will be in that position. But he can aim to be a good general practitioner; he can get it up carefully and explain it in language which he understands and which he intends members of the committee to understand. That is the merit of the system.

It is not enough that officials should know what a bill means or that they should be able to explain it to each other. They should be put to the test of explaining it to a minister in such a way that he can expound and defend it before the Opposition in a committee, clause by clause. It is a severe test, for it is a test clause by clause. The Minister cannot rely upon a general speech, prepared in the department, skating over and round the difficulties. That may suffice for a second reading. It will not do in committee.

Although officials are present in the committee room they are technically not on the floor of the committee. They do not speak nor may they be questioned by members of the committee. Standing committees have no witnesses. What officials have to say in defence of a bill must be said to the Minister; he must translate or transmit it to the committee. Similarly, such views about the bill as other experts may hold cannot be placed directly before the committee. They must approach the Minister or the members of the committee individually. This procedure is in contrast not only to the procedure of select committees of inquiry in the House of Commons or of other committees to inquire or to advise in Britain, but also to the procedure of committees to legislate in the United States and in many continental countries, such as France. There it is accepted as an essential part of a committee's consideration of a bill that the views not only of the Minister and his department should be heard but also of others who wish to express an opinion. Considerable time is given over to 'hearings' when experts for and against the measure attempt to influence the committee in evidence. No such procedure is permitted in the standing-committee stage of legislation in Britain.

Some mention should be made of a further device for making expert advice and leadership available to the standing committees. Questions sometimes arise in the course of debate upon the legal implications of a clause in a bill or of some proposed amendment. Upon a matter of this kind the Minister in charge of the bill commonly feels himself unqualified to express an opinion. Legal advice is no doubt available to him, but that is not enough, for someone must explain that legal advice to the committee in language which can go on record in the committee's *Hansard* as an authoritative statement of the government's view. For this task it is clear that the Attorney-General and the Solicitor-General are best qualified. It is a part of their business as Law Officers of the Crown. They are invariably lawyers of standing, and constitute two of the few exceptions there are in Britain to the general rule that ministers are not expected to be experts in the affairs of the department over which they are called to preside. It is clear, however, that the services of the Attorney-General and the Solicitor-General may be required at any stage in the discussion of any bill in any standing committee, and it follows that the only safe rule is to make it permissible for them to take part in the proceedings of any standing committee. As members of the House of Commons they are entitled, of course, to become members of standing committees, but it would clearly be a great burden upon them if they were obliged to take part in all the proceedings of all standing committees. It is accordingly provided that the Law Officers 'though not members of a standing committee, may take part in the deliberations of the committee, but shall not vote or move any motion or any amendment or be counted in the quorum'.[1] By this means expert legal advice is available for the standing committees, while the Law Officers can participate when required in the proceedings of a committee but are not obliged to be present at other times. It may be mentioned that it was not until standing committees came to be used more widely and for more important bills, in 1945, that this arrangement was made.[2] Previously the amount of work undertaken by standing committees had been such that the Law Officers could carry out their duties by being members of the standing committee concerned.

5

It may be appropriate now to ask whether it is correct to speak of the standing committees as being not only committees of party men but also committees of laymen. The answer to this question needs a little consideration. It may be said to begin with that the standing committees are not specialized committees. That is to say that, unlike the French or American com-

---

[1] S.O. 65.
[2] The change was authorized by sessional order in 1945 and it was embodied in standing orders in 1947.

mittees, they are not set up at the beginning of a session to deal
with specific subjects such as commerce, trade and industry,
health, education, foreign relations, and so on. In this respect,
too, they differ from the select committees on public accounts,
estimates, and statutory instruments,[1] and from the committees
set up by local authorities in Britain.[2] Members of a standing
committee therefore lack the opportunity to make a continuous
study, extending perhaps from one session to another, of a particular branch of policy, as do the members of the select committees just mentioned. Although proposals have been made
from time to time that standing committees should have a
specialized field allotted to each of them—and a notable suggestion to this end was put forward by the Clerk of the House of
Commons, Sir Horace Dawkins, before the Select Committee
on Procedure in 1931[3]—the plan has not been adopted. It is
interesting to notice, also, that before 1907 the standing committees of the House, and the Grand Committees which preceded them, had always been appointed on a specialist basis.[4]
Since that date, however, the procedure is to appoint as many
standing committees as are necessary to deal with bills,[5] and to
allot bills to them when they are free to take them. The 'lay' or
'neutral' nature of the committees is emphasized or illustrated,
perhaps, by the fact that committees are distinguished from
each other by letters of the alphabet and are known as Committees A, B, C, D, E, and so on.

When we look at the record of work which standing committees have carried out in a particular session, the lack of specialization seems further illustrated. In the session of 1948–9,[6] for
example, Standing Committee A considered bills dealing with
wages councils, savings banks, the coal industry, legal aid and
advice, national parks and access to the country-side, and air-
ways corporations; Standing Committee B considered bills dealing with special roads, licensing, war damage (public utility
undertakings), superannuation, and the National Health Service. Although Standing Committee C considered three bills
only, it would be difficult to cover a wider range or to imagine

[1] See below, Chapter VIII.   [2] See below, Chapter VII.
[3] See H.C. 161 of 1931, Appendix 6 and evidence.
[4] H.C. 189–1 of 1945–6. *Third Report of Select Committee on Procedure*, p. xlii.
[5] Subject, as was explained above, to the upper limit imposed until 1945.
[6] See H.C. 334 of 1948–9.

anyone who would be expert in all three subjects. For after the committee had devoted thirty-six days to the consideration of the controversial and technical Iron and Steel Bill, by which time some of its members presumably had become fairly well informed on the subject, it turned to consider first a housing bill and thereafter a coast protection bill. The record of Standing Committee D gives a similar impression. It considered bills dealing with agricultural marketing, agriculture (miscellaneous provisions), milk (special designations), prevention of damage by pests—so far there seems some family resemblance between the bills, but it ceases now—merchant shipping (safety convention), the sea fish industry, and patents and designs.

On one standing committee private members' bills have precedence, and it is apparent that specialization would be difficult to achieve on this committee, since all that private members' bills will be certain to have in common is that they are introduced by private members. In the session of 1948–9 Standing Committee E considered private members' bills; there were ten of them and they covered a wide variety of subjects—hairdressers' registration, adoption of children, law reform, the maintenance of married women, the baiting of animals, analgesia in childbirth, docking and nicking of horses, pet animals, war damage, and the censorship of plays. Yet it may be doubted whether the range covered by this miscellaneous collection of private members' bills was wider than that which Standing Committee A had referred to it.

It may seem at first sight that the business of the Scottish Standing Committee would provide an exception to the general impression so far given of the business referred to the ordinary standing committees. It is composed, predominantly, of members who have all a common interest in Scotland and the business referred to them will, by standing orders, always relate exclusively to Scotland. Yet it must be remembered that these Scottish members will be required to consider all the exclusively Scottish business, and that covers a wide range. In the session 1948–9 the Scottish Standing Committee considered bills relating to education, water, tenancy of shops, slaughter of animals, legal aid and solicitors, and housing, while in addition it devoted six days to the Scottish estimates, covering the Scottish home department, approved schools in Scotland, public education in Scotland, the department of health for Scotland, the National Health Service in Scotland, and the department of agriculture for Scotland. It may be doubted whether many members of the committee had special knowledge on more than one or two of these matters, though it may well have been that many of them were interested in almost all of the topics discussed.

The standing committees of the House of Commons, then, are not specialized committees in the sense of being committees set up to deal with bills relating to particular fields of governmental activity, as are the committees of the United States Congress and of many continental parliaments. But it would be a mistake to conclude from this that the standing committees contain no members with special knowledge of or interest in the subject of the bill which is referred to them for consideration, or that if any members should have such special knowledge or interest, their presence on the committee is purely a matter of chance. Let us recall, first of all, that the standing orders concerning the composition of standing committees provide that the committee of selection has power to add to the nucleus of twenty members of a standing committee up to thirty additional members 'in respect of any bill referred to it, to serve on the committee during the consideration of such bill, and in adding such members shall have regard to their qualifications'.[1] It is possible therefore for a majority of the members of a standing committee to be persons with a special knowledge of or interest in the bill which the committee is considering. It is not certain that all thirty will be of this kind, of course, for the committee of selection will not overlook the fact that the government must have a majority on the committee. Nor can we be certain that the committee will not sometimes select members who are unqualified but who, for some reason, want or deserve to sit on the committee. There are many reasons why the full thirty members may not be the best qualified or even well qualified. But it is clear that there is provision for ensuring that some members of the committee are not merely laymen.

It is apparent from a study of the standing order, also, that when we speak of a standing committee having dealt in a particular session with a wide variety of bills, we must not fall into

[1] S.O. 58.

the error of imagining that the same body of persons has dealt with all the bills. The most that should be assumed is that the nucleus of twenty may have continued unchanged throughout. Let us look at what actually happened, for example, in some of the cases in the session of 1948–9 which have already been quoted. If we take Standing Committee C, which dealt with the controversial Iron and Steel Bill, and thereafter the Housing Bill and the Coast Protection Bill, the first thing we should notice is the nucleus of twenty members which was chosen for this committee. It contained practically all the Opposition members who were expected to play a leading part in the con-duct of the Opposition's case against the bills—Mr. Oliver Lyttelton, Mr. Harold Macmillan, Mr. Osbert Peake, and Mr. Manningham-Buller. These members, though chosen for the nucleus, where, as the standing order prescribes, the committee of selection shall have regard to the composition of the House, were clearly chosen for their qualifications also. It is evident that in choosing the nucleus of a standing committee, the com-mittee of selection does not proceed in the abstract and choose members regardless of the nature of the bill which the committee will first consider. Evidently it waits until it knows what that bill is before it begins the task of selecting members. We must rid our minds of any notion of a set of nuclei for standing com-mittees selected *in vacuo* at the beginning of the session, before it is known what bills will be referred to them, and thereafter being added to when the particular bill is known. It seems fairly clear that so far as the first bill to be considered by a standing committee in the session is concerned, the selection of the nucleus and of the additional members occur after it is known what bill is first to be referred, and that the principle of con-sidering a member's qualifications for membership operates in the selection of the nucleus no less than in the selection of the additional members.

It may be noticed also that the members of the nucleus do not necessarily remain the same throughout the session. Thus in Standing Committee C in the session 1948–9 no less than nine of the original twenty members who formed the nucleus of the committee and who formed part of its membership in the consideration of the Iron and Steel Bill ceased to belong to the committee when it considered the Housing Bill and the Coast

Protection Bill, while two other members ceased to belong to it after the consideration of the Iron and Steel Bill and the Housing Bill.[1] There is nothing particularly surprising in this. It is understandable that members, for a variety of reasons, should not wish to continue to serve on a committee throughout a session. An explanation of why some members do not continue may be seen when we notice that among the members of the nucleus of Standing Committee C who ceased to serve after the consideration of the Iron and Steel Bill were Mr. Oliver Lyttelton, Mr. Harold Macmillan, Mr. Manningham-Buller, and Mr. Osbert Peake. They had done their job and their special knowledge was not required by the Opposition side on the two later bills. Mr. Lyttelton and Mr. Macmillan did not in fact sit on any other standing committees during the session but Mr. Peake was a member also of Committees A and B and Mr. Manningham-Buller of Committees A, D, and E (the last named dealing with private members' bills).[2]

If there is a change in the membership of the nucleus of a standing committee from bill to bill, there is of course almost a complete change in the additional membership. Of the additional members that were added to Standing Committee C, for example, only four (if we exclude ministers) were members of the committee for the consideration of more than one of the three bills it dealt with; none of these four was a member for the consideration of more than two bills. So far as the members of the nucleus were concerned, it may be noted that nine out of the original twenty served on the committee for the consideration of all three bills.

It is not necessary to give detailed figures for all the standing committees. It will be found that in general they all illustrate the sort of position which Standing Committee C has indicated. The personnel of the committees, then, in spite of the notion of the nucleus, differs considerably from bill to bill, and this difference is partly explained by the fact that their membership is altered so as to allow members to get on to a committee which is considering a bill in which they are interested. The first im-

---

[1] They were replaced, of course, by other members nominated by the committee of selection.

[2] Mr. Manningham-Buller was a lawyer and therefore his services would be particularly in demand by the Opposition. As Sir Reginald Manningham-Buller he was Solicitor-General in the government formed by Mr. Churchill in 1951.

pression one has of a constant committee with varying measures coming before it must be put aside, or at any rate considerably qualified. The committees by adjusting their membership to members' interests give much more scope to special knowledge and interest than might seem possible at first sight. In fact, one might say that the essential contrast between the British system of committees and the American and French systems in the matter of bringing special knowledge and interest to bear on bills is that whereas in the French and American systems the bills go to the members with special knowledge and interest, in the British system the members with special knowledge and interest go to the bills, pursuing them to the committees to which Mr. Speaker has referred them.

It would be out of place in this chapter to attempt to illustrate this point at great length. A few examples may be given which show that when members with expert knowledge in some matter are available in the House, they are chosen to sit upon committees dealing with a bill on which they can claim knowledge. Thus, when in the session 1948–9 Standing Committee A considered the Legal Aid and Advice Bill, there were to be found upon the committee such legal men as Sir David Maxwell Fyfe, K.C., Mr. Quintin Hogg, Mr. Hector Hughes, K.C., Mr. Joynson-Hicks, Mr. Maude, Mr. Paget, K.C., Mr. Ungoed Thomas, Mr. Basil Nield, K.C., Mr. Henry Strauss, K.C., in addition of course to the Attorney-General and the Solicitor-General, who were in charge of the Bill. When Standing Committee B dealt with the National Health Service (Amendment) Bill four doctors were among the members added by the Committee of Selection in respect of this Bill. Many other examples could be given.

6

It may well be contended that the examples just given have in them an element not only of the expert but also to some degree of the interested party, however remote that interest may be in particular persons. What about those people whose interests are affected by a bill, the interested parties or 'partisans', those who may be promoting it and urging it upon the government or opposing it because of its effect upon their interests? How do they get their say? It has been explained already that the hearing of evidence is no part of the proceedings on a bill before a standing committee in Britain, whereas before the standing committees of Congress, for example, all interested parties or partisans are expected to urge their views. On rare occasions, it is true, a bill has been committed to a select committee of the House of Commons after its second reading, and when that has happened evidence can be and has been called. But it is an unusual proceeding. The partisan is expected to make his views known in other ways. Something has been said in the previous chapters of some of these ways. Much government legislation has been discussed with the interests concerned before it is introduced. Committees to inquire and to advise, before which interested parties may have given evidence and upon which these interests themselves may have been represented, perhaps considered the problem and made recommendations. Organized interests make representations direct to ministries and propose or criticize legislation. They make representations, too, to members of Parliament while a bill is proceeding through the House. When standing-committee stage is reached the representatives of these interests often attend the sittings in the space reserved in the committee room for members of the public, and are available to discuss matters with members. The Opposition will be ready to use ammunition which can be provided for them in order to make a case against the government's bill. Through these informal ways the interests affected by bills are enabled to bring their views and opinions to bear, and it cannot be doubted that what they do is of influence at the standing-committee stage. But their actions are informal; they do not give evidence; they do not appear, as in the United States, before the committee.

It is to be expected, also, that some members of Parliament will themselves be partisans[1]—that is to say they may either

---

[1] From many examples may be selected Standing Committee C on the Licensed Premises in New Towns Bill in session 1951–2, whose members included varying degrees of interest from a teetotaller (*Standing Committee Debates*, col. 98) to the director of a firm of brewers (cols. 68–69). One member represented Carlisle, where state management of public houses exists (col. 66), another spoke as a resident of a new town (col. 82). There was some argument on the committee about the nature and extent of the brewery director's interest (cols. 165, 166, 216–17), and there were allegations in the House of Commons itself that a place for the director had been found on the committee by inducing a member to resign who happened to occupy the position of President of the Band of Hope, thus substituting one kind of interested party for another. 504 H.C. Deb., 5th ser., cols. 69–70, 105 ff.

themselves belong to some interest which is affected by the legislation or they may represent a constituency which is concerned with a subject upon which legislation is being undertaken. Thus members of Parliament who are miners or officials of a miners' union will have an interest in a coal-mines nationalization bill; members of Parliament who are doctors in a national health service bill; members of Parliament who are owners of or workers in steel plants in an iron and steel bill; and so on. It is certain that, in the course of a session, bills will be referred to standing committees on matters concerning which some members of Parliament are, either through their employment, present or past, or from the nature of their constituency, partisans. As partisans they may also be experts, and they would seem to fall well within the category of those additional members whom the Committee of Selection may appoint having regard to their qualifications. And in fact such appointments are made. It is not considered a disqualification for appointment to a committee that a member represents an interest which a bill affects.[1] He has knowledge which qualifies him to be a member of the committee.

7

Standing committees, then, may contain experts and they may contain representatives of interests, who may or may not be experts. It is certain that they will contain laymen and in many cases they will contain a majority of laymen. It will be rare, however, to find an occasion when the Minister with his expert official advisers is not confronted by an Opposition member whose task it is to conduct the opposition to the bill in the committee and who, for this purpose, has studied the bill and made himself aware of the various criticisms of the bill which can be advanced on behalf either of those directly affected by it or of the party and the public. In this way what may

[1] It should be added, however, that if a member is judged to have a direct pecuniary interest in a bill, he is disqualified from voting upon it, but he may speak upon it. The disqualification is narrowly interpreted—the interest must be immediate and personal, not general or remote. See Erskine May, *Parliamentary Practice*, 15th ed., p. 418. It is customary for a member to declare his interest, although it may not amount to a disqualifying interest.

be, for the most part, a lay committee is given leadership both on the majority side and on the minority side. Party in this respect brings the benefits of order and leadership to the standing committee and ensures that some knowledge and, on occasions, some expert opinion will be brought to the discussion.

It is possible to consider now the use to which standing committees are put and how far this use is a good use or a bad use. The first and obvious reason for the use of these committees to legislate is to secure the passage by the House of Commons of more bills. If all bills had to be considered by a committee of the whole House, obviously fewer bills would pass.[1] There can be only one committee of the whole House sitting at a time and it can only discuss one bill at a time; several standing committees can sit at once and each can consider a bill. When in 1945 the Labour Government proposed to the Select Committee on Procedure, which it had invited the House of Commons to set up, that more bills should be considered by standing committees in future, its main reason was that it thought that Parliament would be obliged in future to pass more bills.

During the period of the transition from war to peace [it said] a really heavy programme of legislation of one kind and another will be required and will be required urgently, for the purposes of reconstruction. . . . The main expenditure of time upon legislation arises at the Committee stage. . . . The first main proposals of the Government are accordingly directed to the Committee stage. In their opinion, it will be necessary during the reconstruction period both to send practically all Bills upstairs and to find means of accelerating their passage in Standing Committee.[2]

As the standing orders stood in 1945 it was the rule that a bill—unless it was a financial bill or a bill to confirm a provisional order—went to a standing committee unless the House ordered otherwise, but the practice had been to keep bills of importance on the floor of the House. The government's proposal was that the provisions of the standing order should be applied generally in future and that only bills of great constitutional importance—in addition to financial and provisional-order bills—should be considered in committee of the whole House. In order to cope

---

[1] Unless, of course, discussion were cut down by the closure to a point never yet contemplated in the House of Commons.

[2] *First Report from Select Committee on Procedure*, H.C. 9–1 of 1945–6, pp. x, xi.

with what was expected to be a much larger number of bills, the government also proposed that there should be no limit on the number of standing committees—it had been fixed at five including the Scottish Committee in the standing orders of 1945 —but that there should be set up as many committees as the business demanded. These proposals, the government believed, would save anything up to thirty days on the floor of the House of Commons in the course of a session.[1] The Select Committee on Procedure approved these proposals and the House adopted them. They have been in operation since 1945.

It is interesting to see what use it has been possible to make of standing committees in this period and to compare it with the use made before 1939. In 1919 standing committees considered 45 bills; in 1924–5 50 bills; in 1929–30 32 bills; in 1934–5 15 bills; and in 1936–7 26 bills.[2] We may compare these figures with those for a few of the sessions since 1946. In the session of 1946–7 standing committees considered 15 bills;[3] in the session of 1947–8 they considered 21 bills;[4] and in 1948–9 they considered 42 bills, though of this large total only 31 were government bills and 10 of these were Scottish bills dealt with by the Scottish Standing Committee.[5] At first sight therefore it would look as if, in spite of the government's intentions, the standing committees had not dealt with an increased number of bills; there was not at any rate any striking increase on the figures for the years before 1939.

But it would give an incomplete picture of the position if we left it at this. Although the standing committees did not deal with a greater number of bills, it is clear that they dealt with a greater number of important bills than they had done before 1939. In the session of 1946–7, for example, four important bills were dealt with by standing committees—the Agriculture Bill, the Transport Bill (which nationalized transport), the Town and Country Planning Bill, and the Electricity Bill (another nationalizing measure). It may be doubted whether any one of these bills would have been sent to a standing committee before 1939. The two nationalizing measures certainly would not. Moreover, without having been sent to a standing committee, it is practically certain that no more than two of them could

[1] Ibid., p. xi. [2] Ibid., p. 39. [3] H.C. 9 of 1947–8.
[4] H.C. 210 of 1947–8. [5] H.C. 334 of 1948–9.

have been passed through the whole House. Certainly two nationalizing bills would have been more than a pre-war House would have been ready to take along with the other two. Any one of these four measures would have been thought to be enough for one session in the years after 1922. Yet all four were taken through standing committee and, by this means, enacted in the session. The other sessions supply further examples. In the session of 1947–8 standing committees considered the Criminal Justice Bill, the National Assistance Bill, the Local Government Bill, and the Gas Bill—the measure by which the gas industry was nationalized. In the session of 1948–9 a standing committee considered the Iron and Steel Bill—a measure which before 1939 would certainly have occupied the time of the Committee of the Whole House throughout the session.

There is little doubt then that the record of the years 1945–50 when the Labour Government had a large majority in the House of Commons shows that by the use of standing committees it was possible for a greater number of important and controversial bills to be passed than would have been possible without the use of standing committees. It must be added, however, that when a conclusion of this kind is stated, it is made on the assumption that no other changes were made in procedure. It is assumed that if major bills were taken on the floor of the House no new form of closure would be introduced, although no doubt some extensive use of the existing forms of closure would be required to get controversial bills through. The argument for using standing committees is that if the government tries to use the Committee of the Whole House it will either not get its bills through or it will do it only by so restricting discussion in the whole House as to make proper consideration of the bill in committee impossible.

This leads on to a consideration of the second advantage which, it is held, comes from the use of standing committees. It is maintained that by using committees it is possible not only to pass a greater number of important bills, but also to ensure that these bills get proper consideration. The two arguments are, in fact, usually regarded as linked together. A government which desires to pass a lot of bills could no doubt use its majority to get them through the whole House, but if it did so a proper consideration of the bills would be impossible. The use of committees meets both points. More bills can be considered and each will be considered properly. Some people would go further and say that even if there were time to take all bills in committee of the whole House, it would still be better to take them in standing committee, where the members are likely to be more interested in the proceedings than a casual majority of members called into the chamber from time to time at a division without having followed the discussion.

But it is proper to notice that there are certain limits upon the extent to which a government can use standing committees to assist it in legislation. In the first place it must be noticed that the number of bills which a government can expect to pass, even with the fullest use of standing committees, has certain limits upon it from the nature and extent of parliamentary business. Let us notice these. To begin with, a certain amount of parliamentary time is allocated to business other than ordinary legislation. Some days are devoted at the beginning of each session to the debate on the address in reply to the Speech from the Throne; certain financial bills must be passed each year and a prescribed amount of time—not less than twenty-six days—must be devoted to the discussion of the Estimates in Committee of Supply; and there are certain debates on the adjournment which must be held. All these activities take up time which is consequently not available for ordinary legislation.

When we consider the use that can be made of what time is available, we come up against the fact that standing committees cannot get to work on bills until the House has given them a second reading. This takes time. It is not until some weeks after the beginning of a session that as many as four or six standing committees could be expected to be hard at work on bills of importance or about which controversy may arise. The second reading of a controversial bill would usually take at least two days. It is a matter of some difficulty, on the present disposition of parliamentary time, to get enough second readings through to keep more than four standing committees going at the same time.[1] But that is only one end of the system. Bills must not only be got into the committees; they must be got out and got through. It is essential therefore that no more bills should be put

---

[1] It was rare even in the Parliament of 1945–50—in Mar. 1947 and Mar. 1949 only was it achieved.

into the committees than can be got out of them in time to allow
for a report and third-reading stage. It will not do to have a lot
of bills through committee unless the House can find time to give
them a report and third-reading stage. A bill that has been in a
standing committee may well seem to members of the House
who have not sat on the standing committee to be a bill upon
which they should be given a good deal of time at the report
stage. But if this view is acceded to, may not some of the time
gained by sending the bill to committee be lost on report stage?[1]

But when we speak of increasing the number of standing
committees we have to take notice of another limiting factor,
and that is the number of members available to serve on committees. It must not be assumed that the whole House is available. We must exclude the members of the government—except
the ministers concerned with a particular bill—the Speaker,
chairman, and deputy chairman of committees. Then, if committees are to meet in the morning, some members will be
engaged upon their business affairs or the affairs of their constituents. Some members will be ill, some abroad, some inactive.
It was calculated in 1945 by the then Clerk of the House that
it would be very difficult to get as much as 50 per cent. of
the membership of the House available for regular work on
committees, so that the notion of, say, six committees of fifty
members, each sitting simultaneously, seemed on the verge of
impossibility. What follows from this is that if more committees
are to be used, then their size must be reduced, probably below
the figure of fifty members each.

It is interesting to notice, therefore, in the light of these considerations, that in the sessions before 1939 the number of standing committees appointed was six in 1919, five in 1924–5, five
in 1929–30, four in 1934–5, and five in 1936–7, while in the
sessions after 1945 the number was six in 1946–7, five in 1947–8,
and six in 1948–9.

8

It is clear that by the use of committees more bills can be
passed by the House than if the committee stage were taken on

----

[1] This point was appreciated by Mr. Herbert Morrison, Leader of the House
of Commons, in his evidence before the Select Committee in 1945. *First Report of
Select Committee on Procedure*, H.C. 9–1 of 1945–6, q. 122.

the floor of the House, and that a full and informed discussion can occur in a committee. But it is necessary to consider what criticisms can be made of the use of committees in this way and whether experience suggests that it is desirable, or whether in fact there should be less use of committees.

A preliminary objection to the use of standing committees as a regular means of legislation is that there are, anyhow, too many bills passed by Parliament as it is, and that anything which increases the output is undesirable. Those who hold this opinion would prefer to see such bills as were passed considered by a committee of the whole House. They would regard the use of standing committees as bad because it facilitates legislation. With an objection of this kind, fundamental as it is, it is not possible to deal here. Nor is it necessary to deal with it. What we are concerned with is, granted that governments propose to pass legislation, does the use of standing committees work well or ill? Is it excessive? Is the consideration given to bills in standing committee sufficient?

Let us begin by asking whether the use of standing committees is excessive. Are bills sent to standing committees which should have been retained for consideration by the whole House? Is it an abuse of the standing-committee system that it removes from the House as a whole matters which should properly remain with it?

What are the rules governing the sending of bills to standing committee? It will be recalled that no financial business is taken in standing committee: it is still taken in committee of the whole House. This means that a very large and important part of what the House of Commons has to do is kept within the purview of the whole House. Through the conduct of its financial business the House undertakes criticism of the whole range of administration; the Opposition obtains most of its opportunities to discuss government policy. These matters are not relegated to standing committee. Nor is this all. It was accepted by the Labour Government when it put forward its plan for making increased use of standing committees in 1945 that it would not refer to standing committee any bill of constitutional importance, but would retain it in committee of the whole House. And in fact when the Parliament Bill of 1947 was introduced to reduce the suspensive veto of the House of Lords from two years to one year, that bill was taken in committee of the whole House in each of the three sessions in which it was passed by the House of Commons. At the same time it has to be remembered that before 1939 it would have been accepted that not only bills of constitutional importance should be kept in committee of the whole House, but also any important and controversial bill.

The position after 1945 was that financial bills and bills of constitutional importance were the only important measures which did not go to standing committee. For the rest it was understood that very unimportant or uncontentious bills might be taken in the whole House; it would be quicker to deal with them in that way than to go through the business of setting up a standing committee. There would be times, too, when the House of Commons was having a slack period, awaiting the return of major measures from standing committees, and at such periods as these it might be found convenient to put small bills through committee of the whole. But apart from these minor matters, everything of importance, except financial and constitutional measures, went to standing committee. Is this an abuse? The short answer is that provided the House gets adequate opportunity to debate the bill on second reading and again on report and third reading, and provided most of those members who have knowledge of or interest in the bill are able to find a place on the standing committee considering it, there is little to criticize in the procedure from the standpoint of the House as a whole being deprived of its proper share in legislation. The record of the Parliament of 1945–50, when this procedure was most fully used, seems to show that these conditions were fulfilled with few if any exceptions. The time allotted to the second-reading debate on controversial measures, though seldom enough to satisfy the Opposition and never enough to allow everyone who wished to speak, was sufficient to allow the principal points to be made for and against the measures. Thus the bills to nationalize coal, transport, gas, electricity, and iron and steel were given three days for second reading, while such important measures as the Planning Bill, the Agriculture Bill, and the Local Government Bill were given two days. On the report stage a similar amount of time was usually given, with, as a rule, a day allowed thereafter for third reading. As a general rule it can be said that at these later stages the House as a whole was given an opportunity to debate the matters which could usefully be discussed at that time.

There were one or two occasions, however, where it looked as if the House was being denied sufficient time at the report stage, and it is necessary to say a word about them. Two Bills particularly came in for this criticism. They were the Transport Bill and the Town and Country Planning Bill, both considered in the session of 1946–7. Both these Bills were subjected to a closure in standing committee, of which more will be said later, and when they came to the report stage, three days were allotted for each Bill. When the time expired, however, the House had, in neither case, finished the discussion of the amendments put down both by the government and the Opposition. The votes were put, in accordance with the guillotine procedure, and, in the case of the Transport Bill, ninety-seven remaining government amendments were passed without discussion—though the Opposition kept the House employed from 9.30 p.m. on Wednesday, 30 April, until 12.50 a.m. on Thursday, 1 May, in conducting divisions—while in the case of the Planning Bill 168 government amendments were put and carried without discussion. It seems a fair comment on these proceedings to say that for the House of Commons to be required to agree, not merely without discussion but actually without even an explanation, to a series of amendments to a Bill which itself has been fully discussed only by a committee composed of approximately one-twelfth of the whole House, is legislation by automatic machine and not legislation by men. It could not fairly be said that the Opposition had been unduly obstructive at the report stage.[1] The real difficulty was that there was not time to discuss even the government amendments. There were good reasons for most of the government amendments, but there was no time for these reasons even to be stated.

If it is believed that the report stage should be taken in the House as a whole—and, as will be indicated later on, not everybody holds this view—it seems clear that the amount of time allotted to this stage of the Transport and the Planning Bills was not sufficient to ensure that the House could carry out its

---

[1] But it might fairly be said that it had chosen to use its time on points which had already been thoroughly discussed at previous stages of the Bill's progress— a procedure which might be politically wise.

duties effectively. Many of the amendments which were moved from the government side at the report stage were the result of discussions and assurances given in standing committee, and it was proper that the House should hear some explanation of them. In many cases this was not done. In the case of these two Bills, then, it may be said that the House had cause to complain. There appear to be no other cases of comparable importance. Generally speaking it can be said that the House had adequate time on second reading and on report and third reading to discuss the Bills which were referred to standing committee, and that to this extent the reference to standing committee did not deprive the House as a whole of what it might properly claim.

But another proviso was suggested earlier, namely, that as many members as were qualified by knowledge and interest should find themselves on the standing committee. Here, generally speaking, it can be said that the condition was satisfied. No doubt there were many members of the House who would have welcomed the opportunity to take part from time to time in the committee stage of these Bills, but whether there were many who would have been prepared to sit through the entire debate on the Bill clause by clause is another matter. And that is what is done by those in standing committee. It may be doubted whether in a debate in committee of the whole House the average attendance of members would be much larger than that in standing committee on these important Bills. The figures for a division might well be larger, but for the continuous consideration of the Bill it is unlikely that they would. Some members undoubtedly failed to obtain seats on a committee dealing with a bill in which they were interested. Some who were fortunate enough to get on a committee might have wished that they could sit on another also at the same time. It may be suggested that few members who really deserved to be on a standing committee for an important bill failed to obtain a place upon it.

It should be remembered, too, that the greater part of the attack on the bill in committee will be carried out by two or three of the leading Opposition members, who are in charge of the operations on their party's behalf. These members can operate just as effectively and perhaps more effectively in standing committee as in committee of the whole House. All the points which it is intended to make will be made in standing committee. The House, considered as a party House—and this is one of its most important aspects—does not lose something which it ought to have by the reference of bills to standing committees.

The general conclusion to be drawn from the experience of standing committees, particularly since 1945 when important and controversial bills began to be sent to them, is that the procedure does not result in the House being deprived of an opportunity to deal with matters which properly concern it. That there can be exceptions to this statement has been indicated. It is also difficult to pronounce upon a matter of this kind, where party considerations are involved. It is certainly impossible to obtain unanimous consent to such a conclusion.

9

We may consider now, not whether too many bills are sent to standing committee, but whether bills are given adequate consideration in the standing committee, whether their work is done well. Two possible abuses are envisaged in this connexion. It is alleged sometimes that the Opposition abuses standing-committee procedure by obstruction, or that even if it does not, the whole procedure is likely to be dilatory and cumbersome to handle, especially when several committees are sitting at once. On the other side, it is alleged that discussion is curtailed in standing committees and that too much closure is applied. We must consider how far experience seems to support these allegations.

It is interesting to record that before 1939 standing committees were seldom used for important and controversial bills not only because members of the House were reluctant to lose their opportunity to intervene in a committee stage if they felt like it, but also because the government thought that standing committees would be difficult to manage.[1] To keep a majority in committee of the whole House is a relatively simple matter, but to keep majorities in several standing committees is much more complicated, and clearly gives the Whips much more work. The majorities are inevitably smaller and every vote counts, and the

[1] See the evidence of Mr. Herbert Morrison, ibid., qq. 192 and 219.

problem is repeated three or four times.[1] Discussion in standing committee, too, was thought to be more searching and to call for more reasoned answers. The Opposition could hold up the bill effectively without actually resorting to obstruction. And it had always been accepted that the guillotine should not be applied in standing committee.

There was a great deal in these views. And it was clear in 1945 that if standing committees were to be used for controversial bills the Whips on both sides, but particularly on the government side, would have a great deal of extra work to do. It was clear also that if the government was to get its bills out of standing committee in time to pass them through the remaining stages in the House it would have to be prepared to limit the time a standing committee might take over a bill. It must be able to prevent obstruction. It was therefore part of the Labour Government's plan that closure should be applied to standing-committee debates, and provisions to that end were adopted by the House of Commons.

In considering whether the abuse of obstruction or the abuse of suppressing discussion has been found in the work of the standing committees, we must remind ourselves that what ought to be achieved is a balance between the right of the Opposition to criticize and the right of the government, having heard the criticism, to take the responsibility of having its way. The chairman of a standing committee, as has already been pointed out, has his own contribution to make towards the achieving of this balance by his power to accept or refuse the motion that the question be put and by his power to select amendments. Both these types of closure were normally operated in standing committees from 1945, and it would be difficult to find a case of

---

[1] The difficulties are well illustrated when a government has a small majority. The use of standing committees for many bills, especially contentious bills, becomes impossible. In the session of 1950–1, when the Labour Government had a small majority, the number of standing committees set up was four, including the Scottish, and they dealt with 23 bills, of which 9 were private members' bills and 8 were Scottish. In the sessions of 1951–2 and 1952–3, when the Conservative Government had a small majority, four standing committees including the Scottish Standing Committee were set up, and they dealt with 26 and 28 bills respectively, of which 13 and 10 respectively were private members' bills. See H.C. 325 of 1951–2 and H.C. 314 of 1952–3. It is interesting to notice that whereas the Transport Bill and the Iron and Steel Bill were taken in standing committees in 1946–7 and in 1948–9 respectively, the Transport and the Iron and Steel Bills of 1952–3 were taken in committee of the whole House.

genuine hardship. But there remained the use of the guillotine closure. This was applied to three Bills in the Parliament of 1945–50—the Transport Bill and the Planning Bill in the session 1946–7 and the Iron and Steel Bill in the session 1948–9. Was its operation an abuse? Let us see first what it was.

The proposal adopted by the House of Commons in 1945 was that when it was decided by the House that a time limit should be placed upon the proceedings of a standing committee, the manner in which the bill should be dealt with in the time allowed should be considered by a business sub-committee of the standing committee. This business sub-committee was to be appointed by the Speaker of the House and would consist of the chairman and seven other members of the standing committee. The business sub-committee would submit to the committee proposals for allocating the time to the various clauses of the bill, and the committee would accept or reject these proposals.[1] This scheme had the merit that it left to the standing committee and in practice to the Opposition leaders on the committee the right to say how much time they wished to spend, out of the whole period allotted to them, on various parts of the bill. The fact that the Speaker appointed the sub-committee meant that the Opposition would be represented on it along with the government. It was a reasonable scheme in this sense that, though the Opposition might object to having a time limit placed on their discussion in standing committee, they were able to say how they wished to spend that time, granted that it was limited. The discussion in standing committee on the three Bills already mentioned was therefore conducted according to a time-table devised by a business sub-committee, and the Opposition knew how much time it had on various groups of clauses.

But should the government have imposed this time limit at all? It should be noticed that whereas the allocation of time order was imposed upon the committee stage of the Iron and Steel Bill as soon as it passed its second reading in the session 1948–9, in the earlier cases in 1946–7 it was not until the two Bills had had some time in standing committee that the government decided to ask for a time limit. Standing Committee B which was considering the Transport Bill had had eleven sittings and had passed five clauses of the Bill, and Standing

[1] S.O. 64.

Committee D, on the Planning Bill, had had four sittings and had reached clause 4 when the guillotine resolution requiring that both Bills should be reported to the House by Easter was passed by the House on 3 March 1947. Now it is clear that with a Transport Bill of 127 clauses and 13 schedules, and a Planning Bill of 108 clauses and 9 schedules, proceedings at this rate would, if maintained, have made it impossible for the Bills to be passed within that session of Parliament. But it was not contemplated on either side of the House that proceedings would continue at that rate; the earlier clauses of both Bills contained the important matters of principle upon which most debate was needed; upon later and less important clauses the pace could quicken. The government spokesmen did not in fact allege that the Opposition had been resorting to obstruction, but it was the view of the government that, in the words of the Minister of Town and Country Planning, 'the business of the Committee has not been conducted with the maximum economy of words or of time' and that it would be wise to take precautions to secure the Bills.[1]

So, for the first time in the history of the House of Commons, the guillotine was applied to proceedings on a Bill in standing committee. In the result 37 clauses and 7 schedules of the Transport Bill were not discussed at all in standing committee, while the discussion on half a dozen clauses was terminated by the guillotine. In the case of the Planning Bill, about 50 clauses and 6 schedules were excluded from discussion. The Iron and Steel Bill contained 58 clauses and 8 schedules, and of these 24 clauses and 1 schedule were fully discussed but, because of the operation of the guillotine, debate on 11 clauses and 1 schedule was curtailed, and 23 clauses and 6 schedules were not discussed at all.

What opinion can we form of this procedure? Were the standing committees being abused by this curtailment of discussion? It is difficult to express a decided opinion. Some points should be stressed, however. It is fair to say that, in all three Bills, no important provision escaped discussion.[2] The time spent on the

[1] *Standing Committee Debates*, session 1946–7, col. 182.
[2] It should be remembered, too, that of the clauses not discussed by reason of the guillotine some had no amendments tabled to them. Thus, of the 37 clauses of the Transport Bill not discussed, 17 had no amendments tabled to them by the Opposition.

Bills was considerable. The Transport Bill spent twenty-five days in standing committee and on some of these days two sittings were held, with the result that the Bill came to be considered in thirty-one sittings for a total of roughly seventy-seven hours. The Planning Bill spent eighteen days, with a total of twenty-five sittings, in standing committee. The Iron and Steel Bill spent thirty-two days in standing committee, with a total of thirty-six sittings. When it is noticed that the debates in standing committee ran to 1,478 columns in the Committee *Hansard* in the case of the Transport Bill, to 1,104 columns in the case of the Planning Bill, and to 1,786 columns in the case of the Iron and Steel Bill, it is difficult to believe that there was much more of importance left to be said. Nor was the talking all on the government side. On the contrary, it is usual in standing committee, as already explained, for most of the talking on the government side to be done by the Minister while most of the other government supporters remain silent; the greater part of the time is taken up by Opposition speakers. On the Transport Bill it would appear, on a rough calculation, that the Opposition speakers did about 57 per cent. of the talking; if we add the Liberals and Independents to this, the total would be something like 62 per cent., leaving 38 per cent. to the government side. On the Opposition side (grouping Conservatives, Liberals, and Independents together) there were about twenty principal speakers; on the government side there were seven, two of whom were ministers, and these two ministers did three-fifths of the talking on the government side. On the Iron and Steel Bill, to take another rough calculation, the government side again did about 35 per cent. of the talking and the Opposition (again grouping Conservatives, Liberals, and Independents together) did about 65 per cent., and the Minister of Supply, in charge of the Bill, occupied one-third of the time taken on the government side.

On the whole it seems fair to say that, so far as the standing-committee stage of these three Bills was concerned, adequate time was available for discussion. The same conclusion may be drawn from the course of proceedings in the case of the fourth and fifth Bills to be subjected to closure in standing committee, this time by the Conservative Government which took office in November 1951. They were the Licensed Premises in New

Towns Bill, in the session of 1951–2, and the Housing Repairs and Rents Bill, in the session of 1953–4. The former was a controversial rather than an important Bill, and it is difficult to see why the government should care so much for it that it resorted to the closure. It was introduced in the standing committee very late in the session (9 July 1952), although its second reading had been secured in February 1952. It proceeded very slowly until closure was applied. Once the closure came into operation, progress occurred, of course, but it is fair to say that adequate time was given to discuss all important points and that the Opposition made the best use of its time.[1] The Housing Repairs Bill was more important. After two days for second reading it was sent to standing committee, which, after ten sittings, had completed only six clauses out of the 44 clauses and 5 schedules which the Bill contained. The Minister of Housing and Local Government, in moving the guillotine in the House, claimed that there had been 'examples of real, old-fashioned obstruction'.[2] Under the guillotine, the Bill was concluded in twenty-two sittings (as compared with twenty-five for the much longer Planning Bill), while two days were devoted to report and one to third reading. It is difficult to see that debate was unduly curtailed by these proceedings.

Needless to say, the Opposition was not prepared to admit this, in the case of any of these five Bills. It would be a bad day, indeed, for freedom of discussion in the House of Commons when an Opposition acquiesced tamely in the imposition of the guillotine. It would seem at times, too, that the Opposition spent longer on the discussion of certain clauses than was necessary. The points had been made more than once; no purpose, other than a party political purpose, was served by repeating them. But generally speaking the proceedings on these five guillotined Bills do not modify the conclusion which can be drawn from the study of the working of standing committees as a whole, namely, that there is adequate opportunity for a good discussion of the clauses of a bill, and that this opportunity is, as a rule, well taken by the Opposition in its conduct of the de-

[1] See 504 H.C. Deb., 5th ser., cols. 49 ff., and Debates of Standing Committee C in session 1951–2.
[2] See 524 H.C. Deb., 5th ser., col. 48, and Debates of Standing Committee C in session 1953–4.

bates. Anyone attending a standing-committee debate will be impressed by the close and careful discussion that occurs on each clause, by the critical attitude of the Opposition, and by the trouble which is taken on the government side to give a reasoned defence of what is proposed. Of course the personal temperament and characteristics of ministers and of Opposition leaders affects the atmosphere of the discussions. On some occasions debates are characterized by the scoring of mere debating points, indulgence in rhetoric, and party propaganda and misrepresentation. These are often entertaining occasions.[1] But as a rule this sort of thing is not found in standing-committee debates; it is left for the House as a whole, partly perhaps because the newspapers take more interest in what is said in the House, but partly also because it is felt to be out of place. On occasions, too, there is sufficient agreement between the government and the Opposition to permit a bill to be passed in standing committee not merely without a division,[2] but even without a word of debate[3] or with a few civilities only.[4]

It might be added that the Opposition's labours in standing committee are conducted without much hope of reward or success, for they can never expect, if the government has a workable majority, to carry an amendment against the government.[5] But it would be wrong to judge proceedings in standing committees by the number of times the Opposition fails to carry a division. It should be remembered that many of the amendments put down by the Opposition are put down in order to obtain information or assurances or explanations from the Minister, and are withdrawn when his statement has been made. On some occasions an Opposition amendment is accepted. On other occasions, a minister will refuse to accept an amendment but will undertake to reconsider the matter and propose an amendment on the report stage. On many occasions, the Opposition's

[1] A good example is the debate in Standing Committee C on the Licensed Premises in New Towns Bill in the session 1951–2.

[2] For example, the War Damage (Amendment) Bill in Standing Committee E 10 Nov. 1949; the debate lasted from 10.30 a.m. to 12.7 p.m.

[3] For example, the Transport Act (1947) Amendment Bill in Standing Committee B on 29 July 1952. The proceedings lasted from 10.36 a.m. to 10.38 a.m.

[4] For example, the Wages Councils Bill in Standing Committee A on 18 Nov. 1948. The proceedings lasted from 10.32 a.m. to 10.40 a.m.

[5] It happens occasionally. In the session 1953–4 the government was defeated twice in Standing Committee A on the Mines and Quarries Bill.

amendment is clearly unacceptable to the Minister and is moved and resisted in order to bring into the open the difference of political opinion which is involved. It must be emphasized always that the standing committees like the House itself are party organizations; they are based on the principle of party government. If the government cannot command a majority in the House or in the Committee something is wrong. If it continues in this state for long, it should resign and make way for others. On British parliamentary principles, it is not merely the usual thing but also the normal thing for the government to win.

But it is sometimes asked whether party discipline could not be relaxed a little in standing committee. Should not the government be prepared to accept amendments there more freely than, as a rule, it is? It may be admitted that there is a tendency for governments to be too rigid in refusing to reconsider their proposals, though this differs a good deal from one minister to another. On the other hand, if controversial bills are to be taken in standing committee, it cannot often happen that a government will be able to give way on a point of importance, at any rate to the Opposition's criticisms. It may find itself obliged to modify a bill in response to the complaints of members on its own side. But this rigidity and unwillingness to accept amendments applies throughout the stages of legislation in modern Britain, and it is possible that if amendments were accepted in standing committee, they might be rejected later in the whole House at report stage. The strength of Whitehall has no doubt some effect upon this also. The combination of strong party discipline with strong official support for a minister makes it relatively easy for him to refuse to give way. He can be supplied with an armoury of arguments with which to resist every criticism that is made. Yet considered as a whole it seems fair to say that the proceedings in standing committee, little as they may change a bill in important details, ensure a reasoned defence of it and reasoned criticism of it. They are seldom, if ever, reduced to mere voting machines, nor is the government's majority used with cynical disregard of the Opposition's case. Both government and Opposition behave responsibly—and indeed it may be suggested that for the efficacy of standing-committee proceedings a responsible Opposition is even more important than a responsible government. Standing committees provide a valuable element in the British system of government by discussion.

10

It remains to discuss certain suggestions which have been made upon the ground that the best use is not yet made of the standing committees in the legislative process. The first is that the committees would be of greater use if they were specialized, if, that is to say, there were allotted to each committee a part of the field of public business, and if any legislation in relation to that field were referred to the committee upon that subject. It might well work out that there would be a standing committee for each government department or for a group of related government departments. It is sometimes suggested that these specialized committees should not only deal with bills in their respective spheres but also should exercise some degree of scrutiny and control over the administrative work of the departments concerned, as in fact is the case with the committees of the United States Congress and of the French Parliament. But their usefulness may be judged here by considering the plan solely upon the basis of their taking a part in the legislative process.

It has been emphasized already that the British standing committees exhibit more of the qualities of a system of specialized committees than may appear at first sight. There is a tendency for those members with special knowledge and a special interest in a bill to get themselves placed upon the standing committee which is dealing with that bill. Moreover, as the discussion of the bill is very largely the responsibility, in the British system, of the government and the Opposition, and as the committees are so constituted as always to contain those members of the two sides who are in charge of the defence and attack on the bill, an organized and informed discussion is likely to be conducted. What must be conceded, however, is that the British system does not provide, through the standing committees, a steady education to members in a particular sphere of public business, such as would be provided if members belonged throughout a parliament to one or two specialized committees. If members have special knowledge or interests they are usually able to employ them on an appropriate standing committee, but after they have finished with the bill they do not have any reason to continue in their study of this field. And if they have no special knowledge they have no incentive through the standing committee system to begin to educate themselves. In a parliament where specialized committees exist, on the other hand, members find themselves given a field of public affairs in which they are to interest themselves, and they may proceed to acquire special knowledge or to extend what they know.

This argument should not be exaggerated. Let it be remembered that under a system of specialized standing committees, while members placed upon some specialized standing committees such as finance or foreign affairs will get a great deal of interesting and important work, those on others will get hardly anything to do, and they may well not feel inclined to acquire knowledge of mere academic interest. It is only in a system where the specialized committees extend their interest to the administration of the departments that they can be certain of having some material upon which to use their minds in the course of a session and so acquire some specialized knowledge. There is a fundamental difference in this respect between standing committees dealing with bills in the House of Commons and administrative committees in local councils in Britain. The council committees always have some work to do; their members have a chance to acquire and extend specialized knowledge. But specialized standing committees would operate only when bills upon their subject were introduced into Parliament. It may well be doubted whether under a system of specialized standing committees many more members of Parliament would take advantage of opportunities for using their specialized knowledge or for acquiring it than do so at present under the system whereby the man of special knowledge seeks out the bill he is interested in, rather than waits for the bill to be brought to him.

It is worth while to add, perhaps, that some criticisms of specialized standing committees, based upon experience of them in foreign parliaments, should not be accepted as inevitably applicable to Britain. This is true particularly of the assertion that a system of specialized standing committees is likely to weaken the control by the government over the House of Commons. This assertion appears to be based upon the experience of the French Parliament and the American Congress particularly. It may be conceded that in France and the United States the committees do weaken the government, but they weaken a government which is already inherently weak in its relation to the legislature. The committees provide, indeed, just one more illustration of the weakness of these executives. The weakness of the French Executive is primarily the result of the French party system—a system which itself is not easily explained—and the weakness of the American Executive is the result of the independence of Congress, which enables it to defy the Executive if it chooses. There can be no doubt whatever that if a system of specialized standing committees were set up in Britain and were composed in proportion to the party strengths in the House, the government would control the committees, just as it controls the House. If its majority in the House were small, the business of controlling the committees would be all the more difficult; but it would not be more difficult than it is under a system of non-specialized standing committees. Governments with small majorities will always be reluctant to use standing committees where a majority of one or two is very difficult to keep in being. But specialization will not make the difficulties any greater. It must be remembered also that French and American committees deal with administrative matters, which gives scope to harry the Executive that is not possible when legislation only is under consideration.

The case against specialized standing committees cannot be founded upon any supposed weakening of the Executive's control over Parliament. Nor should it be based upon some extreme dogma of the infallibility of the layman, which would frown upon those with special knowledge finding their way on to committees dealing with matters which they understood. On the contrary, it would seem that the British system, with its flexible provisions for adding and removing members to and from a committee in respect of a given bill, does in practice give considerable opportunities for members to get on to committees for bills about which they know something. The discussion comes down in the end to a question of which is the better method for ensuring that the greatest use is made of members' knowledge while at the same time making it possible for all members who wish it to acquire some specialized knowledge. Under the British system no member need be relegated for a whole Parliament to an obscure field of public affairs; he has a chance of getting on to a committee dealing with an interesting bill. It is true that the process of steady education which specialized committees can provide is not ensured in the British system, but at the same time there are greater opportunities for using and acquiring specialized knowledge than are often realized. On balance it may be doubted whether a change to the specialized system would be an advantage.

II

A second suggestion which has been made with a view to making better use of standing committees is that they should be so organized that they can take not only the committee stage of a bill, after its second reading, but also the report stage. It is admitted that a great deal of the time of the House is taken up with the report stage, and that the more standing committees are used the greater will be the pressure on the government to allow more time for report. Yet a great deal of the report stage is unintelligible to the majority of the members of the House, and from time to time there is the spectacle of dozens of amendments being pushed through on report under the guillotine. Considerations of this kind led to suggestions in 1946 that standing committees should be so organized that they might break up into sub-committees, of about forty members, each of which would deal with the committee stage of a bill, while the report stage would be taken by the whole standing committee. A general proposal of this kind was put before the Select Committee on Procedure in 1946 by the then Clerk of the House of Commons, Sir Gilbert Campion, who calculated that it might save ten days or so of the time of the House in an average session.[1] The suggestion was quite unacceptable to the Select Committee, which felt that the notion of taking away the report stage from the House as a whole was quite repugnant. And yet, as Sir Gilbert pointed out,[2] if the House desires to spend so much time 'considering what is largely the details of legislation, it runs the risk of finding itself short of time to discuss more important matters of principle or policy'.

There can be little doubt that the present use of the whole

---

[1] H.C. 189-1 of 1945-6, pp. xxxix-xlii.   [2] Ibid., p. 351.

House for report is unsatisfactory both in the consumption of time that might be used for other purposes, and also in the quality of the discussion that is possible in such a body. Report should be dealt with by a body of members who have some knowledge of what is being done, and this can seldom be expected of any except those who have been with the bill in the committee stage. The debate in the whole House on report is usually conducted by the same party leaders as conducted it in the standing committee, for they alone, for the most part, know what the amendments signify. No doubt there would be objections to leaving the report stage to the ordinary standing committee itself which has already dealt with the bill in the committee stage, but in many cases such a proceeding would not be foolish, for many of the amendments moved on report are the result of the Minister's reflection upon discussions and assurances in the committee stage, and with these the members of the standing committee are familiar. If, however, it is desired to bring in other members at the report stage, some proposal on the lines advanced by Sir Gilbert Campion should be considered. What is clear is that much of the discussion on report does not require or deserve the attention of the members of the whole House. It would seem worth while to adopt a procedure by which the report stage could be taken in standing committee, organized either as at present or extended in size as Sir Gilbert Campion suggested, but to provide that if a certain number of members objected the report stage should be taken in the whole House. There might well be occasions when a wider audience should hear and participate in the report stage, and the rights of the whole House could be safeguarded. But on many occasions it would be a wise use of standing committees to leave the report stage with them.

12

It is not easy to say what should be done about a third suggestion for the better use of standing committees, namely, that more second readings should be entrusted to them, rather upon the model of the Scottish Standing Committee to which, by standing orders,[1] the second reading of a bill dealing exclusively with

[1] S.O. 60 (2).

Scotland is remitted unless ten or more members of the House object to the proposal. Could this not be extended to other bills, say bills affecting England only or bills of minor importance? A standing Committee would thus take the second reading of a bill and then proceed to the committee stage and, if the proposals concerning the report stage were adopted, would also go on and deal with report, the House itself coming in at the end to give a third reading.

It may be conceded that, if such an arrangement as this were adopted, a number of unimportant bills might well be remitted without objection to the standing committees for their second reading. But it cannot be expected that bills of any importance would be so treated. In the result, therefore, no great saving of time can be expected from such a change. There is, however, a much deeper objection to any reform of this kind. The task of the House as a whole is surely to debate the general principles of a bill and to leave details to a committee. The case for confiding the report stage of bills to some sort of committee is to be justified on the ground that the work is closely related to the type of discussion that has gone on in the committee stage. But second readings are on a very different footing. There should be an opportunity at this stage for any member to express his views. If few members are interested, then the second-reading stage will be quickly concluded.

But, it may be asked, why is it considered proper to allow second readings to be taken in the Scottish Standing Committee and not in other standing committees? The answer is that the Scottish Standing Committee is on a very different footing from others. If we are to follow the analogy of the Scottish Standing Committee we must propose, not that the second readings of bills should be taken in standing committee, but that the second readings of bills relating exclusively to England must be taken in a standing committee consisting of all the members for English constituencies, or if, as is usual, the bill relates to England and Wales, all the members for English and Welsh constituencies. Such a committee would consist of over 500 members. It is, indeed, the body which in practice now does take the second reading of bills dealing with England and Wales, for Scottish members do not take a large part in such discussions. But a standing committee of over 500 is not what we intend when we speak of saving the time of the House of Commons by sending the second reading of bills to standing committee.

Let us consider why it is that it was agreed that second readings should be taken by the Scottish Standing Committee. The reason was not primarily the desire to save the time of the whole House of Commons; it was to satisfy the desire of Scots to regulate their own affairs. The conferring upon the Scottish Standing Committee of the power to take second readings of exclusively Scottish bills, as well as to take Scottish estimates, is an attempt to make a kind of little Scottish House of Commons inside the House of Commons of the United Kingdom. It is true that what has been done falls short of a Scottish House of Commons—for English members are also found on the Committee—and it is true also that the arrangement fails to satisfy the demands of many Scots for autonomy. The important point for our consideration is, however, that the Scottish Standing Committee is composed upon the principle of nationality. Because it is proper that the second reading of purely Scottish bills be confided to a standing Committee upon which all the Scottish members sit, it does not at all follow that it is proper to confide the second reading of purely English bills to a standing committee upon which only a fraction of the English members sit, or that the second reading of bills relating to the whole United Kingdom should be taken in a standing committee on which again only a fraction of all the members of the House of Commons sit. The Scottish Standing Committee is not strictly comparable with the other standing committees, whose primary purpose is to save the time of the House as a whole and to ensure a more informed and educative discussion of the details of the bill. The Scottish Standing Committee has these objects, too, but they flow from its primary object of ensuring that purely Scottish affairs shall be decided more and more by the Scottish members. It happens that the number of Scottish members, though not small, is not so large as to make the Scottish Standing Committee too numerous to be compared as an institution with the other standing committees. Similarly, a Welsh Standing Committee would be of a comparable size. But that is a fortuitous circumstance. The great bulk of legislation, and especially of the important or contentious legislation in the House of Commons, relates either to England and Wales or to the whole

United Kingdom, and it would not be practicable to refer it to a standing committee upon the same basis as purely Scottish bills are referred to the Scottish Standing Committee. It would be a breach with accepted doctrine and, it is submitted, a bad breach. For the purpose of the House as a whole is to discuss policy and principles and this duty should not be confided to a standing committee. In the trivial cases where no great harm would be done if a second reading was so transferred, no saving of time worth speaking of would be achieved in compensation for the breach of an important principle.

CHAPTER VII

Committees to Administer

I

WRITERS on political theory have sometimes discussed
the question whether it is better to entrust the process
of administration to single individuals or to groups of
individuals, whether the unitary executive is preferable to the
plural executive.[1] In Britain we have examples of both systems.
In the central government, the responsibility for the administration of the departments is entrusted to single individuals—the
ministers—each one of whom is responsible to Parliament and
to the electorate for the proper conduct of the affairs of his
department. It is true that we do not stop at this. We provide
also that these single individuals shall be members of a team—
the Cabinet and ministry—so that they do not act in complete
isolation from each other. Their individual responsibility is
supplemented by a collective responsibility. It may well be that
this particular mixture of the unitary and the plural systems of
administration in Britain—and in other countries where the
cabinet system is adopted—provides as good a solution as you
can get to the problem of how to organize central administration. It appears to combine the advantages of the two
systems.

Be that as it may, it is a fact that central administration in
Britain is the responsibility of individual ministers,[2] and that the
notion that responsibility for running a central department
should be entrusted to a committee, whether of the House of
Commons or not, would be firmly rejected by most of those con-

---

[1] It is discussed in *The Federalist*, No. lxx, by Alexander Hamilton, who argues
strongly that unity in the executive can only be achieved by granting the executive
power to one man.

[2] Thus even where, as in the Admiralty, the Air Ministry, and the Army, the
administration is conducted through a board or council of which the Minister is
chairman, the responsibility to Parliament rests upon the Minister alone, and he
can therefore override the board or council.

cerned with central government.[1] In the sphere of local government, however, the opposite doctrine prevails, and prevails not only with the approval of the central government, but in some cases at its positive behest. Local authorities in Britain are administrative bodies; almost all the functions they perform are concerned with carrying into effect services which the central parliament has decided shall be provided. They carry out these duties by the use of committees. It is the rule rather than the exception in Britain for administrative functions in local government to be made the responsibilities of plural rather than unitary institutions. Local administration in Britain is administration by committees.

2

There are about 9,000 local councils in the United Kingdom. They are all empowered by Act of Parliament[2] to conduct their affairs by the use of committees. In some matters, indeed, they are required by statute to use committees. Thus the sixty-two county councils and the eighty-three county borough councils in England and Wales, being local education authorities, are required by the Education Act of 1944 to use an education committee.[3] They are required by the Children Act, 1948, to have a children's committee,[4] by the National Health Service Act, 1946, to have a health committee,[5] and if they are police authorities—and they usually are—they must exercise their functions through a committee, the watch committee in a borough[6] and the standing joint committee in a county.[7] County councils are obliged to appoint a finance committee.[8] Quite apart from the statutory requirements to use committees, all local councils set up such committees as they think necessary. It would be rare to find a council in England and Wales among

[1] Mr. Balfour's words to the Select Committee on Procedure of 1914 may be recalled: 'The idea of managing great Departments of State by a Parliamentary Committee is perfectly futile, and I do not think it is really worth consideration.' H.C. 378 of 1914, p. 78, q. 1168.
[2] Local Government Act, 1933, sections 85 and 90.
[3] 1st Schedule, Part II.   [4] Section 39.
[5] 4th Schedule, Part II.
[6] Municipal Corporations Act, 1882, section 190.
[7] Composed half of county councillors, half of justices. Local Government Act, 1888, section 30.
[8] Local Government Act, 1933, section 86.

the 309 municipal boroughs, the 572 urban district councils, the 475 rural district councils, or the 7,000-odd parish councils, or in Scotland among the 33 county councils, the 195 town councils, and the 201 district councils, which did not have, for example, a finance committee, whether called by that name or not. And most councils, according to their functions, will have a highways committee, a libraries committee, a parks committee, a cemeteries committee, a baths committee, a sewage committee, an allotments committee, a health committee, a planning committee. Most councils of any size will usually have an establishment committee to consider staffing questions which affect different departments of the council and a selection committee to make recommendations about appointments by the council to its committees. From time to time various special committees will be set up for particular purposes.

Before we can get a complete idea of the multiplicity of committees in local government, we must remember that in some of these services a host of sub-committees is set up around one committee of the council. The education service in counties and county boroughs illustrates this as well as any. Education committees break up into sub-committees each charged with the control of a part of the service and reporting to the main education committee. Primary schools have their boards of managers, secondary schools their boards of governors by the dozen. Indeed, no notion of committee work in local councils is adequate which neglects to notice that council committees have a strong tendency to break up into sub-committees. One important part of the study of committees in local government is the investigation of the use and abuse of sub-committees.

Although it is not necessary to be very precise in counting up the number of committees it is interesting to make a rough calculation of their quantity. If we assume that, on an average, a county council or a county borough council sets up twenty committees, that metropolitan borough, municipal borough, and urban and rural district councils set up ten committees, and parish councils two committees, and if we assume that each of the 145 local education authorities in the country has on an average about fifty boards of governors and managers attached to it, and if we put the number of joint committees and boards set up by two or more councils at about 2,000, then we find that the grand total of committees in local government is round about 50,000. This, it must be emphasized, is a conservative figure, for it excludes sub-committees, which in many cases have so independent an existence that they operate like committees.

3

Who are the people who sit on these committees? And what part do our seven characters play in committee work? Since most councils are elected on party lines, and since most committees are composed entirely of council members and all have at least a majority of council members, it follows that most committee members are party men. The strength of their party spirit varies from place to place, but it is usual for the party in the majority upon a council to secure a majority of seats on the important committees. Where the Labour or the Communist parties are in a majority this principle is strongly enforced; when Conservative or Liberal parties are in the majority it may be weaker, though here again a good deal will depend upon the strength of the Labour or Communist opposition.

Among the exceptions to the general conclusion that committee members are party men are, of course, those councillors[1] who describe themselves as Independent, and perhaps a certain number of those who, though nominally Conservative, permit themselves or are permitted a good deal of freedom of action. Where Labour is strongly represented on a council, however, those opposed to it, whether they call themselves Conservative or Reform or Progressive or Liberal or even Independent, are more and more obliged to take on the role of the party man.

Upon some committees of a council it is required and upon all except the finance committee[2] it is permitted that some co-opted members may sit. Their number may not exceed a third of the total membership of a committee, for it is provided that at least two-thirds must be members of the council.[3] In practice councils have made little use of their permissive power to co-opt, and co-opted members are usually only to be found upon committees

---

[1] The word 'councillor' is used here and throughout to mean alderman as well as councillor.
[2] And the watch committee of a borough. Municipal Corporations Act, 1882, section 190.   [3] Local Government Act, 1933, section 85.

when their presence is obligatory, as, for example, upon education committees and allotments committees.[1] In the education
field, indeed, the use of co-opted persons is particularly widespread, for they are found not only upon the main education
committee and its sub-committees but also upon the boards of
governors and of managers of schools. These co-opted members
of council committees are not chosen as party men; for the most
part, indeed, they are intended to represent interested parties or
partisans. Thus upon education committees certain important
interests in education—the churches and the teachers—are represented by co-opted members, and it is usual that the persons
appointed are suggested or nominated by the interest which they
represent. It is common to find representatives of the Church
of England, of the Roman Catholic Church, and of the Free
Churches upon an education committee, along with representatives of primary teachers, of secondary teachers, and of teachers
in institutions for further education. Upon allotments committees it is obligatory to place representatives of allotment
holders who are interested parties.

Upon some committees it is provided, either by Act of Parliament[2] or by the rules of a council, that women must find a place.
Whether they should be regarded as representatives of interested parties or not is hard to say. It is perhaps a correct
description. Their compulsory presence was justified on the
ground that the education or other services so far as they
affected girls or women required special protection and might
be overlooked. Such requirements are almost out of date now,
for the number of women who take part in local government or
are selected by organizations to represent them upon committees
is so great that no special steps need be taken to ensure their
presence. The 'statutory woman' is now almost an anachronism.

It is well, in speaking of the inclusion of interested parties in
the membership of committees by the use of co-optation, to make
it clear that the term is not used in the narrow sense in which
it is employed for some local government purposes. It may well
happen that a member of a council sitting upon a committee

[1] Education Act, 1944, 1st Schedule, Part II, para. 5, and Allotments Act, 1922,
section 14 as amended by section 12 of the Allotments Act of 1925.
[2] See, for example, National Assistance Act, 1948, 3rd Schedule, Part I,
para 3.

may have a financial interest, direct or indirect, in the business being transacted by the committee. In such a case special rules apply to him. They would apply equally to a co-opted member of a committee if he found himself an interested party in the narrow financial sense. Such interested parties in this sense are required to disclose their interest and are forbidden to take part in the discussion or in the voting of a committee or of the council on a matter in which they have such an interest.[1]

In speaking of the co-optation of interested parties in the broader sense, it is well to remember too that among the ordinary elected members of a council, sitting upon its committees, may be found representatives of interests. They may be party men, also. The significance of the co-opted members is that, as a rule, though they are partisans they are not party men.

Another reason why members are co-opted to council committees is that they possess some knowledge or experience, sometimes of an expert kind, which it is thought would be valuable. It may be suggested, indeed, that the reason why teachers are co-opted to education committees is not only or even mainly because they represent interested parties, but because they have knowledge and experience of education. On many education committees, also, and upon the governing bodies of council schools, representatives of universities are often co-opted in order to bring some expert knowledge to the problems of administration. As with the interested party, however, so with the expert, although he is often found among the co-opted members upon a committee, he is not exclusively there. It is not uncommon for councillors to have some special knowledge and experience which is of value in the work of some committee.

It is because councillors, however, are likely as a rule to be laymen in regard to a great deal of a council's functions, that the co-optation of experts is permitted in the rules regulating the composition of certain committees. The system of choosing councillors by elections conducted on party lines is unlikely to secure and is not intended to secure in local government, any more than it secures in central government, councils of experts. Just as the House of Commons is the great house of laity of the realm, so in the town and county halls of the country, the coun-

[1] Local Government Act, 1933, sections 76 and 95; Local Government Act, 1948, Section 131.

cils are councils of laymen, and the committees as a general rule have a majority of laymen upon them.

Stated in summary form, then, the committees to administer in British local government are predominantly committees of party men and of laymen; they contain interested parties and experts, but the latter two characters find their place more among co-opted members than among the elected council members. It is over committees of this kind that chairmen must preside and it is with committees of this kind that officials in local government must work. It is the higher officials, of course, who have most contact with the committees, for they deal with regulatory and administrative matters, which are a committee's chief concern. They attend committee meetings and present business to the committee and take part in discussions. The members of a council, through their committee work, have a contact with the official and share responsibility for administration with him in a way quite unknown to members of the House of Commons.

4

It is time to consider now whether this system of administration works well. At the outset it is proper to draw attention to certain advantages which may be expected to accrue from administration by committees just because they are committees. The first of these advantages may be expressed in terms of the old sayings that two heads are wiser than one and that in the multitude of counsellors (and even of councillors) there is wisdom. This is not a proposition which commands universal assent. Everyone can think of examples where one man was right and a committee was wrong. Many people would maintain, however, that though a committee can be wrong and often is, it is good that questions should be considered and decided by more than one person. They would agree with John Stuart Mill that 'a man seldom judges right, even in his own concerns, still less in those of the public, when he makes habitual use of no knowledge but his own, or that of some single adviser'.[1] A committee is an institution for ensuring that this consideration will occur.

But not only may a committee ensure a wiser decision from

[1] *Representative Government* (Everyman ed.), p. 333.

the discussion of a subject by different people of knowledge and experience, it ensures also that the interests of a wider variety of people are represented. Council committees, being composed largely of elected councillors or indirectly elected aldermen, representing different areas of town or country, bring together persons who represent different interests and classes and, what is more, different political parties. They can speak with some authority of the way in which a proposed administrative action affects the people in the area they represent and the party to which they belong. Under a system of administration by a single person or local minister this would not be impossible, of course —members of a council or a committee could make representations to him and question him just as members of Parliament question a minister of the central government. But it would not be so easy. For one thing the Minister would belong to one party and probably to the majority party. Under the committee system it is certain that a number of representative people are associated with the administration from the inside and from the outset. While a decision is being sought, they are in a position to express the views of their constituents.

Closely linked with this advantage of administration by committees is another which can also be expressed in terms of an old saying—that many hands make light work. A single minister has only one pair of hands; more important, he has only one pair of eyes and ears. If the control of administration is to be placed effectively in the hands of a body of elected persons, is it not better to have more than one pair of eyes and ears to see and hear what is going on? No one local minister for education can see and hear all that should be seen and heard. It is true that complaints could be brought to him by other councillors. But is it not better that there should be a body of people whose responsibility it is to see that the education service is wisely administered and whose inquiries and criticisms will be linked with this responsibility? The oversight of the administration of local services is too large a task for a group of local ministers. If it is their responsibility alone, it may be assumed that it cannot be done effectively by them and that if it is to be done at all, it will be done by officials themselves. The committee system widens the responsibility and authorizes a number of people to make it their business to see that what is done is well done. In this respect the committee system is one of the greatest safe-guards against mere bureaucratic administration. A good local minister could do something but a good committee can do so much more.

The use of a committee instead of one man may be justified, too, on the ground that the exercise of power by one individual tends to be abused and that it is usually better for it to be shared with others. It is a safeguard against what John Stuart Mill called 'the evil effect produced upon the mind of any holder of power, whether an individual or an assembly, by the consciousness of having only themselves to consult'.[1] There would be a tendency for a local minister to associate himself closely with his officials, if only for reasons of safety and self-preservation, and to develop a method of administration which was characterized by arbitrary decisions, undue secrecy, delay or denial of justice, corruption, and nepotism. If what is to be done must be considered by a group of people and if their consent must be obtained, the opportunities for abuse of power may be diminished.

Again, the committee system ensures that a considerable number of people get some administrative education, some education in political life. Under a system of local ministers the number of people who would be informed about adminis-trative problems from the inside would clearly be much less. In a committee system it is ensured that all the members of a council, and a considerable body of co-opted members from outside also, are in a position to take part in the administration of the council's services. At a rough guess there are probably something like 70,000 people sitting upon the councils of the local authorities of the United Kingdom. They do not only learn about officials and local departments. They are brought into close contact with the workings of central government. It is not really an exaggeration to say that a member of a local council is in a position to know more about the workings of Whitehall than is a private member of Parliament. But it is not only knowledge of what is going on that committees make possible for a large number of people. They give them an opportunity to learn how joint discussion and consultation takes place; they give them practice in the art of self-government. If there is to

---

[1] *Representative Government* (Everyman ed.), p. 325.

be any reality in the idea of democratic government, it is essential that as many people as possible should have an opportunity of taking part in governmental processes. Committees provide this opportunity.

Administration through committees not only does good to the committee members—and it may be remarked in passing that if this were all that could be said for it, it would not be quite enough—it does good also to the officials. Bureaucratic sense must justify itself before the questioning of common sense. It is true that a system of local ministers would go some way towards achieving this object, but the committee system goes further. If officials are acting in the knowledge that they must be prepared to explain and justify their actions to a committee composed of people of very different interests and capacities, they will feel obliged to act with care and responsibility. What is more—and this applies particularly to those officials whose duty it is to prepare documents for committees and to take committee work directly—the process of thinking out and expounding some problem, in such a way that the committee can grasp it and be qualified to make a decision upon it, is most valuable for officials. In trying to make the problem intelligible to the committee, you find that at last it seems to be becoming intelligible to you. The old departmental jargon no longer suffices; the old excuses for inaction prove inadequate; the old answers cease to convince. All this must make for better administration.

5

These are some of the advantages which administration by committees could bring, and especially in comparison with administration by individuals. It will be apparent, however, that before any judgement can be advanced upon the performance of committees, it is essential for us to know what we believe the proper functions of a committee to be in the conduct of administration. This raises at the outset the whole question of how much power should be exercised by the committees of councils. For it is certain that a cardinal rule for their right use is that they should possess and exercise the right amount of authority—not too little and not too much. If we are to consider whether, generally speaking, committees of councils do possess adequate authority, we are led to consider, on the one side the relation between the committees and their council, and on the other the relation between the committees and the officials with whom they work. Do councils confer upon their committees the proper amount of authority? Do committees, in relation to the officials, exercise that authority in the right way? Some general observations upon the working of this system may be offered under these two heads.

If we consider first the adequacy of the authority which councils confer upon their committees, we must notice that this raises the whole question of the adequacy of the authority which councils themselves possess. It raises, that is to say, the whole question of the relations between local and central government. For if the powers of councils can be exercised only subject to approval by the central government, then the actions of their committees are similarly restricted. If no real discretion is left to local councils, the task of their committees tends to lack reality; they become less and less committees to administer and more and more committees to advise the central government, through their local council. The relations of central and local government are of prime importance, therefore, for the proper use of committees to administer. Too much central control may well be a fundamental cause of the ineffectiveness of committees. This is, of course, too large a subject for investigation here.[1] All that can be attempted is a general statement upon the position, based so far as possible upon the authority of those who have investigated the question in detail.

Put shortly and without exaggeration, it must be asserted that local councils have certain substantial powers, but it must be asserted at the same time that the exercise of these powers is subjected to a greater degree of central control than is necessary or than is compatible with making the fullest use of the capacity of local councils' committees to administer. That this position was recognized in 1949 is shown by the appointment of the local government manpower committees and by the reports which those committees have put forward.[2] Too often, council committees found that they were powerless to take decisions or to exercise discretion because of the detailed control, through

[1] See D. N. Chester, *Central and Local Government.*
[2] See above, pp. 96–7.

regulations or approvals, of the central government. Although greater freedom has been achieved by the carrying into effect of the recommendations of the local government manpower committees, it is certain that the position always needs watching. If there is to be an opportunity assured for council committees to obtain adequate authority, it is essential, in the words of the first report of the local government manpower committee,

to recognise that the local authorities are responsible bodies competent to discharge their own functions and that, though they may be the statutory bodies through which Government policy is given effect and operate to a large extent with Government money, they exercise their responsibilities in their own right, not ordinarily as agents of Government Departments. It follows that the objective should be to leave as much as possible of the detailed management of a scheme or service to the local authority and to concentrate the Department's control at the key points where it can most effectively discharge its responsibilities for Government policy and financial administration.[1]

If we turn next to consider the degree of authority which a council should grant to its committees, we see that there are two extremes which should be avoided. One is to refuse to grant authority to a committee to decide matters itself and to require it to refer all matters for decision to the full council. To do so is to use committees for advice and not for administration. So extreme a position can scarcely be found in any British council. Administration could not proceed if every matter had to be referred to the full council, for the council meets infrequently— county councils meet once a quarter, and most other councils only once a month. Inevitably, therefore, all councils delegate some authority to committees and empower them to decide certain things on behalf of the council, while reserving other matters for the decision of the council itself, subject to a recommendation from a committee. In some cases, however, councils go almost to the opposite extreme from that first discussed above. They grant to committees power to decide almost all questions, subject only to a report to the council itself. There is, indeed, a limit beyond which even the most enthusiastic council cannot go in delegating its powers to its committees. It is forbidden to delegate to a committee the power to raise a loan or

[1] Cmd. 7870 (1950), Appendix I, p. 6.

levy a rate.[1] But with this exception, some councils hand over administration almost entirely to their committees. This again, however, is not administration by committees, but administration by what are in practice independent *ad hoc* bodies. Committees must bear some sort of subordinate relations to the body which creates them.

The problem, therefore, is to strike a balance between these extremes. It is usual in most councils for committees to have certain powers delegated to them which they may exercise on their own authority, and to have certain other matters referred to them upon which they may make recommendations to the council as a whole. In this matter councils are not entirely free. In relation to the police, for example, the powers of the police authority in a county are conferred directly upon the standing joint committee, appointed by the county council and the county justices,[2] while in a borough which is a police authority the watch committee exercises the power, subject to a report to the council and to the provision of finance by the council.[3] This delegation of executive power is required by Act of Parliament; the councils have no discretion in the matter. In other matters, such as education,[4] allotments,[5] and health services,[6] however, councils are required (unless the issue is urgent) to refer all matters to their committee before taking action upon them, but they are not required to delegate the power to decide such matters to the committees. They are left free in these cases as in others to determine what powers to decide and what powers to recommend shall be conferred upon their committees.

It is most important that a right balance should be struck between the powers of a council and the powers of its committees. If too much power is given to committees, they will begin to act as independent bodies; they will be reluctant to co-operate with other committees of the council; there will be a lack of co-ordination in council work; and there will be attempts at empire-building or committee imperialism at the expense of each other. This is, indeed, the great danger in ad-

[1] Local Government Act, 1933, section 85.
[2] Local Government Act, 1888, section 30.
[3] Municipal Corporations Act, 1882, section 190.
[4] Education Act, 1944, 1st Schedule, Part II, para. 7.
[5] Allotments Act, 1922, section 14.
[6] National Health Service Act, 1946, 4th Schedule, Part II, para. 1.

ministration by committees, as will be seen in later pages. There are many reasons for it, but it is certain that a good foundation upon which such difficulties and tendencies flourish is the grant of delegated powers of administration to committees of councils. It encourages them to believe that they are little councils in themselves.

Before this subject can be explored further, however, it is necessary to complete the discussion of the proper powers which a committee should exercise by looking at the relations it should have with the officials with whom it works. Granted that there is an area of power in which a committee is authorized by the council either to decide upon action or to recommend action, what part should be played by committees and what by officials in making these decisions or these recommendations? Though we speak of administration by committees we do not imagine that all administrative decisions which a committee is authorized to take can or should be taken by the committee. We know that a hierarchy of officials will be there not merely to carry out a committee's instructions, but itself to take the initiative at the higher levels. In practice the administrative function will be shared between the committee and the higher officials. It may be that in law the committee could make every decision and give every instruction; in practice it cannot be done. And it cannot be done, not only because no committee could give the time to cope with such detail, but because no good official could be expected to tolerate a situation in which he had no discretion, initiative, or responsibility.

If we do not expect the committee to do all the administration itself, what matters should remain within its competence? Some officials appear to think that a committee should be in a position, in relation to its officials, comparable to that which Bagehot described as appropriate for the sovereign in relation to his ministers. On this view a committee would have three rights, 'the right to be consulted, the right to encourage, and the right to warn'. Now there is no doubt that if committees were guaranteed the full and free exercise of these rights, they would have considerable power, more indeed than many of them exercise at present, for some officials are reluctant to give any very generous interpretation to 'the right to be consulted'. Large as these powers could be, if fully exercised, however, they are not enough. If we are to preserve any notion that administration in this country is not to be the concern merely of the bureaucracy, we must go further.

One thinks next of Sir George Cornewall Lewis's dictum about the proper relation of a Cabinet Minister to his department. 'It is not the business of a Cabinet Minister to work his department', said Sir George. 'His business is to see that it is properly worked.'[1] There is obviously some truth in this, more particularly if it is phrased in the form that a minister's business is *not so much* to run his department as to see that it is run well. Even so, may it not work out that if a minister is to see that it is run well, he must himself run some of it, he must himself take certain decisions? But whatever truth there may be in this dictum so far as ministers of a central government are concerned, it does not follow that it applies to the work of a committee in local government. To begin with, the committee has the advantage, already discussed, that it consists of several people and not one; it can share the work out among sub-committees and among individuals. In the second place the committee's sphere of action is narrower than the minister's. It is concerned with a small locality and within that locality it is confined to the administration of that residue of matters which has not been decided by Parliament or by the Minister and his advisers in Whitehall. The job is more manageable and there are more managers.

If I am to hazard a statement on the proper functions of committees in relation to officials I would say that it is the job of the committee, within the limits of the powers conferred upon it by the council, and by Parliament, to decide what shall be done, to appoint those who are to do it, and to see that they do it well; and that it must reserve to itself the right to receive all such information, to make all such decisions and appointments, and to take all such actions as are necessary for the proper and efficient performance of these functions. We should not say that these functions are the exclusive responsibility of the committee and that, in particular, chief officials have no concern with them. Chief officials are entitled to express their views about what services should be provided and how a service is to be administered and we know that in practice committees rely on their advice tremendously in this repect. But in this matter, the

---

[1] Quoted in Bagehot, *English Constitution*, p. 177.

official advises; the committee decides. Chief officials, again, will advise upon who shall administer the service, but the committee must decide. It may indeed authorize an official to make appointments at a certain level—in clerical or manual grades— where no administrative principle seems to arise. There can be no quarrel with this. Finally, chief officials are concerned to see that a service is run well. That is one of their responsibilities, but they are responsible to the committee, and the committee therefore has an oversight of them. Some chief officials like to claim that they should be left free to control the service as they think fit; that the committee should leave it to them and hold them responsible; that, in particular, members of the committee should not themselves go about looking into administration. This is an understandable point of view. The wandering, probing, or snooping committee member or sub-committee can cause more trouble than they cure. But it would reduce a committee's functions to futility if its members were confined to contact only with chief officials. They should, through a regular procedure, be authorized to observe the work of their officials and to concern themselves with the day-to-day running of a service.

One general remark must be made about the power of a committee to control its officials. It is subject to one important limitation in the permanence of the officials. Committee members and chairmen come and go, but officials go on. It is true that officials can be dismissed for disobedience or incompetence. In practice it does not work out like that: officials seldom wilfully and openly disobey. They obstruct or delay or forget. So far as incompetence is concerned, it would be difficult in these days to dismiss an official in local government service for incompetence unless it amounted to gross and almost criminal negligence. In the national civil service transfers may be arranged to move people from a place where their incompetence does a lot of harm to one where it does less. In the local civil services, this is much more difficult. Chief officials who are incompetent can seldom be 'unloaded' upon another council; it is extremely difficult to arrange a transfer. Committees must continue to suffer the shortcomings of their officials. At a lower level in the hierarchy some translations may be possible, and promotion, of course, need not occur. But there is a general belief that dismissal for incompetence is too extreme a step to take. Here there is a strongly limiting factor

upon the extent to which a committee can see to it that the
service it administers is run well.

6

It was suggested earlier that one use of a committee to administer, in contradistinction to administration by the single
individual, was that many hands make light work. But one
abuse to which it may be prone may also be expressed in terms
of a proverb—too many cooks spoil the broth. If these dangers
are to be avoided, a committee must have leadership. It is an
accepted principle of British local government that leadership
is not only the legitimate function of a chairman, but that it is
the mark of a good chairman, and the lack of it the mark of a
bad chairman. When we come to consider how well the task is
performed, it is necessary to set down at once certain respects
in which chairmen make bad use of their position of leadership
in a committee.

There is first the practice, common in some areas and never
quite escapable anywhere, of regarding the chairmanship as the
perquisite of the senior member or senior alderman of the committee. This practice can obviously produce bad results.
Seniority may well be one of the qualities which should be
considered by members of a committee in selecting their chairman. Seniority can bring wisdom; but it can also bring senility.
Yet it is a very tenacious principle. It commends itself to many
committees because it involves 'no damned nonsense about
merit'; it therefore saves troubles and heartburnings and em-
barrassing decisions which many members of local authorities
are anxious to avoid. It must be admitted that since it is important that people should work together with as little personal
and petty friction as possible on a committee, the choice of a
chairman by seniority has a certain value. Room for intrigue
and jealousy is reduced to a minimum. Yet it cannot be pretended that it is a good principle of selection. It must deny
opportunities to others as well or better qualified, with the result
that men of ability are not willing to enter local councils or that,
if they are, their chance of giving a lead as a chairman comes
when they are probably past or passing their best. If it be true
of a council that the adoption of the principle of selecting chair-

men by merit could not replace the principle of selection by
seniority because of the discord and ill-feeling it would cause,
then we may say that in such a case selection by seniority is the
best that can be done. But the best in that case is not very good.

Somewhat similar remarks may be made about a second
abuse, namely, that of chairmen holding office, in practice, for
an indefinite period. The merits of a long term for a chairman
are obvious. He gets a chance to learn his job. And it is probable
that no chairman of an important local government committee,
such as an education committee, a housing committee, a planning committee, or a finance or establishment committee, has
really learnt his job effectively until he is in his third year as
chairman. But after that time dangers beset him. He has got
into the saddle; he can answer any questions about his committee's work; he has his chief officials where he wants them or,
at any rate, he thinks he has, and they too cherish the same
belief about him; the council knows him and he understands
their ways. This is the picture of the successful chairman. Two
dangers in particular must be guarded against. The first is that
he has so acquired the administrative point of view that he may
have become in practice almost an official himself. And he may
have lost the layman's attitude and have become almost an
expert. Now, efficient as all this is in one way, it is dangerous in
another. A chairman of this kind is liable to get out of touch
with his committee and his value as a leader decreases. The
second danger is that the chairman who proposes to hold office
indefinitely blocks the prospects of all other aspirants for the
office on his committee. There is no point in their throwing
time and energy into a committee in which, so far as anyone
can see, they have no chance of being anything more than members of the rank and file. This suppresses initiative and discourages enthusiasm in a committee and can be another cause
why good men do not see anything worth while for them to do
on local councils. Generally speaking there should be a time
limit of something like five years on the holding of a chairmanship of any committee in a council. With all its drawbacks, it
has great merits. And what could be more valuable on a committee than the presence of a few ex-chairmen with some experience of the work of the committee and of a chairman's functions, role, and difficulties?

The criticisms that have been made of the selection of chairmen by seniority and their holding office for an indefinite period can be applied also to the practice by which one person acquires a collection of chairmanships, and sometimes of the most important chairmanships, of a council. Here again, even if such a man is a capable chairman and gives his whole time to council work, it discourages the others. If there are no prospects of promotion, how can a council expect to get good recruits? And if a man spends all his time as chairman of committees, he gets that official point of view to which reference has already been made. There is, too, only one way in which people can show their capacities as chairman, and that is by actually holding the office. Men in office are inclined to think that nobody else on their committee could really take the chair effectively. But there are many examples that disprove this view.

Committees may be badly used by their chairman, too, in the matter of talk. Some chairmen apparently cannot talk, others apparently cannot stop talking. Either type is a mistake and it is difficult to say which is worse. Neither provides leadership. The silent or dumb chairman—not to be confused with the taciturn chairman who is one of the best—clearly gives no lead; he may have to be prompted, indeed, even to put the question. The talkative chairman, however, treats his committee as a sounding board. He bludgeons them into unconsciousness with words and in self-defence they cease to listen attentively to what he says. He kills discussion, for people feel either that there is nothing left to discuss, or that if a discussion begins, another outpouring will be precipitated from the chairman and they will never get home. There are undoubtedly chairmen of this kind. They prepare their agenda carefully, expound each item to the committee, suggest the pros and cons, and perhaps (though not so commonly) suggest a line of decision. But this is the death of government by discussion. The good chairman will prefer to share the work of expounding the agenda with the secretary and the other officials and he will remember that the members of the committee prefer to conduct a discussion themselves and not to be a mere audience at a monologue. Chairmen are sometimes jealous of their position in this respect and anxious to show in particular that they are independent of the officials. But there are other and more effective ways of showing this independence.

The greatest disservice which a chairman can inflict upon his committee, however, is that of becoming a mere echo or a sworn companion-in-arms of the officials. It is an understandable development, though more understandable in the case of a minister, facing the House of Commons single-handed and relying so much on his officials to see him through, than in the case of a chairman who is not solely responsible for administration but can share his responsibility with his fellow members on the committee. A chairman, however, who wishes to lead may find himself insensibly relying more and more on the chief officials who have all the answers and arguments ready to support him. He may not be a weak man, and he will not necessarily be a mere tool of the officials—though he could be both—but he may wish to assert himself and to have his way with his committee, and if he and the chief officials can work together, each supporting and influencing the other, soon they stand together, sometimes dominating a committee, sometimes in constant warfare with it. This is an abuse to which chairmen who hold office indefinitely may become prone, although there are plenty of cases of capture or surrender within the first few days or weeks of a chairman's term of office.

It is hardly necessary to argue at any length that this alliance of chairman and officials is treason to the whole idea of government by committee. Such a chairman loses his power and his right to lead his committee. He may dragoon them but he can do no more. Yet it is a common spectacle in the operation of committees in British local government, and it deserves a little consideration. It is as well to look at the matter, first of all, from the point of view of the officials. It commonly happens that an official finds that the chairman of a committee is quite unable to provide even a minimum of leadership to the committee. If the chairman is aware of his deficiencies and remains silent, there is nothing left for it but for the official as secretary to conduct the business of the committee, presenting each item of the agenda and indicating to the chairman what questions should be put and when they should be put. Many an official finds himself saying to his chairman: 'Shall we proceed to the next item, sir?' or 'Will you put that question to the committee, sir?' Depressing as this spectacle may be to those who believe in the value of the committee system of administration as a school of self-government, it must be acknowledged that an official who behaves in this way is not behaving improperly. He is doing his duty and no more. The committee's business must be carried on. An official is entitled to try to rescue or to protect a committee from the consequences of its chairman's incapacity.[1] In so doing he must exercise a gift for ventriloquism. Not all officials have this gift, and not all those who have it realize what a dangerous gift it is. Many may exercise it when it is not necessary, giving the impression that the ventriloquist's doll is their idea of the ideal chairman. In their impatience to get things settled they find themselves prompting a chairman and taking the reins out of his hand and running the committee. Sometimes they may do it better than he does. But they are acting improperly. They should go no further than is absolutely necessary.

More difficult is the case of the chairman who is anxious to give a lead to his committee and to take part fully in all discussions, but who relies entirely upon his chief official for his information and ideas. He is not captured; he surrenders. And he is thereafter a voluntary mouthpiece of the official. In such a case an official is in a difficult position. But it would be absurd to say that he should not supply his chairman with all the ammunition he asks for. An official in such a case, however, is subject to great temptation. He has a chance to influence a committee considerably; he sees an opportunity to get his way. But although in some cases this may happen, he should remember that a committee may be quick to realize that its chairman is no more than the mouthpiece of the official and may come to resent and to resist it.

There are cases, however, where a chairman does not surrender willingly to the official, but is captured, perhaps by slow degrees. An official sees in the chairman the instrument by which he can control the committee. He goes through the agenda with him privately and seeks to suggest to him the right solution. He mentions things to the chairman in confidence and suggests that perhaps they need not 'bother' the committee with this 'at this stage'. Close contact between chairman and

---

[1] Let it be noted that while it is common to find officials rescuing committees from a chairman's incompetence, it is extremely rare, if not unknown, for a chairman to be able to rescue a committee from the consequences of its officials' incompetence.

official breeds a feeling of alliance and comradeship; they face the foe together; they plan how to get things past the committee. And after a while the chairman has in effect gone over to the enemy. Not all chairmen go quietly, however. It can happen that an official spends a great deal of his time attempting to win his chairman over to his side, but that the chairman resists, and attempts to retain for himself some independence, some freedom of action, some initiative, which will enable him to lead his committee. The relations between such a chairman and such an official can deteriorate into wearisome private battles in which a chairman loses confidence in the official. There can be no doubt that such action by an official is improper. It is not the task or duty of an official to win his chairman over to his side. He should explain his point of view to his chairman; he may indicate what, in his view, would be the right course for the committee to adopt; he should give all the information at his disposal to the chairman. But beyond this he should not go, if he has a chairman who is able and ready to give leadership to the committee. It is an official's duty to say what he thinks is the right decision for the committee to come to; he is not failing in his duty if, after he has explained and justified his point of view, his chairman and later his committee reject his advice. That is the difference between administration by bureaucracy and administration by committees. In a bureaucracy it is an official's duty not only to express his view about what should be done, but also to see that is it done; under a system of administration by committees, the official proposes, but the committee disposes.

7

It is not enough for a committee to be wisely led; it must also be wisely fed. While the chairman has the primary responsibility for wise leading, the secretary has the primary responsibility for wise feeding. In council committees the secretarial function falls largely within the province of the town or county clerk and his department, save in the case of the education committee for the chief education officer or director of education is often also secretary of the education committee. Thus the principal official of the council is the secretary of council committees, and his secretarial function is one of his most important tasks.

He and other officers of his department are in charge of the arrangement of committee business and the recording of committees' decisions. They do not present all the business to a committee—the officials of the other departments concerned are, of course, present at committee meetings and expound matters which fall within their purview. But the clerk's department must always be represented, and it is entitled to a say in any question which involves the presentation of business to a committee. The great influence of town and county clerks in local government and their pre-eminence in the official hierarchy arise in large measure from the fact that they exercise a controlling function over the conduct of business. They are, indeed, the secretaries-general of council committees. The nature of their secretarial function gives them a priority over the work of other officials. It is interesting to note, in passing, that whereas in the central government it is the head of the Treasury who is the head of the civil service, in local government (as in colonial government) it is the head of the secretariat who is head of the local civil service.

The task of an official in presenting business to a council's committee is extremely difficult—more difficult indeed than is often realized by councillors themselves, or even by officials. The task of the official in Whitehall advising his Minister is in many ways much simpler. He deals with one man only, supported by a party majority; the official in the town or county hall has a group of people of all parties to deal with. The difference in technique required is tremendous; the art of committee management is a distinct and difficult art.

In considering how to present his business to a committee an official will be aware of certain weaknesses which council committees exhibit, and his duty will be to make the best of those weaknesses, while his temptation will be to exploit them for his own ends. Committees, for example, are ready to talk, but they are reluctant to read; even if they are able and willing to read, they are unable to write—they cannot draft. Committees prefer to go round a difficult point rather than to go at it; committees are anxious to finish, and consequently are ready to postpone. From these general qualities there arise those desperate attempts to shelve responsibility—the setting up of a small sub-committee, the calling for a further report or more information, the seeking of information about what is done in other authorities, the calling for consultation with other committees or other interested bodies. Now these tendencies and the devices to which they give rise are not always bad, but they can lead to abuse. What an official has to consider is how to present his business to the committee in such a way that these abuses do not arise. He must try to present questions for decision when they are ripe for decision, not before and not after. He may find it wise to inform his committee at an earlier stage that a question will be coming up for decision, and explain to them how it is developing and what will be involved when the time for decision comes. A discussion at this stage may help him to see on what lines his committee may wish to consider the question, and what information he should have ready for them. But it will always be unwise, of course, to ask for a decision before the question is ripe for decision. It may be doubted, however, whether an official is often tempted to make this mistake. His temptation is more often the other way—to postpone consulting a committee until the eleventh hour. This particular abuse of committee administration deserves a few words.

It is a common failing of officials to bring questions to a committee for decision at the last possible moment. A committee is then told that it must act or it will be too late. No proper discussion is possible in these circumstances and none seems desirable. Such action amounts to contempt of a committee, and it makes good committee work impossible. The fault in these cases does not lie always with a local official. It may arise from the action of some central official who calls for a reply at short notice, a call which may be the result either of delay and incompetence at the centre or of the mistaken idea that the demand for an immediate reply gives an impression of efficiency. But in many cases the fault lies with a local official, and it is a mark of incompetence. This incompetence may be the result of an official's inability to see in time that a problem is ripe for a committee's decision, or it may arise from an official's reluctance to consult his committee until the very last moment, when he may hope that it will feel obliged to accept his proposals at the point of the pistol. The latter case is the mark of the worst official in the sphere of committee administration, for he is deliberately undermining the system.

Closely linked with the abuse of presenting the committee with a pistol is that of presenting it with a *fait accompli*. When this is done, it is often made to appear respectable by obtaining the chairman's approval for the action and seeking the committee's retrospective approval. Now it is admitted that there are actions which cannot await a committee's approval, but it is apparent that if there is to be any reality in committee administration, the *fait accompli* must be genuinely exceptional. The matter concerned must be so urgent or so trivial that the committee's approval can be taken for granted. The principal safeguard which a committee can have in a case of this kind must be its chairman, who should be careful and reluctant about giving his consent to actions unless he is satisfied that they are so urgent or so trivial that the committee's freedom of action is not really being infringed. The most pernicious form of the *fait accompli* is that in which officials have allowed a matter to develop so far along certain lines, without consulting the committee, that it is impossible for the committee, when the matter comes before it, to reverse the course of events. In practice the decision has already been taken, though formally the committee itself has not acted. As a regular instrument in the hands of officials, the *fait accompli* is an abuse of administration by committees.

It has been remarked already that committees are willing to talk but unwilling to read. For the conscientious official, anxious to guide his committee wisely, it is a problem to know how to present his information and how much information to present. He must ask himself whether he will address himself to the slowest or to the quickest intellects on the committee, and he will be wise if he decides to strike somewhere between. He must consider how far he will present the agenda in writing, circulated in some detail beforehand, and how far he will rely upon oral exposition of the points in the meeting, circulating only brief headings in writing before the meeting. No hard and fast rules can be laid down. So much depends upon the personalities and capacities of officials and committees. But it may be suggested that it is perhaps easier to err by choosing the side of circulating written matter in some detail beforehand. There are at least two difficulties. One is that a concise statement of an issue is extremely difficult to set down in writing; the other is that, as indicated already, councillors, though usually able to read, are usually also unwilling to do so. A great many points may be more effectively grasped by a committee if expounded orally in committee by an official. Obviously some matters require treatment at length and in advance in a written document; some decisions must be based on information; appointments can be made only after perusing particulars of the candidates' qualifications and experience. But it seems certain that the amount of paper circulated to members of a committee should be kept to a minimum. Administration by committees is administration after discussion, and the oral method of presentation is more effective in provoking and guiding discussion than the written.

Officials, too, must avoid the temptation to smother or choke their committees with too much information. It is difficult, in advance of a discussion in a committee, to know what information is required. The response of some officials to a situation of this kind is to produce all that they know about the question, and particularly about the history of the question, and place it before the committee. This is often wasted effort. Worse still, it prevents an official from having the time or feeling the necessity to think about his problem; and it has the same effect on his committee. The very minimum of information should be circulated in writing; enough to make clear what the question is and what considerations are involved. Let the rest of the information be held back until the discussion in committee, when it will become clear what further information is needed and what is relevant to the course of the discussion. And as at this stage information will be presented verbally, it will become clear from a committee's reactions whether the official is giving them more than they can take or not. If, after such a discussion, further information is needed in writing, it can be circulated. Let the stress always be upon verbal exposition.

On some subjects, an official cannot expect his committee to understand at all fully the grounds upon which they are asked to decide a question. The subject-matter may be so technical or so complicated that it is incomprehensible to the layman. There are matters in the spheres of law, finance, technology, and even of labour relations where this situation commonly arises. Who can understand the intricacies of the Private Street

Works Act, of the housing subsidies, of the scientific disposal of sewage, or of the proper grading of a partially qualified trench inspector, to mention a few examples of an elementary order of complication? The consent of committees is needed to courses of action which cannot be explained to them in a way which they can understand. Let it be admitted, too, that not all officials can understand the mysteries of each other's special crafts. In cases like this it is clearly desirable that a committee should be told, if at all possible, what the consequences of its decision are likely to be. Even that, however, is not always possible. In certain matters a committee is, in practice, entirely in the hands of its officials, and its action in coming to a decision is purely formal.

On the other hand, officials are often inclined to exaggerate the extent to which a committee is unable to grasp what is put before it, and to make that the excuse for telling it very little. Committee members, it is true, often get the wrong end of the stick; they often go off at a tangent; they are often prejudiced, wrong-headed, soft-hearted. But anyone who has sat upon a committee composed entirely of officials will have found similar characteristics exhibited, and in any case the job of the official is to do his best to get the best out of the committee. Too often officials regard a committee's inability to agree with their proposals as a proof that the committee has not understood those proposals. The reverse is sometimes the case.

8

A particularly delicate aspect of an official's relations with a committee is the problem of his position in relation to any experts who may be members of the committee. Part of the officials' task is to advise the committee upon policy and administration, and if they are to be good officials, they must know something about it. They need not be experts—indeed, they are more likely to be general practitioners. But like all general practitioners, they wish to have the right to decide what expert advice is to be called in. They feel entitled to claim that expert advice should be put to the committee through them. Now in spite of the fact that, generally speaking, committee members are laymen, occasionally experts will find a place there. Thus a builder or an architect may be on a housing committee, a town planner on a planning committee, a doctor on a health committee, a headmaster or a psychologist or even a parent on an education committee. Experts find their way on to committees by different routes. Thus the fact that people sometimes choose to enter local councils upon retirement means that people of experience and expert knowledge, based upon a life's work, can find their way on to council committees. Apart from this, however, there is positive provision, as was explained earlier, that upon education committees, for example, there should be teachers with experience of primary, secondary, and further education, and persons with knowledge of the work of voluntary schools.

Naturally officials find relations with these experts a delicate matter, and all the more delicate when, as in some of the cases just mentioned, these members are not merely experts but also interested parties. It is not untrue to say, perhaps, that officials prefer not to have these potentially rival experts on the committee, though in a matter of this kind personality and temperament play so large a part that it is possible to find cases where an official and an expert produce the happiest of combinations, even when the expert happens to be chairman. What is the true doctrine in this matter? It would seem to be this. The requirement of a member of a committee is that he should be capable of understanding the issues before his committee, of learning about the work it does, and of taking part in the control of that work. He is not required to be an expert or even to be capable of becoming one. He need not be educated in his subject, but he must of course be educable. For the rest, however, what is needed for a good committee member is intelligence, sense, application, judgement, and decision. Now although a committee member may be an expert already in the subject-matter of his committee, he may or may not have these good qualities. But knowledge is the least of the prerequisites for membership. If he has the other prerequisites, the fact that he is an expert is not a disqualification; it is perhaps an additional qualification, but it is the least of the essential qualifications.

It may seem perverse to state the doctrine in this form. In particular it may be objected: Would it not be a good idea to have a few experts on a committee, so that the committee should not be wholly in the hands of its official experts? Will not the official have it all his own way unless there are some other experts to contradict him from time to time and remind the laymen present that experts differ and can be wrong? There is truth in this. It is undeniable that if a member of a committee is not only well qualified to be a member of a committee by his qualities of intelligence, sense, judgement, and the rest, but is also an expert on the subject, he is a valuable member of a committee. It follows, of course, from the fact that he is, by definition, a good member of a committee, that he will use his expert knowledge wisely and that he will not attempt to usurp the position of the official as adviser to the committee. Even so a difficult situation is liable to arise, and a battle of expert opinions leaves the majority of a committee bewildered.

On the whole the balance of advantages seems to lie with the opinion that if a committee has no lack of good laymen upon it, the introduction of expert members raises more problems than it solves. Better still, if a committee has a good official, it can be sure that he will present the expert advice to them with a full regard to the pros and cons involved; that he will indicate where experts differ, and that he will try to give the committee such full and fair information as will enable them to make up their minds. Good lay members of a committee also will be sufficiently sceptical to know that no expert is infallible, and that where expert sense flies against common sense in the sphere of administration, something must be wrong with the official's expert advice. In the sphere of administration it cannot be too strongly emphasized that the role of the expert is advisory; he should not be on the committee but by its side. In more general terms, the place of the expert is on committees to advise, not on committees to administer.

9

It is time to say something now of the committees as a whole, having dealt at some length with the way in which three characters—the official, the secretary, and the chairman—may help or hinder its work. What is the position of a committee as an administrative body in British local government? There is one first misuse of committees which deserves attention. It may be introduced with some words which Jeremy Bentham used in speaking of boards. 'A board, my Lord,' he wrote, 'is a screen. The lustre of good desert is obscured by it; ill desert, slinking behind, eludes the eye of censure.'[1] What Bentham said of a board may be said also of council committees. Where many are responsible, no one is responsible. How can we find out where authority and responsibility lies, so that we may initiate proposals or apportion praise and blame? There can be no doubt that this is one of the weaknesses of administration by committees. It shows itself in a variety of ways.

In the first place a committee may be a screen for an official. To the ordinary citizen or to the employee of a local authority this aspect of a committee's action often reveals itself. The official, often as secretary, speaks on behalf of the committee; he receives its letters and writes its replies. Behind the screen of the committee he is tempted to pursue his own policies and to express his own ideas of how a service should be conducted. He holds up the committee as a vague body which would be 'reluctant to do this' or would be 'unhappy' about that; a body which 'had not contemplated action on these lines' or 'would be unwilling to re-open the question on the present facts'. In this way citizens are held back from the committee, fended off, kept at bay, and not always, as is often said, so as 'to avoid bothering' the committee, but so as to avoid holding up the administrative process which the official is carrying out. The official becomes a high priest through whom alone citizens can speak to a committee and through whom alone the committee's answers can be transmitted. Chairmen and committee members are discouraged by official frowns from writing letters to citizens; all communications must pass through the proper channels, and the whole essence of the transaction is that it must be impersonal. Committees become even more impersonal than the Minister in Whitehall, that remote figure who 'directs' his officials to acknowledge receipt of our communications and to regret that no action is possible in the matter.

In both central and local administration this tendency of the official to shield himself behind the Minister or the committee is well established. It is obvious that not all matters can be placed before a minister or a committee, but so far as local officials are concerned there can be no doubt that they succumb

[1] *Letters to Lord Grenville* (1807), Works, v. 17.

at times to the temptation to invoke the committee on their side, to speak for it, and to interpret its mind in order to support their own views of proper administrative action. Many matters which should go to a committee for decision, clear as that decision must often be, are held back or suppressed by an official nervous, perhaps, lest a committee may not agree with him. Local administrative committees owe part of their justification for existence to the fact that, being local, people can be brought into contact with them and can put their case to their fellow citizens. It is no part of the duty of local officials to prevent this happening.

But it is not only the official who uses the committee as a screen or a shield. The individual committee member does the same. The councillor, harassed by his constituents, assures them that he has raised their grievances or suggestions on the committee, but that he has been unable to prevail. And in many cases this is true. Not even the chairman can be charged with responsibility, for though he may have greater authority than other members, he must carry his committee with him. There is no doubt that many councillors are relieved of responsibility only too easily by the fact that their proposals are killed in committee. They find themselves either advocating weakly what they do not believe in or advocating strongly what they do not expect to see done, because they know that the responsibility for decision will rest upon the committee and not upon them as individuals. The reformer is nonplussed, for he cannot tell by what handle to take hold of the committee. It is an elusive, many-headed body.

Nor are these difficulties made much easier by the fact that, generally speaking, council committees meet in private. It is true that one or two committees—the education committee of a county or county borough council is one example—are required by law to meet in public, but this requirement is rendered of less effect by the practice of meeting in sub-committees in private and transacting formal business in public. Even so, it can be said that when committees do meet in public, there is some opportunity for individual members to make their views known and to indicate to their constituents the extent to which they concur with the committee's actions. Upon the whole, however, it is clear that a great deal of the work of council committees must be conducted in private, if there is to be free and informal discussion, and it follows that individual members will find themselves using the committee like a screen.

It is not only the official and the individual councillor who use the committee as a screen. The tendency of almost all committees to set up sub-committees means that in many cases committees are but screens behind which sub-committees do their work. To such an extent does this process go, indeed, that it seems clear in some cases that the power has gone so far to the sub-committees that the committees themselves are not merely screens but also shams. A study of the use and abuse of sub-committees is an important part of the study of the use and abuse of committees. It is clear, of course, that most committees must make use of sub-committees for the same reasons of administrative convenience and efficiency which justify councils in making use of the committees themselves. Labour must be shared, details must be delegated, questions must be investigated before coming up for discussion and decision by the full committee. On many occasions progress is possible only if problems can be referred to sub-committees for consideration and report. But some curious tendencies soon begin to show themselves. Difficulties are avoided, decisions postponed, discussion shortened or prevented by the use of sub-committees. And the process of referring matters to smaller and smaller bodies seems at times to have no limits—sub-committees have their sections, sections their sub-sections; there are panels and working parties and informal groups and drafting sectors and segments. There is a sort of law of gravity in committee work by which things are referred farther and farther back and down. Along with this tendency, there goes the tendency for each small group to feel a sense of its own importance and to conspire against the body to which it is nominally subordinate. It holds as much power in its hands as it can; it tells its parent as little as possible and what it tells, it tells as late as possible. Within every committee which makes use of sub-committees and other subordinate bodies, there are parties of conspirators, all engaged in the ludicrous task of keeping things from each other. Thus arises the expression 'wheels within wheels' in regard to committee work, and there can be no doubt that it describes a common human characteristic displayed in the use of sub-committees.

The result of this kind of behaviour is that a committee's meetings can become mere formalities. Decisions have been taken in sub-committees and only those who have sat upon the sub-committees have had any real share in making the decisions or have any real knowledge of what is going on. This is the common experience of members of education committees, whose wide range of duties and functions makes the use of sub-committees necessary. If committee work is to have any reality, however, it is clear that sub-committees and their subordinate bodies must show confidence in their parent bodies. The tendency towards oligarchy, which the use of smaller and smaller bodies within a committee exhibits, makes committees at the best a screen and at the worst a sham.

It is not the use of sub-committees only which can make committees a sham. The workings of party can produce the same result. The party man in local government as in central government can do good and he can do harm. Something will be said later on in this chapter of some of the uses of the party man in committee work, and it is enough to say here that, on the whole, he does more good than harm. But a word must be said here of the harmful effects upon committee work of one abuse of the party system. In some councils it is a feature of party organization that all important decisions are taken at a private party meeting whose decisions are then binding upon all the members of the party. When this system is operated to excess, committee meetings are no more than a formal ratification of what has already been decided in private. Discussion is not worth while; the issue is a foregone conclusion. When the majority party on a council adopts this method, the minority may as well not express its views. It is confined to the task of an impotent opposition, with no function but to protest—a situation which can soon produce an irresponsible opposition. There is no room for dealing with issues on their merits.

There can be no objection, of course, to parties deciding the line to be taken on major issues of principle in local government, and this must be expected to show itself particularly in the important debates in the full meetings of the council. But on a great deal of committee work it is proper to allow freedom of discussion to all members. Where this is denied, and the private caucus of a party decides all questions beforehand or binds its members to follow the leader in committee on all questions, then power has left the committee altogether. The situation becomes particularly unsatisfactory when the chairman of a committee is a party man under orders in the same way. Party discipline has its value in committee work, as will be suggested later on, but when carried to excess, as it is in some councils in the country, it robs committee work of its value. There is no exchange of views, no sharing in administration, no collective consideration.

10

Not less serious as an abuse of committee work than the treating of the committee as a screen or as a sham, is what may be called the treating of the committee as an empire, as a council within the council, as a self-contained *ad hoc* authority, keeping itself to itself. This is perhaps the commonest besetting sin of committees in local government.

An outstanding defect of committee administration is the isolation in which committees tend to work, insulating themselves from the activities of other committees and refusing to co-operate with them. This departmentalism is not due solely to officials. Chairmen and committee members develop these self-contained, self-sufficient, and self-important attitudes as well, and resent attempts by others to encroach upon their authority. But officials often foster this feeling, and encourage their chairmen and committees to protect the department against encroachment and to defend all its claims against those of other committees. There is nothing peculiar to local government in this, of course. Central departments are often at war with each other; departmental jealousies and territorial disputes are a regular feature of central administration, and ministers are expected and urged by their officials to fight for the department. Nor should it be suggested that the disputes need never arise or that they necessarily concern trivial matters only. Sometimes no doubt the issues are petty, and often they are made acute by considerations of personal prestige. But in many cases an important matter of policy is involved. Disputes about the distribution of functions between departments are bound to arise and are not necessarily simple to solve. In committee administration no matter how carefully functions have been distributed some questions will involve more than one committee and can only be dealt with by co-operative action between committees. This co-operation is hard to get; the seeking of it delays administration, for it is harder to get committees to meet together and decide things than to get two individual ministers to do so.

Yet it is essential that co-operation should occur. Committees in local government are committees of the council; they are not themselves separate councils. Yet at times chairmen and committees and their officials talk and act as if they were self-sufficient councils, acting on their own, unmindful of the responsibility they bear to the council which has appointed them and of which they are only a part.

There seems little doubt that one cause of this tendency to independence in committees is the presence upon them of interested parties who are not themselves members of the council. This is particularly noticeable in education committees where representatives of teachers and of religious bodies usually occupy a strong, though minority, position, extending from the main committee through sub-committees, governors, and managers of schools. These interested parties combine a strong enthusiasm for education, and particularly for that section of it with which they are identified, with no direct responsibility as members of the council for the provision of the other services for which a council is responsible. As a result they often conceive their duty to be no more than pressing hard for what they are interested in, and they resent interference by the council in what their education committee proposes. This tendency to separate action is encouraged by the fact that the law makes compulsory upon local authorities the setting up of an education committee and the reference to it of any matter in the sphere of education before the council itself may act upon it. It is true that there is no compulsory delegation of functions to an education committee, but such a committee is given a certain independent status by law.

Watch committees are even more independent, and in the counties police functions are conferred upon standing joint committees, only half of the members of which are members of the county council, the other half being justices. It is the law, however, rather than the presence of interested parties which gives watch committees their independence, and there is no doubt some case for suggesting that, in a matter like this, debates in a council might be bad for good police administration.

II

The problem of ensuring co-operation between council committees is perhaps the most important problem in British local government. In particular it is difficult to find just the right method and just the right degree of co-operation. The question of degree is particularly important, for it is a fact that if committees can err by a failure to co-operate, they err also by going to the other extreme and co-operating too much. Chairmen and officials, whose business it is to see that consultation takes place between committees, may find that consultation, joint discussion, and co-ordinating committees develop so much that they become almost an end in themselves. Decisions are held up while a committee consults everybody else who is likely to be concerned. Members constitutionally incapable of taking decisions, or anxious for some reason to avoid a decision or to frustrate a policy, show a passion for consultations between committees which can soon become an abuse. It requires a constant drive on the part of the chairmen and the officials concerned, and a genuine willingness on the part of all to get a decision and push ahead with it, before joint discussions between committees can expedite the conduct of business. Otherwise they do no more than produce delay, deadlock, confusion, dissipation of energies, and frustration.

It is difficult to know how best to mitigate—for it cannot be overcome—the inefficiency that arises from the tendency of committees to become either excessively unco-operative or excessively co-operative. It is apparent that the co-ordination of committee work is a proper function of the town clerk, aided by such officials as the treasurer and the planning officer. Their authority will depend to a large extent on their personal skill, and of course on the support they get from the chairmen of the principal committees. A town clerk is not charged with the sort of authority to co-ordinate the council's activities which is given to a city manager in certain American cities. Nor has he usually at his disposal a committee or a chairman charged with co-ordinating functions, with whom he could work regularly upon this problem. He can achieve something in certain aspects of a council's work by the activities of a finance committee, an establishment committee, or a planning committee, committees which are not themselves providing a service directly but are concerned with certain aspects of the work and activities of all committees. In local government as in central government co-ordination and control can come through finance as effectively as anywhere. But it is not enough. It is a limited approach to common problems. Something more comprehensive is clearly needed.

Would there not be some value in having in every council a sort of 'steering' committee, composed of the chairmen of the principal committees of the council? Some councils, indeed, do make use of this device. One can foresee the difficulties of such a body. It would be a committee of prima donnas, each deter-mined to defend his committee to the last, and many of its decisions would be taken on the principle of log-rolling, by which one chairman supports another in return for that other's support. But there would always be some chairmen upon it who, either because their committees were concerned with a wider range than others, such as finance, establishment, and planning, or because their committees were not directly involved in the argument before the steering committee at the time, would be capable of assisting the steering committee to a decision upon the question. Such a steering committee, too, would provide a town clerk with some kind of instrument or institution through which the task of co-ordinating committee work could be achieved.

In this connexion it is interesting to observe the experience which the London County Council has had in framing an instrument to ensure co-operation between council committees. Alone among the councils of the country it has a leader of the council, who works along with a conference of the principal chairmen of committees and thus provides a sort of steering committee for the council's work. In a sense this committee is a sort of cabinet and the leader of the council a sort of prime minister, but the analogy should not be pushed far. It is only in so far as the Cabinet is a co-ordinating body that the steering committee of the L.C.C. resembles it. That and one other point of importance—the steering committee of the L.C.C. is composed of party members. It was indeed the invention of Mr. Herbert Morrison and the Labour party when they obtained a majority in the L.C.C.[1]

The mention of party draws attention to a factor which can be of great importance in the co-ordination of committee work. There has been a good deal of criticism about the introduction of party politics into British local government. Whatever its drawbacks—and they are often exaggerated—it brings a unifying factor into the work of council committees. More particularly is this found, of course, in a party where discipline is strong and members can be relied upon to vote together. It assumes also that the party in a majority will have a majority on the principal committees, and that in many cases it will ensure that the chairmanships are held by its members. The discipline in the L.C.C. was even stronger. The chairmen of the committees were nominated by the Leader of the Council, and the party majority on the committees saw to it that they were elected. There is no doubt that a policy committee of this kind is a valuable institution for co-ordination and control in a council's work. A council with a Conservative majority might not be amenable to such strict discipline, but it would gain something by the adoption of the system.

But the value of party is not confined to its possibilities of counteracting the abuse of the committee as empire. It has a value in relation to the abuse which was described as the committee as screen. It was remarked, when this abuse was being considered, that one difficulty in the use of committees to administer was that where so many are responsible, no one can be responsible. Party can mitigate this tendency to irresponsibility. Just as party can organize a council by holding its committees together, so it can bring some organization into a committee. What the committee does, whether it does well or not, comes to be thought of as a mark of the party's success or failure. Where members of a committee are linked together by a party tie, they are no longer isolated individuals advocating a course of action alone or criticizing alone. They belong to an organization which can give them machinery for action. Whether in opposition or not, the party man is in a more effec-

[1] See Herbert Morrison, *How London is Governed.*

tive and more responsible position than an isolated independent. With all its faults party brings the opportunity for fixing responsibility in committees in a way which the non-party committee cannot achieve.

It must be admitted, of course, as has been pointed out already, that if the party organization is overdone, a committee becomes a sham. There is the danger. Party, if wisely used, can do much to prevent the irresponsibility which arises from the fact that committees can be screens; if overdone, party can make the situation much worse by exploiting the fact that a committee is a screen and making it a sham. The right use of party in local government is therefore at the very root of its effective working. On it, probably more than on anything else, depends the answer to the question whether committees are used wisely or unwisely.

12

From what has been written in the preceding pages, it is clear that if committees to administer, in town and county hall, are to work well, it is necessary to maintain the supply of two types of person—the good layman and the good official. There will not be a supply of good laymen unless there is a demand for them, unless, that is, local councils offer opportunities for them to exercise their talents, to show initiative and leadership, and to obtain some positions of power and influence. To a large extent today the scope open to the local councillor is restricted, not because of any action or intention on the part of the local council, but because of the intervention of the central government. If most matters of importance are settled, in the last resort, in Whitehall, there is nothing worth while for a man of energy and ability in the town hall. The proper allocation of functions between local and central government is a pre-requisite of obtaining good local councillors, as it is of many other important feature of good local government. But even if this allocation were settled well, it remains to emphasize that if chairmanships go by seniority, or are held for life, and if officials treat chairmen and committees with slight regard, then a supply of good laymen cannot be expected.

It is important too that councillors should be drawn from as wide a range of persons as possible. Administrative ability and common sense are characteristic of many different classes of people and are produced in many different walks of life. Yet because people cannot afford the time and money to serve on councils, it has often happened that councillors are drawn largely from the ranks of the retired or the leisured or the wealthy. The wage earner or the person actively engaged in business has felt unable to serve. The position was improved a good deal by the coming of women into local government, for in many cases women were able, when their families had reached school age, to give time to local government at an earlier age than men who waited until retirement. But until it became accepted that service on a local council or its committees should not involve financial loss to an individual, and that councillors might claim expenses for loss of income through attendance at council or committee meetings, there were considerable difficulties in the way of service in local government by wage earners and by a large number of salaried workers. Very many of these classes of people had had considerable administrative experience and had a wide knowledge of how a council's services appeared to the consumer, and their presence on committees could be most valuable. It was not until 1948, however, in England, that as a result of the report of an inter-departmental committee,[1] legislation was passed to authorize expenses for loss of pay as a result of attendance at council and committee meetings.[2]

There is a case for arguing that chairmen, at any rate chairmen of important committees in large authorities, should get some sort of salary. In many cases, such as that of education committees, a chairman's work, if he is to do it at all well, is a full-time occupation. In a county area he must travel about a great deal to be in personal contact with the people his committee serves. Unless some remuneration is given in a case of this kind, a chairmanship can only be held by a retired person, or a person who can afford to give all his time to the work. There is a good deal of reluctance among many people to accept a proposal to pay chairmen. They speak of the professionalization of local government. Yet if the office is full-time and the work is impor-

---

[1] Cmd. 7126 (1947). *Report of the Interdepartmental Committee on Expenses of Members of Local Authorities.* The chairman was Lord Lindsay of Birker.
[2] Local Government Act, 1948, Part VI.

tant, should it not be paid for? Can it be well done on a part-time basis? It is thought proper to pay a mayor a salary; should the chairman of an important committee be treated differently?[1]

Some would go further and suggest that councillors should be paid, just as members of Parliament are paid. They suggest that the numbers of councillors might be reduced, so that there would be more work for the others to do and that they would be able to devote themselves full-time to it. Such a proposal would apply, of course, to county councils particularly, where the amount of time required for a councillor to get round his district and to get to his county town frequently is very considerable and comes near to being a full-time job if it is done effectively. This is one of the reasons why the great proportion of county councillors belongs to the wealthier or retired classes. It would be difficult to decide whether the payment of councillors, on the lines of the payment of members in the House of Commons, would be justifiable or desirable yet. It is best to wait, perhaps, to see what effect the system of expenses introduced by the Act of 1948 has upon the situation.[2]

So far as the supply of good local officials is concerned, the emphasis, in this chapter, must be placed upon the recruitment and training of higher or chief officials who will have the capacity and the inclination to develop the peculiar technique needed for dealing with committees. What is needed is not a narrow specialization nor any special technical ability, nor the pedestrian devotion to executive detail, but a capacity to understand issues, to expound them to a committee lucidly and fairly, and to draw out from the committee the best sense that the members can offer. It cannot be stressed too strongly that his task is not like that of any ordinary official. He is in a very different position from officials whose daily work brings them in contact either with other officials or with the public in the capacity of customers or applicants. The administrative technique required of an official dealing with committees is distinct and peculiar. He must be something of a hybrid. He must be able to talk a

---

[1] The matter was considered by Lord Lindsay's Committee, but it felt that the difficulties were insuperable. Cmd. 7126, p. 34.

[2] Lord Lindsay's Committee took the view that 'local government must not even look like a salaried service'. Cmd. 7126, p. 23.

language which officials understand or speak, but he must also be able to speak the language of the committee member. And this phrase must be taken almost in a literal sense, for his dealings with his committee must usually be oral and not written. He must be able to discuss things with them and see (though not necessarily share) their point of view. He must understand that if a committee disagrees with him, he need not construe that to be a vote of no confidence in himself. He must possess some political capacity, too, in addition to administrative capacity, which enables him to see how a committee may approach a question and how its mind is working during a discussion. An official must at times be a committee's nurse, at times its tutor, at times its conscience, at times its candid friend—yet always its servant, never its master. These varied roles call for special qualities which can be learned, but are hard to teach. So far as the most important of them are concerned, it is likely that the good official is born, not made.

CHAPTER VIII

Committees to Scrutinize and Control

I

MIDWAY between committees to advise and committees to administer or to legislate come committees to scrutinize and control. Their task is not themselves to take part in the process of administration or legislation nor to advise others about what should be done. They are entrusted with the task of seeing whether or how a process is being performed, and by their conduct of this task they serve to provide the means of some sort of control over the carrying out of the process. From the variety of committees performing this function in modern British government, it is proposed to choose for discussion in this chapter four select committees of the House of Commons—the Select Committee of Public Accounts, the Select Committee on National Expenditure, the Select Committee on Estimates,[1] and the Select Committee on Statutory Instruments.[2]

There have been proposals from time to time that the House of Commons should be given an opportunity through the use of committees to exercise some sort of control over what Whitehall does. It is admitted that while the House has important and valuable opportunities to criticize administration through debate, it lacks any chance of close and continuous examination of what is being done. Its standing committees set up to consider bills, as we have seen, are confined purely to that function, and though in the course of debates on a bill some discussion of administration may be in order, there is not much scope for it. There is no allocation of particular subjects to committees, as in the Parliament of France or in the Congress of the United States

---

[1] The standard work on these committees is B. Chubb, *The Control of Public Expenditure* (1952), to which the author is greatly indebted.
[2] This Committee's work was examined in 1953 by the Select Committee on Delegated Legislation. See H.C. 310–1 of 1952–3.

or in the town and county councils of this country. It has seemed to some students of the working of standing committees in Britain that their functions should be extended from the consideration of bills to the study of administration, and that they should be organized according to a division of subject-matter and authorized to deal with both legislation and administration in their allotted field.[1] Though proposals of this kind have been put forward and supported by people of authority and experience,[2] they have always been rejected, and usually emphatically. The Cabinet will tolerate no rivals to its authority in the House of Commons. Whether it is justified in its attitude or not, the outcome has been that standing committees have been confined to the consideration of bills. The only opportunities which members of the House of Commons have for inquiring into administration have arisen through the establishment of the four select committees which have been mentioned.

The oldest of these four committees is the Public Accounts Committee. It was first set up in 1861; it is firmly established and indeed it actually finds a place in the standing orders of the House of Commons.[3] The youngest is the Select Committee on Statutory Instruments which, under a different name, was first set up in 1944[4] and has been continued each session since, but has not yet been accorded the relatively permanent status of recognition in standing orders. The Estimates Committee has had an intermittent existence. It was first set up in 1912 and reappointed in 1913 and 1914. It lapsed during the war, but was reappointed in 1921 and 1922 and thereafter each

---

[1] For example, Ramsay Muir, *How Britain is Governed*, 4th ed., 1933, pp. 220 ff.

[2] See, for example, evidence of Mr. David Lloyd-George before the Select Committee on Procedure of 1930. H.C. 161 of 1931, pp. 43 ff.

[3] Standing Order 90 reads: 'There shall be a select committee to be designated the Committee of Public Accounts, for the examination of the accounts showing the appropriation of the sums granted by Parliament to meet the public expenditure, and of such other accounts laid before Parliament as the committee may think fit, to consist of not more than fifteen members, who shall be nominated at the commencement of every session, and of whom five shall be a quorum. The committee shall have power to send for persons, papers and records, and to report from time to time.'

[4] It was known originally as the Select Committee on Statutory Rules and Orders. By the Statutory Instruments Act, 1946, which came into effect on 1 Jan. 1948, the term 'statutory rules and orders' was replaced by the term 'statutory instruments', which was, incidentally, to cover a wider range, and the name of the select committee was accordingly changed.

session until the outbreak of war in 1939. Once again it lapsed during the war years, but it came to life again in 1946 and has been reappointed annually ever since. The relative insecurity of its existence may be illustrated also by the fact that it, like the Statutory Instruments Committee and unlike the Public Accounts Committee, is not provided for in standing orders. The Select Committee on National Expenditure has been a wartime institution. One such select committee was set up in 1917, during the First World War, reappointed in 1918, and continued in 1919 and 1920; at the very outset of the Second World War in 1939 it was set up again, and it was reappointed each session until 1945.

All four select committees have one point in common—they are not authorized to formulate or criticize policy. What they scrutinize is the application of policy—its forms and its results. To this extent only are they concerned with policy. This has been made clear, as a rule, in their terms of reference. When the Select Committee on Estimates was first set up in 1912 it was authorized 'to examine such of the Estimates presented to this House as may seem fit to the Committee, and to report what, if any, economies consistent with the policy implied in those Estimates should be effected therein'.[1] Although this exclusion of policy from the discussion was omitted when the Committee was reappointed in 1913 and 1914, it was reinserted when the Committee was revived in 1921 and continued until 1939[2] and from 1946. A similar explicit restriction was inserted in the terms of reference of the National Expenditure Committee set up in 1917 when it was authorized 'to examine the current expenditure defrayed out of moneys provided by Parliament and to report what, if any, economies consistent with the execution of the policy decided by the Government may be effected therein', and the same thing was done with the Committee set up in 1939.[3] So far as the Public Accounts Committee is concerned its exclusion from the formulation of policy is implicit in its task, for it is investigating accounts, so that the money is already spent and policy, good or bad, is

[1] See H.C. 122 of 1944, *Eleventh Report from the Select Committee on National Expenditure*. The terms of reference of the various financial committees are conveniently set out in Appendix 2 to this report.
[2] Ibid., pp. 21 and 22.
[3] Ibid.

already decided and applied. Finally, in the case of the Statutory Instruments Committee also, the terms of reference by implication exclude consideration of policy.[1] The nearest they come to it is when they authorize the Committee to bring to the notice of the House of Commons any Statutory Instrument that appears to make some unusual or unexpected use of the powers conferred by its parent Act or that, from its form or purport, calls for elucidation. Under these heads, perhaps, the Committee might introduce some element of the discussion of policy.

What these four committees are authorized to do and what they do in practice are not always the same thing. The line between scrutinizing the application or legalization of policy and discussing the formulation of policy is not easily drawn, and indeed it is sometimes quite genuinely impossible to discuss the one without encroaching upon the other. More particularly is this true in the case of the financial select committees, where wise spending, economy, waste, and misappropriation of funds can hardly be discussed without some discussion of policy. It will be seen in fact that they have not always in practice kept

---

[1] The terms of reference of the committee when it was set up on 4 November 1953, for example, were as follows:

'To consider every Statutory Instrument laid or laid in draft before the House, being an Instrument or Draft of an Instrument upon which proceedings may be or might have been taken in either House in pursuance of any Act of Parliament, with a view to determining whether the special attention of the House should be drawn to it on any of the following grounds:

(i) that it imposes a charge on the public revenues or contains provisions requiring payments to be made to the Exchequer or any Government Department or to any local or public authority in consideration of any licence or consent, or of any services to be rendered, or prescribes the amount of any such charge or payments;

(ii) that it is made in pursuance of an enactment containing specific provisions excluding it from challenge in the courts, either at all times or after the expiration of a specified period;

(iii) that it appears to make some unusual or unexpected use of the powers conferred by the Statute under which it is made;

(iv) that it purports to have retrospective effect where the parent Statute confers no express authority so to provide;

(v) that there appears to have been unjustifiable delay in the publication or in the laying of it before Parliament;

(vi) that there appears to have been unjustifiable delay in sending a notification to Mr. Speaker under the proviso to sub-section (i) of section four of the Statutory Instruments Act, 1946, where an Instrument has come into operation before it has been laid before Parliament;

(vii) that for any special reason its form or purport calls for elucidation.'

clear of the discussion of policy. In estimating the use of these committees, it will be necessary to consider how far their exclusion from discussing policy or 'the merits' reduces their usefulness, and whether an authorization to consider them would increase their usefulness.

2

Let us consider in some detail the membership of these four select committees. First of all it should be noticed that the committees are composed exclusively of members of the House of Commons, and these members are, almost invariably, party men. Occasionally, no doubt, one or two of the few independent members of the House of Commons may find a place on one of these select committees, but generally speaking the committees are composed of party men. What is more it is accepted that membership will be distributed among the parties roughly in proportion to their strength in the House. This means that the government will have a majority on all these committees. Although the members are appointed to the committees formally by the House itself, they are in practice nominated by the party Whips, whose proposals are always accepted. These four committees are thus quite different from the overwhelming majority of the committees to advise, to inquire, and to negotiate which were discussed in previous chapters. They resemble rather, so far as their composition is concerned, the committees to legislate or the committees to administer which have been discussed in the last two chapters.

When we reflect that these select committees are composed of party men we begin to realize why it is that considerations of policy are excluded from their purview. If it were not so, the committees would tend to become little more than another debating chamber within the House. This probability was well expressed in 1946 by Sir Charles MacAndrew, then chairman of the Statutory Instruments Committee, in his evidence before the Select Committee on Procedure of the House of Commons. In a memorandum submitted to the Committee by the then Clerk of the House of Commons, Sir Gilbert (later Lord) Campion, it was proposed that the terms of reference of the Statutory Instruments Committee 'should be extended to enable it to report also on the merits of a Statutory Instrument, as an exercise of the powers delegated. . . . Consideration might also be given to empowering the select committee to inquire into and report on any grievances arising out of Instruments *actually in operation.* . . .'[1] When these suggestions were put to Sir Charles MacAndrew and to Sir Cecil Carr, the adviser to the Statutory Instruments Committee, they were both quite emphatic that such an extension of the Committee's powers would be unwise.[2] It would be unwise because, as Sir Charles MacAndrew put it, 'its deliberations would be changed from being semi-judicial to wrangles on party lines'.[3] 'Anyone coming into our Committee', he said, 'would not have the slightest idea to which party the various Members belonged. . . . As soon as merits arise, policy must be discussed and the Committee must be divided into the Government and Opposition.'[4] 'Any Government would have a majority on the Committee; so the possibility of an adverse report on its merits would be unlikely. Even if one were made, it is difficult to see what good would result.'[5]

What is said here about the Statutory Instruments Committee applies to the other three. As soon as policy is approached —and on the Estimates Committee, for example, it is often difficult to keep quite clear of it—the party division begins to show itself, and the Committee becomes a debating body and not a scrutinizing and controlling body. If a committee composed of party men is to perform successfully the function of scrutinizing the performance of governmental processes, it must keep away from the discussion of policy. In so far as it cannot avoid such discussions, it must change its nature and the function it is performing.

A second feature of the membership of these four select committees is that, generally speaking, the members are all laymen and not experts. That is not to say that they are ignorant of or uninterested in the subject-matter of the committees' scrutiny. They may have expressed a wish to sit on the committee, and may have some knowledge of its work. Moreover, if they continue to sit upon the committee for several sessions they may come to acquire a good deal of knowledge of the subject. But it

[1] H.C. 189–1 of 1945–6. *Third Report of the Select Committee on Procedure*, p. xlv.
[2] Ibid., pp. 242–61.　　　　　　　　　　　　　[3] Ibid., p. 243.
[4] Ibid., p. 246.　　　　　　　　　　　　　　　[5] Ibid., p. 243.

may be suggested that save in the case of the Statutory Instruments Committee, where a keen legal member might conceivably become something of an expert in the subject, the field over which the committees must range is so wide and technical (and the knowledge required is in any case locked up in the departments and only disclosed in evidence) that it would be impossible for the members to become experts. Conceivably, if a member devoted a great deal of time to it, he might become something of a general practitioner. This is particularly likely to happen to the chairman, about whom something must be said.

The chairmen of these select committees, like the chairmen of the administrative committees already discussed but unlike the chairmen of the committees to advise, to inquire, to legislate, and many of the committees to negotiate, are elected by the committees themselves and are not appointed by an outside person or body. But one or two conventions have grown up concerning the choice of chairman. It is accepted that the chairman of the Public Accounts Committee should be chosen from among the members of the Opposition party on the Committee.[1] Thus although the Committee will contain a majority of government members, its proceedings will be in charge of an Opposition member. The Estimates Committee, however, appears to have established a usage of choosing its chairman from among the members of the government party.[2] It is possible to see a reason and perhaps a justification for the difference in practice between the two committees. As the Public Accounts Committee is looking at what is past, the government is prepared to tolerate the choice of a chairman who will not be disposed to see mistakes glossed over or whitewashed. When it comes to estimates, however, and current expenditure, not yet voted, is being discussed, the majority party feels safer perhaps with a chairman of its own way of thinking. None the less it sometimes happens that the chairmen of the sub-committees into which the Estimates Committee breaks itself up, and through which it does most of its work, are drawn from the

[1] 'Only twice before 1916 was the chairman a government supporter. If the war years be excepted, he has always been an Opposition member since that date.' Chubb, op. cit., p. 182, n. 1.

[2] With the exception of the years 1912–14, when Sir Frederick Banbury, a Conservative, was chairman, though the Liberal party was in power.

Opposition party. They may easily conduct an unsympathetic inquiry into some aspect of government spending.[1]

Of the remaining two committees it is not possible to speak so definitely. The Committee on National Expenditure was set up in time of war and at a time also when coalition government was in operation. The chairmen were members of the party with a majority in the House of Commons[2] though naturally there were among the chairmen of the sub-committees, which were a leading feature of its way of working, members of the minority party. When there was no Opposition, it was not possible to consider whether the chairman should be chosen from the government side or from the Opposition side. It is clearly impossible to say whether any usage has been established for a committee of this kind. The choice in each case appears to have been determined largely by the interest and ability of the individual concerned in the subject of national expenditure.

So far as the Statutory Instruments Committee is concerned, it is possible to go a little farther. It was first set up in 1944, in a Parliament in which, though coalition government was in operation, the Conservative party had the majority. The first chairman was a Conservative member, Sir Charles Mac-Andrew. Yet there can be little doubt that his choice was made largely on personal grounds. He was an experienced and respected member, who had held the impartial office of Deputy Chairman of Ways and Means in the previous Parliament. When the Committee was set up in 1945, after the General Election, at which the Labour party gained a large majority, Sir Charles MacAndrew was again elected as chairman, although the Committee over which he was to preside contained seven Labour members, three Conservatives (including himself), and one Liberal. Yet it would not do to conclude at once that the choice of Sir Charles meant that it was accepted that the chairmanship must go to an Opposition or minority-party member. His personal qualities no doubt again played the largest part in his selection. On the other hand, it may well be that these personal qualities assisted to establish the view that

[1] Sir Herbert Samuel maintained in 1931 that it would be better if the chairman of the committee was an Opposition member. See H.C. 161 of 1931, q. 2587.

[2] Mr. Herbert Samuel (as he then was), in 1917 and 1918; after the election of Dec. 1918, when the Conservatives became the largest party, Sir Frederick Banbury in 1919 and 1920. From 1939 to 1945 Sir John Wardlaw-Milne, a Conservative.

an Opposition member might be chosen to preside over the Committee, and to commend the idea to the majority. Be that as it may, when Sir Charles MacAndrew resigned from the chairmanship of the Select Committee in 1949 on his election as Deputy Chairman of Ways and Means once more, he was suceeded as chairman by another Conservative member, Mr. Godfrey Nicholson. When the new Parliament assembled after the General Election of 1950, and the Conservative party was still in opposition, although very close in numbers to the government party, Mr. Nicholson was again elected to the chair. Then after the General Election of 1951, when the Conservative party obtained power, the select committee chose as its chairman a member of the Labour party, Mr Eric Fletcher. So far it seems that a usage is being accepted that the chairmanship should be placed in the hands of an Opposition member.[1] So long as the Committee keeps clear of discussing 'the merits' of Statutory Instruments, one can see that the majority party would be ready to tolerate this position. As it is the task of the Committee to scrutinize the legislative actions of government departments, it is right that it should be led by a chairman who has no conflicting loyalties to embarrass or hinder him in the conduct of his duties.

Party is not the only consideration which is taken into account in the choice of chairmen. In the case of the Public Accounts Committee, at least, it is understood that not only should the chairman be a senior member of the Opposition party, but also if possible he should have some idea of the way in which government departments work on the financial side. Often the chairmanship is taken nowadays by a member of the Opposition who held the office of Financial Secretary to the Treasury when his party was in power, but such a member is, of course, not always available, nor is a rigid convention established on the point.[2] There are, indeed, disadvantages in having an ex-Financial Secretary, for he is an important Opposition member with duties in the House which may prevent his giving sufficient time to the Committee's work.[3] It may be remarked in passing that the choice of a former Financial Secretary to the Treasury

---

[1] See *Report of Select Committee on Delegated Legislation*, H.C. 310-1 of 1952–53, p. xii, para. 47.
[2] H.C. 161 of 1931, qq. 3753 ff.   [3] Ibid., qq. 3751, 3752.

as chairman of the Public Accounts Committee does not necessarily ensure that he will be completely free from party bias
when he comes to preside over the inquest into the government's
accounts for it may well happen that, with a change of government, he is considering in the first year or two of his chairmanship the accounts of the departments while his own party was
in power. The same would be true indeed of most Opposition
members in such a case. The inquest which the Public Accounts
Committee conducts is, inevitably, a couple of years behind the
times, and it will be the former government's spending which
is in question. No charges of partiality could in fact be pre-
ferred against chairmen of the Public Accounts Committee
on this ground, but it is worth while to mention the point
because it is often assumed that to put an Opposition member
into the chair necessarily means that the government's spending
is going to be scrutinized with no special tenderness.

In the other three select committees, as in the Public Accounts
Committee, there is evidence that, in choosing a chairman, members consider whether he has some taste or gift for or knowledge
of the subject-matter of the Committee's scrutiny, or whether,
even if he lacks knowledge or experience, he is the right sort
of man to pick up all that he needs to know. He is not required
to be an expert. If he should qualify by experience and practice
to become a general practitioner, that may be an advantage,
but it is not essential.

Finally, as will have been apparent, all the members on these
committees are back-benchers. They may have held office but
they do not hold it now. It is not thought necessary or proper,
as it is, for example, on many advisory committees and on all
committees to legislate, that the department concerned should
be represented on the committee. If a department's accounts
or actions or estimates are the subject of a committee's scrutiny,
then it appears as a witness before the committee or submits
written observations to it. The Minister and his parliamentary
assistants never appear before the committees.[1] The departments are represented by officials. These committees, in their

[1] The practice of Financial Secretaries of the Treasury attending meetings of
the Public Accounts Committee appears to have been maintained regularly up to
1908, but it declined after that date and was discontinued in 1922. See Chubb,
op. cit., Appendix 10.

scrutiny, come directly into contact with officials. Whereas in the House of Commons or in a standing committee officials can speak only through a minister, before these select committees they speak for themselves and defend the actions of their departments. The layman is confronted by the official. Now this official is, in relation to the members of the select committees, an expert; what is more he is there to defend his department, and he is therefore an interested party, a partisan. How are these lay committees effectively to scrutinize and to examine the work and the evidence of these expert officials? This is a central question in the discussion of scrutinizing committees.

3

It can be said at once that if these committees are to cope with their work, they will need some permanent staff. The members of the committees cannot be expected to devote more than spasmodic and intermittent attention to the committees' work. As members of Parliament they have many other and more pressing claims on their attention. Someone must keep a continuous watch over the subject-matter with which the committees deal.

This introduces, to start with, the character of the secretary without whom the committees could not operate. Like the standing committees to legislate, the committees to scrutinize have the services of clerks on the staff of the House of Commons. There is a clerk of financial committees under whom come the Public Accounts Committee and the Estimates Committee (or the National Expenditure Committee in time of war), each of which has its own clerk, together with clerks for the sub-committees of the Estimates Committee. There is, indeed, a sort of secretariat to look after the financial committees to scrutinize. So far as the Statutory Instruments Committee is concerned, it too has a clerk to act as its secretary. These clerks arrange the business of the committee and keep its records. Whether they should do more than that, and whether other officials are needed in order that the committees' work should be effectively carried out, is one of the questions which is constantly under discussion when the work of these committees to scrutinize is being reviewed.

Some idea of the task confronting the officials who assist the committees may be given. The Statutory Instruments Committee has less material to deal with, in point of sheer bulk, than the financial committees, and yet its proportions are by no means negligible. Whereas the statutes passed by Parliament in 1947 were published in two volumes and occupy nearly 2,000 pages, the statutory instruments for that year required three volumes and occupied 4,397 closely printed pages. In 1952 Acts of Parliament were published in one volume of 1,437 pages (which included over 900 pages of merely consolidating statutes) while the statutory instruments occupied three volumes of 3,980 pages. Not all the statutory instruments printed and published fall within the purview of the Committee. It is confined to the scrutiny of instruments 'upon which proceedings may be or might have been taken in either House in pursuance of any Act of Parliament'. Certain Acts of Parliament in granting delegated powers of legislation provide that the rules made under such powers must be laid before Parliament, and that they will have effect either upon the passing of an affirmative resolution, or if no negative resolution is passed within a specified time. It is the exercise of delegated powers of this kind which the Committee may consider.

It has been calculated that, roughly speaking, not quite 70 per cent. of the public general instruments (leaving out of account, that is to say, the numerous orders of local application only) come within the purview of Parliament and thus of the Statutory Instruments Committee. In the period from 1944, when the Committee was first set up, to the beginning of 1953, about 7,000 instruments were examined by the Committee, out of a total of roughly 10,250 public general instruments.[1]

But although the Committee does not have to look at all the statutory instruments registered, someone must, if the Committee is to make a serious scrutiny. For its task is to look not only at instruments which are laid before Parliament but also at those which, as its terms of reference say, 'might have been' laid. It must not be assumed that all those instruments which should be laid will in fact be laid. Each must be scrutinized to see whether

---

[1] H.C. 310–1 of 1952–3, p. 6, para. 30. Evidence of Sir Cecil Carr. The total of all instruments registered in the period, general and local, printed and not printed, was approximately 19,400.

it should or should not have been laid. And when all this is done the resulting bundle of instruments which the Committee must consider is still quite formidable. The Committee cannot be expected to meet very frequently. Its meetings are, on an average, once in three weeks during the times when the House is sitting. After a recess a good deal of business has accumulated, for the process of making statutory instruments goes on unceasingly. The output is round about ten a day in a five-day week. One member of the Committee in 1946 appeared in the House of Commons one day with his bundle of statutory instruments, ready for the Committee's meeting, and assured his colleagues that he had had it weighed and found it amounted to one pound seven ounces.[1]

What is clear, however, is that with a constant stream of instruments appearing, and with the need for scrutinizing each one to make sure whether it should be placed before the Committee, advising the Committee is a considerable job. What is clear, also, is that it is a specialized job. The language of statutory instruments is legal language and it is seldom the simplest of legal language. To understand the purport of the instrument it is necessary to look not only at the enabling Act but also at other statutory instruments which may have been made under this Act or other Acts. And thereafter it is necessary to consider whether the instrument is of such a kind that it should be brought before the Committee's attention on the ground that it comes within the Committee's terms of reference. Sometimes this may not be very difficult. It should be fairly easy to discover whether an instrument has been made 'in pursuance of an enactment containing specific provisions excluding it from challenge in the Courts'—one of the grounds upon which the Committee is entitled to bring an instrument to the attention of the House of Commons. But even this may not always be easy. And it may clearly be more difficult to decide whether *prima facie* some of the other grounds upon which the Committee may act appear to be involved. Does the instrument appear to make an 'unusual or unexpected use' of the powers conferred by the statute? Does it purport to have retrospective effect without specific statutory sanction? Does there appear to have been 'unjustifiable delay' in publication of the instrument

[1] Dr. Haden Guest on 24 Jan. 1946. 418 H.C. Deb., 5th ser., col. 311.

or in laying it before Parliament? Or are there any special reasons for which the form or purport of the instrument calls for elucidation? These are all questions upon which members of the Committee have the right to express an opinion. No official of the Committee is entitled to do it for them. But it is his duty to see whether there are instruments which, at first sight, look as if they need scrutiny with these questions in mind.

There can be no doubt that expert legal advice is needed on this subject. If a layman glances at the volumes of statutory instruments he will see at once that only a specialist can find his way through them, even for the limited purpose of finding out where they stand in relation to the terms of reference of the Statutory Instruments Committee. This fact has been recognised from the outset in the working of the Committee. Indeed, it was provided with an adviser, in the person of Sir Cecil Carr, who is the greatest authority upon the whole subject of statutory instruments. While it cannot be pretended that the Committee needs the greatest expert in the world to assist it if it is to perform its work adequately, there is no doubt that it was tremendously fortunate to be able to start its work with Sir Cecil Carr's advice, and that its success is very largely due to his knowledge and wisdom. But while the Committee need not and cannot expect always to have the greatest expert to advise it, it must clearly have an expert on its staff, able to cope with the legal intricacies of delegated legislation. This expert will assist the members of the Committee also in judging the value of the explanations or defences which departments put before them when they are asked to give evidence upon the instruments about which the Committee is exercised. In the end, of course, it will be for the Committee to form an opinion whether the use of the statutory powers has been unreasonable or unusual, but in many cases it must rely a great deal upon the advice which its expert gives it. To be effective the Statutory Instruments Committee must have its own experts, to cope with the departmental experts whose work it is attempting to scrutinize and control.

If this is true of the Statutory Instruments Committee, we should quite certainly expect it to be true of the Public Accounts Committee, for surely the scrutiny of accounts must present to the lay mind even greater difficulties than examples of delegated legislation. The task laid upon the Public Accounts Committee is to examine 'the accounts showing the appropriation of the sums granted by Parliament to meet the public expenditure, and of such other accounts laid before Parliament as the committee may think fit'. Now these accounts are printed in a series of volumes and they run to hundreds of pages. Clearly someone must be able to guide and assist the Committee, not only in selecting those branches of the accounts which deserve attention but also in scrutinizing those which are selected. And although for the first few years after it was set up in 1861 the Public Accounts Committee did not have an expert staff to assist it, quite soon this was remedied by the establishment of the office of Comptroller and Auditor-General under the Exchequer and Audit Departments Act of 1866. It is not necessary to describe in full here the wide and varied and important functions which this officer and his department carry out.[1] It is enough to say that he is responsible for a great deal more than acting as the expert adviser of the Public Accounts Committee. But all that he does qualifies him in a very special way to be that Committee's expert adviser and it is with that aspect of his work that we are concerned.

The existence of the Comptroller and Auditor-General and of his department is an important and indeed rare example of the setting up of a body of officials to assist the House of Commons in controlling the Crown's officials. For the Comptroller and Auditor-General is spoken of and regarded as an officer of the House of Commons or, more properly, of Parliament. He is not in fact appointed by the House or by officers of the House, but by the Crown; on the other hand, his tenure is not, like that of a civil servant, during the pleasure of the Crown but, like that of a judge, during good behaviour, and he is removable only on an address from both Houses of Parliament. In this way he is made as independent of the government as possible, and as his task is to audit accounts on behalf of the House and to report direct to the House—not, be it noted, to the Treasury—he may fairly be described as an official of the House. Needless to say his task is one which can be carried out only by and through a staff. He has a department of his own, numbering about 500, of whom the greater part are posted in the various departments

[1] See, for example, W. I. Jennings, *Parliament*, chap. ix, and B. Chubb, op. cit.

and are engaged in a continuous audit as the year's transactions proceed.[1]

But they are not only officials, they are experts as well. It should be emphasized, however, that they are not supposed to be experts in the work of the departments whose accounts they audit. They are experts in accounts, and in particular in government accounts, which are not presented in the same way as ordinary commercial accounts and are subject to special safeguards.[2] Officers in the Comptroller and Auditor-General's Department may find at times that their work of audit cannot be effectively done unless they obtain some further expert knowledge of the way in which a department works, and this can be provided by the officers of the department itself. An explanation of this kind sometimes provides a satisfactory answer to a question of audit which has been raised. It may be added, also, that in the Comptroller and Auditor-General's department, as in other departments, it is likely that the officers at the top will be less narrowly expert than those lower down. They will have a broad knowledge of departmental accounts, but they will rely on their subordinates for specialist advice. In this connexion it should be recorded that when the Comptroller and Auditor-General himself attends the meetings of the Public Accounts Committee he is often accompanied by members of his staff, who are there to advise him on the particular matters under discussion. The Comptroller and Auditor-General himself, too, has usually had some experience in other departments before his appointment. He is not a professional auditor. Sir Frank Tribe, Comptroller and Auditor-General in 1954, had been Permanent Secretary to the Ministry of Food and to the Ministry of Fuel and Power before his appointment, and his predecessor, Sir Gilbert Upcott, had been a high official in the Treasury.

Although it is true that the Public Accounts Committee is assisted by its own expert officials, it is proper to add that it receives assistance also from Whitehall's officials in the person of certain officers of the Treasury. They are present when the Public Accounts Committee meets; they sit at one end of the

[1] See evidence in 1953 of Sir Frank Tribe, Comptroller and Auditor-General, before the Select Committee on Nationalized Industries, H.C. 235 of 1952–3, pp. 8–9.

[2] It may be mentioned that the members of the Auditor-General's staff are not usually chartered accountants.

horseshoe-shaped table, while the Comptroller and Auditor-General and his assistants sit at the other end. Of them, a Comptroller and Auditor-General said: 'They are not, of course, as I am, independent, but I do not think they have ever found difficulty in reconciling their duty to the Chancellor of the Exchequer with their duty of giving assistance to the Public Accounts Committee.'[1] Nor is this surprising. The Treasury would certainly have an interest in seeing that money had been spent in the way in which it had been authorized and in no other. Little conflict could be expected to arise in this sphere. The predominant share, however, in advising and guiding the Public Accounts Committee rests with the Comptroller and Auditor-General and his staff.

4

If permanent, professional, and expert assistance is needed to assist select committees scrutinizing statutory instruments and public accounts, surely it will be needed in the fields of national expenditure and estimates. The estimates are not less complicated than the public accounts, and the layman confronted with them is at a loss where to begin and what to look for. Surely he must have some expert to guide him. It is interesting to see what attitude was adopted towards this matter as these select committees developed.

When the Select Committee on Estimates was set up in 1912, and reappointed in 1913 and 1914, it was given no expert assistance and no permanent staff beyond, of course, a clerk to arrange and record its proceedings and to perform the secretarial functions. In 1918, when some thought was being given to the control of expenditure after the war, it was suggested that two, and perhaps later three, Select Committees on Estimates should be established, but it was emphasized that if these committees were to be really effective, they must have expert assistance. It was maintained that the pre-war Estimates Committees had not been successful and that one of the reasons was that whereas the Public Accounts Committee had the expert assis-

[1] Sir Gilbert Upcott in his evidence before the Select Committee on Procedure, 1946. See *Third Report of Select Committee on Procedure*, H.C. 189–1 of 1945–6, qq. 4172, 4174.

tance of the Comptroller and Auditor-General and his staff, the Estimates Committee had no expert assistance. It was proposed that an office should be established of Examiner of the Estimates, who would be not an officer of the Treasury but an officer of the House of Commons, on the analogy of the Comptroller and Auditor-General. He would have a staff to assist him, and they would form a small Westminster bureaucracy in the field of estimates.[1] This proposal is understandable. It is based upon the analogy of the Public Accounts Committee. It recognizes the fact that the Estimates Committee needs some staff to guide it. It recognizes clearly, too, that an officer of the Treasury is not really appropriate or effective as an adviser of the Committee. If the Treasury has done its job properly in scrutinizing departmental estimates, there is nothing for him to add. He should not be able, theoretically at any rate, to do more than explain and justify the estimates. The Treasury should have left to itself no scope for further scrutiny.

The essential elements in this plan were, then, that for an effective scrutiny of the estimates the committee needed a staff, it needed an independent staff, and it needed an expert staff. The proposals were not accepted by the government. No select committees on estimates were set up in 1919;[2] instead estimates were referred to standing committees which debated them like miniature committees of supply—a procedure now adopted for the Scottish Estimates, but not followed for others.[3] Discussion went on, however, and an informal committee of members, set up by the Chancellor of the Exchequer to advise him upon the right course to pursue, reported in 1921 that an Estimates Committee should be set up and that

there should be attached to the Committee an experienced member of the staff of the House of Commons, whose function it would be to prepare material for the Committee's deliberations and to render advice and assistance to the Committee and the Chairman in particular. Being a servant of the House of Commons this official would occupy an independent position in relation to Ministers.[4]

[1] These were the proposals put forward in the *Ninth Report of the Select Committee on National Expenditure* in 1918, H.C. 121 of 1918.
[2] It should be mentioned that the Select Committee on National Expenditure was still sitting in 1919 and continued in 1920.
[3] See above, p. 120.
[4] 141 H.C. Deb., 5th ser., 1692–4.

It was recommended further

that this official should not be empowered to call for information from Government Departments except on the instructions of the Chairman of the Committee, nor have the right of access to Departmental papers, but the Committee shall have the ordinary right of sending for persons, papers and records. That no further staff should be appointed at the present time, and that the Committee should decide by experience whether the creation of any additional staff was required.[1]

This proposal clearly recognized the need for a staff and for an independent staff; but it is evident that it did not contemplate an expert staff. There is a suggestion in the wording, rather, that someone more like a good general practitioner was in mind than a specialist. It was a proposal for an efficient secretariat. The Estimates Committee was set up again in 1921 but, in spite of protests by experienced members of the Public Accounts Committee and the National Expenditure Committee, no expert adviser was attached to it. Instead it was given no more than a clerk to assist it.[2]

In 1926 a further step was taken. The Estimates Committee, in its First Report for that year, suggested among other things that its size, which had been increased from 24 to 28 in 1924, should be further increased so that it could break up into subcommittees to which it could co-opt experts from outside.[3] The government rejected this suggestion at once, but conceded a point by agreeing that an official of the Treasury should be placed at the Committee's disposal. Here then was a recognition of the need for staff and for expert staff, but not, be it noted, of independent staff. From 1927 a Treasury official was in attendance. This was the position in the Estimates Committee until the outbreak of war in 1939, when it was not reappointed. There was general agreement that, throughout that time, the Committee was not very effective;[4] it was certainly markedly ineffective by comparison with the Public Accounts Committee.

What was the reason for this? The answer, some people thought, lay largely in the fact that though the Committee had

[1] Ibid.

[2] On its reappointment in 1921 its numbers were increased from 15 to 24.

[3] It was already empowered by its terms of reference since 1921 to break up into sub-committees consisting entirely of its own members.

[4] See Chubb, op. cit., pp. 129 ff.

assistance and expert assistance, it was inadequate and it was not independent assistance. An official of the Treasury would be bound to take the Treasury's point of view. Moreover was it not superfluous? Had not the Treasury already said its say? There was a good deal of argument about this question, and the difference of opinion is well illustrated by the opinions expressed in 1946 before the Select Committee on Procedure by Mr. Osbert Peake, at that time Chairman of the Public Accounts Committee, and Sir Gilbert Upcott, then Comptroller and Auditor-General. Mr. Peake said:

> I sat on the Estimates Committee for some years. They must have expert guidance if they are going to be effective. The form that expert guidance should take is a very difficult question indeed, because the best adviser they are likely to get is a Treasury official, probably, but a Treasury official is, to some extent, advising them on questions which the Treasury have already considered and have satisfied themselves about. In the second place, of course, a Treasury official, who is going back to the Treasury after concluding his period of attachment to the Estimates Committee, has got his future to think of, and he cannot afford to make too many enemies in his own department. Of course, there is a very, very high standard of conscientiousness among Government officials, to which we can all pay a tribute, I think, but it seems to me that the Estimates Committee should have somebody who is not a servant of the Executive, to guide them in their labours, and that they could not probably do better than to take somebody from the Treasury from time to time, for that office, who is getting towards the end of his public career, and who, therefore, is not going back into the department.[1]

Mr. Peake's idea was that this officer would be as independent of the Treasury or any other government department as the Comptroller and Auditor-General, and that he would also have the assistance of an expert costing staff to enable him to check estimates. That is one point of view. There must be staff, independent staff, and expert staff. Treasury staff is expert, but it is not independent and moreover it can contribute nothing new.

Sir Gilbert Upcott expressed a different opinion, and it is all the more interesting because Sir Gilbert was himself once the Treasury officer attached to the Estimates Committee. 'I never felt, in my mind,' he said, 'any difficulty about divided allegi-

---

[1] *Third Report of Select Committee on Procedure*, H.C. 189–1 of 1945–6, qq. 3979–81.

ance. I do not think the Chancellor of the Exchequer used to be at any rate at all unwilling to have the assistance and support of a Parliamentary Committee. 'When it was put to Sir Gilbert that, as the Treasury had been all through the Estimates already, it was difficult to expect that they would prove very good searchers, he answered: 'The Treasury is not as all-powerful as is sometimes suggested, and I think that is rather more a theoretical than a practical difficulty. Only the Treasury can tell the Committee what are the fruitful fields of inquiry.'[1]

The position had thus been reached in the development of the Estimates Committee, at which people asserted that it must have expert assistance, but that that expert assistance could not be independent, nor, in the opinion of some, though not of others, much more than superfluous. And it was generally felt that, for this reason, the Estimates Committee was really of very little use. It might do no harm, but it could hardly do much good.

Through all these discussions, however, it is interesting to notice that one assumption had hardly ever been seriously questioned, namely, that the assistance must be expert assistance. And yet the House of Commons had had experience of a select committee in the sphere of finance which had done valuable work and which had had a staff, but which had not had a staff of experts, and this was the Select Committee on National Expenditure. From 1917 to 1920 and throughout the Second World War, this select committee had investigated Estimates, along with other aspects of national expenditure, and people believed that it had been a success. But its staff was not expert. The Select Committee in the Second World War had the assistance of clerks of the House of Commons, the total number of whom was never more than eleven: some were recruited from the permanent staff and others were temporary clerks. They composed, obviously, a secretariat for the Committee.

They were [said the officer who was in charge of the Committee's work] people we could get hold of and who seemed to have suitable qualifications, and they were extremely useful. . . . We did appoint two economists; I think it is important that I should develop that, because it was pressed on us that we should have some people with economic knowledge. The men we appointed were extremely

---

[1] Ibid., qq. 4171, 4173.

valuable to us, because they happened to be good men with clear minds, but their economic knowledge was practically never used at all, because it was not wanted.[1]

Along with this use of House of Commons clerks went the association with the National Expenditure Committee, and especially with its sub-committees, of liaison officers from the departments whose estimates and expenditure were under discussion, and through whom inquiries with a department were conducted.

When the Estimates Committee was set up in 1945 in the new House of Commons after the General Election, there was available therefore a recent experience of the working of the National Expenditure Committee through a staff of House of Commons clerks and with no suggestion of an expert officer. The work of financial committees had been reorganized, too, by the creation of the post of Clerk of Financial Committees, under whom was placed a small body of clerks whose duties would be concerned with these committees. As a result of the work which the National Expenditure Committee had done during the war, the House of Commons itself was better equipped and better organized to conduct the work of an Estimates Committee. So it came about that when the Estimates Committee was re-established, its work was placed in the care of the Clerk of the Financial Committees, who had, as it happened, been in charge throughout the war of the National Expenditure Committee. He believed that expert assistance was not what was needed to make the Estimates Committee effective.

In my view [he said] any efficient and experienced officer of the House can certainly learn (if he does not already know) his way about the Estimates and Accounts. He can acquire the information that I think a committee properly can ask him to supply them with. His duties are to know how to get the information that the Committee wants, not to conduct the inquiry for them, but to get the stuff before them and present it to them in the form in which they want it. Also he has another primary duty, and that is, he is, or is supposed to be, an expert on Parliamentary procedure, and he has to advise them on that.[2]

These 'House-trained' clerks,[3] as they were called, acting with departmental liaison officers, could ensure, it was believed, that

---

[1] Evidence of Captain Diver, ibid., 1946, H.C. 189-1 of 1945-6, q. 4589.
[2] Ibid., q. 4543.　　　　　　　　　　　　　　　　　[3] Ibid., q. 4592.

the Estimates Committee was well advised about what it should look for and that it should find what it was looking for. It could call departmental witnesses before it, including witnesses from the Treasury. That is where its expert advice and assistance would come from. The experts would be in the witness chair, not at the table.

Since 1945 the Select Committee on the Estimates has worked in this way. Whatever opinion may be expressed about its work, no suggestion has been made that its inadequacies are due to not having an expert examiner of the estimates. It is clear, indeed, that with its staff of House-trained clerks it succeeds in getting the information it wants, and it has organized itself effectively to produce reports and to exercise an influence. We shall discuss the value of its work shortly, but at the moment the point of interest is that, after the Committee appeared to have reached a stage where it was generally regarded as almost useless because it could not get effective independent expert assistance, it became an institution which is generally regarded as useful at the time when it dropped the search for the expert and set about organizing for itself an independent and non-expert staff. Though this staff is non-expert, it is perhaps misleading to think that it is completely lay. Its members approach, surely, the class of general practitioners, who by experience and study have a more than lay knowledge but a less than specialized knowledge of the problems of the estimates.

We must not rush to the conclusion that what success the Estimates Committee has had since 1945 is due entirely to the fact that it has given up the search for the expert. There are, as will be seen, some other reasons. But there can be little doubt that the putting aside of the search for the expert, and the organizing of a body of general practitioners who were officers of the House, made it possible for the Estimates Committee to do useful work, if some other prerequisites for success were also present.

What the experience of the Estimates and the National Expenditure Committee shows, of course, is that it is unwise to assume that if a select committee of the House of Commons is to exercise effective scrutiny over administration, it must have its own experts. It is probably certain that it must have its own officials or secretaries, but they need not be experts. It all depends on the field which the Committee is to study, and what is already done by officials and experts in Whitehall to scrutinize administration. The point was well put by Sir John Wardlaw-Milne who was the chairman of the National Expenditure Committee throughout the Second World War.

I think [he said] that the results that the Public Accounts Committee get are achieved in the correct manner. They are, as you have said, largely a judicial body on the accounts of past expenditure, and they must have expert people to advise them. I think, when you are getting down to the question whether you are getting value for money, it is not a question of expert advice of that kind or taking a judicial function; it is a question of a common-sense attitude to a public problem, which can only be achieved by the combined abilities of a group of men with different aspects, coming from different walks of life, with different ideas; and that examination is not going to be materially helped by a body of expert auditors or accountants. . . . It might be advisable, if it were possible, to have technical advice on all kinds of subjects, but in practice you cannot have that; you cannot get it; and the best way, so far as my experience goes, is to work through the House of Commons' own staff, who can from the Departments call up to the Committee the people who can give definite answers as to the why and wherefore of different measures and different contracts which were made, and that in fact is what has to be achieved.[1]

5

Before we proceed to consider what has been the use of these four select committees in the scrutiny and control of administration, it is worth while to say a word about the position and function of their chairmen. The chairmen, as has been explained already, are not experts but laymen; they are party men, in the sense that they are members of a political party in the House, and the fact that they are members of the government party or the Opposition party has a relevance in the case of each committee; but although they are party men, they are not 'partisans' or interested parties in the sense in which we use this term, for they are back-benchers, not ministers; and those who are interested parties in the committees' inquiries find a place in the witness chair and not on the committees themselves.

These select committees, like most other committees, must, if

[1] Ibid., q. 4457.

they are to work effectively, be wisely led and wisely fed. The task of feeding them rests primarily and predominantly with their officials, the Comptroller and Auditor-General and his staff for the Public Accounts Committee, the Counsel to Mr. Speaker for the Statutory Instruments Committee, the Clerk of Financial Committees and his staff for the Estimates Committee. The task of leading the committees rests primarily and predominantly upon the chairmen. In each case, however, there is something left over which neither the officials alone, in the case of feeding the committees, nor the chairmen alone, in the case of leading them, can achieve. They supplement each other. On many occasions a chairman's advice will assist the committee's staff in presenting material. He can help them to talk the language which laymen understand. At times it may be valuable if he takes a hand in explaining their material to his fellow members. In the same way the committee's officials can give great assistance to a chairman in leading the committee. In a field like public accounts and estimates, for example, it is clear that the chairman must be given some guidance about the lines of fruitful inquiry so that he in turn may lead the committee. The officials must show him the way before he can lead his committee along it. This is all that a good chairman should need. If a chairman cannot find the way, however, the official himself must lead the committee. It is undesirable perhaps and regrettable, but it must be done.

Officials of the committees and chairmen are therefore in close contact all the time. In between meetings it is natural that officials will discuss with chairmen what should be done in the prosecution of inquiries and the collection of material, and what line should be taken if difficulties have arisen. The general plan of a committee's work, and the plan for a particular meeting, are usually discussed with the chairman by its officials before the committee sees them and discusses them. It is accepted, too, that when the time comes for a committee to make a report, the chairman places a draft before them. This draft has invariably been drawn up first by the committee's officials—and here the clerks will play an important part—and then discussed with the chairman. He takes responsibility for it and is prepared to back it. To this extent he has the added weight and influence in the committee which comes from presenting a draft which holds the field and which others must try to amend or reject if they can.

In the conduct of the committee's meetings when witnesses are examined, the chairman takes the major part. He asks questions first and he puts the major points to the witnesses. He has the added advantage which always attaches to a chairman, of course, of being able to intervene and supplement when witnesses are answering the questions of other members of the committee. It is the chairmen, too, who must see to it that the committees do not stray beyond their terms of reference, and that, for example, they keep off questions of policy, if they are forbidden to deal with them. He can discourage a certain line of questioning. He can do a good deal to make the witnesses before the committee feel unhappy or relieved. To a very large extent he can set the whole tone of the committee's relations with Whitehall.

A chairman's authority is increased, too, by the fact that, if he is willing to be re-elected, and there has been no change of government in the House which might affect his position, he is usually re-elected. Thus Sir John Wardlaw-Milne was chairman of the National Expenditure Committee throughout the Second World War; Sir Charles MacAndrew was chairman of the Statutory Instruments Committee from 1944 to 1950; Mr. Osbert Peake was chairman of the Public Accounts Committee from 1945 to 1950. In addition to his continuity by re-election, the chairman has the advantage of continuity in attendance at the meetings of the committee. He must be there. In practice very few other members are anything like so regular in their attendance, and those who are recorded as attending do not, of course, necessarily spend long at the meeting of the committee. The chairman, too, has always read his papers; he cannot function unless he has. Other members are seldom so well prepared.[1] Generally speaking the chairman exercises a great influence in determining the success or failure of a committee; on the other side, if a committee is not of much use, it is unlikely to attract a good chairman. He is something of a symbol of the use of a committee. It was indeed symbolic of the position of the Estimates Committee between 1921 and 1939 that it had frequent

[1] See some comments on this topic by Sir John Wardlaw-Milne before the Select Committee on Procedure in 1946. *Third Report*, H.C. 189-1, qq. 4396, 4397, 4398.

changes of chairman, and that its least ineffective period was from 1932 when, first in Sir Vivian Henderson and later in Sir Isidore Salmon, it had chairmen of vigour and enterprise who guided its inquiries into fruitful paths.[1]

6

It is not easy to know how the usefulness of these committees may best be judged.[2] At first sight it might seem reasonable to argue that, as they are committees of the House of Commons and as they are charged with the duty of reporting to the House, their usefulness can be judged by asking what notice the House takes of their reports and activities. If we follow this line, we shall almost certainly conclude that the committees have very little effect or, at least, very little effect that can be accurately assessed. Their reports and, quite often, their minutes of evidence are published and presented to the House. Some members study them; some members ask questions based upon what the reports have said; some members make use in their speeches of material found in the reports and evidence. But the practice is not widespread.

It is rare, too, that debates take place in the House upon the reports. There is no requirement that reports should be considered and either adopted or rejected by the House. Consideration of the Estimates in Committee of Supply, for example, does not have to await the report of the Estimates Committee. The government is not required to make some statement upon them. It is left as a rule to the private member of the House to take action. It is particularly interesting to notice that the chairmen of these committees, generally speaking, feel that they ought not to put down motions drawing attention to the report of their committee, and that this self-denying ordinance extends to members of the committee also. Some of them feel diffidence even in joining in a debate which has been initiated by other private members. This attitude was well expressed by Sir Charles

[1] See Chubb, op. cit., p. 133.
[2] No attempt is made here to undertake a full discussion of the work of the committees. The reader is referred to Chubb, op. cit. See also A. H. Hanson, 'The Select Committee on Estimates', in *Yorkshire Bulletin of Economic and Social Research*, vol. iii, No. 2, July 1951. For the Statutory Instruments Committee see A. H. Hanson in *Public Administration*, vol. xxvi, winter, 1949, and *Report of the Select Committee on Delegated Legislation*, 1953, H.C. 310–1 of 1952–3.

MacAndrew, in relation to the practice of the Statutory Instruments Committee, when he was discussing whether the members of the committee should see to it that an attempt was made to annul a statutory instrument upon which the committee had reported unfavourably. '. . . I have myself made it a practice', he said, 'never to have anything to do with making a prayer. I do not think it is my function to attack or to defend a Minister. After we have drawn attention, my work is finished, although I am perfectly happy to help any Member who wants information.'[1] Some members of these select committees appear to doubt whether debates in which a minister is to be censured as a result of a committee's report are wise at all. Mr. Wilfred Roberts, a member of the Estimates Committee and chairman of a sub-committee whose report, after being adopted by the full Estimates Committee, was being debated in the House, expressed his regret at the debate, and said he thought it 'likely to make the work of the Estimates Committee very much more difficult in future'.[2]

In these circumstances it is not surprising to discover that there have been hardly more than half a dozen debates on a report of the Public Accounts Committee since its inception;[3] that there was only one debate on reports of the Estimates Committee between 1921 and 1939,[4] and only two between 1945 and 1950; that there were only three debates on the reports of the National Expenditure Committee between 1939 and 1945, though these three were admittedly long and important. Debates were more frequent upon reports by the Statutory Instruments Committee, and this was largely due to the fact that there is a procedure available for the discussion of those instruments upon which parliamentary proceedings must be taken, viz. the moving of a motion to approve or the moving of a prayer to annul an order. In the period between 1944 and 1950, too, a group of active Conservative back-benchers took full advantage

---

[1] *Third Report of Select Committee on Procedure*, 189-1 of 1946, qq. 4719–21, p. 256.
[2] 470 H.C. Deb., 5th ser., cols. 2206–7.
[3] Chubb mentions debates in 1873, 1905, 1907, 1908, 1910, 1916, 1942, and 1947. An attempt to organize regular debates was made in 1905–10 but was dropped thereafter. Chubb, op. cit., p. 193.
[4] This was arranged by its chairman, Sir Frederick Banbury, who did not hold the views of Sir Charles MacAndrew on this subject. 1 Aug. 1922, 157 H.C. Deb., 5th ser., cols. 1362–1416.

of these opportunities. In 1944–5 the Statutory Instruments Committee drew the attention of the House to four orders; prayers were moved against all four.[1] In 1945–6, thirty-three instruments were brought to the attention of the House, twenty-seven of them for unjustifiable delay. A debate was held on thirteen of these instruments on 12 February 1946, and the action was sufficiently effective for it to be unnecessary to hold further debates on the remaining fourteen and for the Committee to be able to report later that very few cases of unjustifiable delay were now occurring.[2] The remaining six instruments reported to the House by the Committee on other grounds were each made the subject of a debate.[3] In 1946–7 six instruments were brought to the attention of the House,[4] and prayers were moved against three of them.[5] Two of the remaining three cases involved unjustifiable delay, but a perusal of the explanations given in each case by the government department concerned makes it clear that no serious fault had been committed and that no further action in the House of Commons would seem necessary.[6] In the session 1947–8 ten instruments were brought to the attention of the House; prayers were moved against four of them.[7] On one of these prayers—that against the Registration for Employment Order—a full dress debate occurred involving the whole policy of the government. Of the remaining six instruments, there were two concerning which a satisfactory explanation was offered by the government department concerned;[8] but in spite of the full explanation offered by the Foreign Office of the other four, each of which involved the same point, a discussion in Parliament would have been justified.[9] On the whole it

[1] 25 Jan. 1945 (Defence Regulation 68D); 14 Feb. 1945 (Defence Regulation 60 C AA); 25 Apr. 1945 (Ploughing Grants); 29 May 1945 (Acquisition of Land).

[2] H.C. 187 of 1945–6, Third Special Report, para. 2.

[3] 18 Dec. 1945 (Defence Regulations); 10 Feb. 1946 (Air Navigation); 12 Feb. 1946 (Bakehouses); 15 Apr. 1946 (Rules of Supreme Court); 6 June 1946 (Food Points, two orders).   [4] H.C. 141 of 1946–7, Special Report, para. 1.

[5] 22 Jan. 1947 (Road Haulage); 30 Jan. 1947 (Coal Industry); 14 May 1947 (Raw Cocoa).

[6] H.C. 141 of 1946–7, Second Report, Appendix II, and Sixth Report, Appendix.

[7] 3 Dec. 1947 (Registration for Employment); 22 Apr. 1948 (Seizure of Food); 6 May 1948 (Directed Persons Appeals); 26 and 29 July 1948 (Poisons).

[8] H.C. 201 of 1947–8. Fifth Report (Leather Charges Order)and Eighth Report (Public Health, Venereal Disease).

[9] Orders concerning the Treaties of Peace with Bulgaria, Hungary, Italy, and Roumania, respectively. See Sixth Report in H.C. 201 of 1947–8, Appendix.

can be seen that in this period, the reports of the Statutory Instruments Committee were frequently made the subject of debates in the House of Commons.[1]

It is apparent, however, that if we are to judge the use of the committees by the extent to which their reports are debated or noticed in the House of Commons, we should have to decide that they are not very effective. Even the debates on reports of the Statutory Instruments Committee are not as effective as their numbers suggest, for they almost always take place late at night, just before the adjournment, before a small House, and too late for any full reporting in the newspapers next day. But it is possible to mention other uses to which the committees' work is put. Their reports have an educative value. They educate the public, and in particular the informed public which takes an interest in or studies the working of government. More important, perhaps, they educate the members of Parliament who sit on them, most of them back-benchers who through inexperience of office would have no opportunity of finding out at first hand, from the high officials themselves, how departments are run. As we read the evidence before these committees, and see the process of question and answer go forward, we can realize what valuable educational work is going on. This is no small advantage. Finally, the newspapers and serious journals can find information from the committees' reports which might not otherwise come to light.

7

But when all this is added up, it still fails to touch, in my view, the most important service which these select committees to scrutinize administration can perform. This service can best be discovered if we ask the question: Do these committees do something or enable something to be done which, if they did not exist, would not or could not be done by officials—the Comptroller and Auditor-General and his staff, the Treasury, the Counsel to Mr. Speaker, and so on? The best short answer to this question can be found in some words which were used by

[1] It may be useful to note that, of the 6,938 instruments scrutinized by the Committee from its inception until Feb. 1953, the attention of the House was drawn to ninety-three. H.C. 310–1 of 1952–3, p. 6, para. 30.

Sir Malcolm Ramsay, then Comptroller and Auditor-General, to the Select Committee on Procedure in 1931. He said: 'Without the Public Accounts Committee I would be quite ineffective, or more ineffective than I am now. They are the sanction on which it all depends.'[1] Although this statement was made only of the Public Accounts Committee, it may be taken as a statement of the most important use to which these committees to scrutinize can be put, and their effectiveness can be judged by the extent to which it is possible to say in practice that they live up to this test. Without them the work of such officers as the Comptroller and Auditor-General would be no more than a discussion and perhaps an argument between officials, conducted at the official level and as an official secret. It is just conceivable that Parliament might authorize such an official to publish an annual report on his work, but it is almost certain that it would not authorize or require him to publish the minutes of evidence of his inquiries. Nor is it conceivable that an official would be given power to examine high civil servants in the way in which the Public Accounts Committee does. The whole process of calling heads of departments to explain their accounts, and of publishing their evidence and the awkward cross-examination to which they are sometimes submitted, can only occur because a committee of the House of Commons is conducting the inquiry. The whole nature of the scrutiny is altered in this way, too. It is one thing for the officials of a department to have to face an inquiry from another official, for officials to answer an official's questions. It is quite another to have to answer the questions of critical and uninstructed laymen. In a system of government where the official is intended to be the servant and not the master, this is an essential exercise.

It is fairly easy to see that the Statutory Instruments Committee will serve much the same purpose in relation to its official advisers as does the Public Accounts Committee. It gives publicity to what might otherwise remain an official secret; it requires the makers of delegated legislation to explain themselves to critical laymen, impatient of the law's intricacies and entanglements. It may not be so clear that the two committees dealing with current expenditure and estimates can be so useful. It takes us back to the old question: What can there

[1] H.C. 161 of 1931, q. 3758.

be to discover that the Treasury has not already discovered? Or, in another form, who can discover something, if the Treasury has not or cannot? As Sir Gilbert Upcott has indicated, we must not exaggerate the Treasury's powers. But even if we accept this view, it remains to be emphasized that there is a value in calling upon officials to justify to a select committee of critical laymen what has already been explained to officials. And it is good for the Treasury also to have to justify what it has approved. Nor should it regret an opportunity of saying to a select committee: 'We did not like this and we will tell you why. You may not like it and you should inquire into it critically. It is not the sort of thing to encourage.' No civil servant likes his department to figure largely, even if not very unfavourably, in the published reports and evidence of a select committee of the House of Commons. This fact must strengthen the hands of the Comptroller and Auditor-General and even of so strong a body as the Treasury in their dealings with departments. Perhaps no other select committee could achieve the position of respect and effectiveness which the Public Accounts Committee has attained. It is still true, as was said in 1903, that ' the Spending Departments stand more in awe of the Public Accounts Committee than of the House itself, probably because there is less chance of escaping its close scrutiny'.[1] But this is becoming true, though in a less degree, of the other three select committees we have discussed.

It is perhaps most surprising that the Estimates Committee should be achieving this sort of position. It is possible to explain the success of the National Expenditure Committee partly by saying that it sat in war-time when there were no detailed estimates before the House, when the normal checks on expenditure were harder to enforce, and when opposition was largely silent, and that as a result the Treasury and the government as a whole must clearly have welcomed and assisted its activities as an additional check upon departmental extravagance. The members of the Committee clearly saw that there was a job for them to do much more obviously than there would be in peace-time, when Treasury control over expenditure was much tighter. Why has the Estimates Committee since 1945 been so successful? It has been suggested already that its success was partly due to

[1] Mr. Gibson Bowles, M.P., quoted by Sir Malcolm Ramsay in 1931. H.C. 161 of 1931, p. 365, para. 10.

inheriting the methods and the staff of the National Expenditure Committee of 1939–45. That is true. It had found a more effective way of setting about its business, and what is more it had a clearer idea of what its business was. In particular it had come to concentrate less upon doing again what the Treasury had done already, and more upon a review of current expenditure upon the lines of the National Expenditure Committee. This was not the least valuable lesson it learned or legacy it inherited from this Committee. It behaved indeed much less like an estimates committee.[1]

The reform in its method of working was not confined, however, to the realization that it should have a staff of general practitioners and not experts. It extended to adopting the system of working through sub-committees, a method which the National Expenditure Committee had relied upon strongly. In this way it was able to cover a much wider range of subjects; some members were able to make journeys abroad and investigate matters on the spot while others conducted inquiries at home. The output of reports was consequently higher. There was always something new and interesting to look forward to from the Estimates Committee. The members of the Committee, too, work harder in sub-committees than they do on a larger committee. There is more interest in what is going on. Each sub-committee has a chairman, and that in itself gives more scope to members to hold office and feel that they are doing something important.[2]

It must be suspected, however, that some part of the interest which the Estimates Committee has aroused since 1945 is due to the fact that, in spite of the limitations in its terms of reference, it does in fact encroach, from time to time, upon the field of 'policy'. It is difficult, of course, to know where policy begins. It has long been accepted that the Public Accounts Committee is entitled to scrutinize expenditure not only from the strict point of view of audit but also from the point of view of waste and extravagance.[3] Does not that lead them into questions of

---

[1] Mr. Chubb's analysis brings out this point clearly. See op. cit., chaps. viii and ix.

[2] Sir John Wardlaw-Milne, the chairman of the National Expenditure Committee, testified that this was a noticeable feature on his Committee. See H.C. 189–1 of 1945–6, qq. 4397, 4398.

[3] Sir Malcolm Ramsay, H.C. 161 of 1931, p. 364.

policy? It must be admitted that it can. Even more likely is
it that the Estimates Committee in considering proposals for
expenditure is likely to be led into judgements upon waste and
extravagance, which are bound to lead to judgements upon the
wisdom of the policy which led to this expenditure.[1] The
National Expenditure Committee had a similar experience.
Mr. Herbert Morrison expressed the opinion in 1945 that it
'got asking questions which . . . were . . . running rival with the
executive responsibility of the Minister himself'.[2] It has been
seen how reluctant the chairman of the Statutory Instruments
Committee was in 1946 to accept the suggestion that that Committee might extend its inquiries into 'merits'.

It is not possible to argue in detail here the case for and
against allowing or encouraging the committees to consider
policy or merits.[3] It may be asserted, however, that much of the
usefulness and reputation of the Public Accounts Committee,
which is regarded as the model of the scrutinizing committees of
the House of Commons, comes from its interest in questions of
wastefulness, which certainly trespass upon questions of policy.
It is certain, too, that a great part of the usefulness of the Estimates Committee comes from its freedom in interpreting its
terms of reference. There has been too much theoretical dogmatism about the proper functioning of these committees. Policy
does not necessarily mean party policy, nor high policy. There
are many questions of policy which members of a select committee, of differing parties, could investigate without dividing
themselves into Government supporters and Opposition supporters. The experience of the National Expenditure Committee
and the Estimates Committee has demonstrated that already.
It is wise, no doubt, not to widen the terms of reference of the
committees by empowering them in express terms to consider
policy. It is much better that these discussions of policy should
arise necessarily from discussions of economy and value for money
and efficiency, rather than that they should be raised directly.
Thus on the Statutory Instruments Committee the terms of
reference permit the Committee to draw the attention of the

---

[1] This is well brought out in Mr. A. H. Hanson's article, already cited.
[2] H.C. 189-1 of 1945-6, q. 3229.
[3] It is discussed well in Mr. Hanson's two articles, one on the Estimates Committee and one on the Statutory Instruments Committee, already cited.

House of Commons to any 'unusual or unexpected use' of the statutory powers delegated to the department. As Sir Cecil Carr pointed out, this 'permits the consideration of aspects not far removed from policy and merits'.[1] This is undoubtedly the better way to approach the scrutiny of policy.

Yet there can be no doubt that some discussion of policy should be permitted, and that the objections to it, based sometimes on supposed analogies from French and American government, are not relevant. Some of the wisest words upon the proper use of these scrutinizing committees are those which Sir Gilbert Campion, then Clerk of the House of Commons, wrote in 1946.

Committees of the House of Commons on administrative matters are, in fact, advisory bodies used by the House for inquiry and to obtain information, and they generally inquire into definite happenings and criticise after the event, though as a result of the lessons they have learnt they may make suggestions for the future. It is difficult to see how such bodies could impair ministerial responsibility, even if matters of 'policy'—a very indefinite word—were assigned to them. If the House is not free to use them as it wishes, it is deprived, or deprives itself, of the most natural means of obtaining information and advice.[2]

8

The accumulated experience of the four select committees to scrutinize is clearly relevant to a discussion of proposals which have been made to set up a select committee of the House of Commons to examine the nationalized industries. These proposals were considered by a select committee of inquiry established by the House of Commons on 4 December 1951 and reappointed in the new session on 6 November 1952, over which Mr. Ralph Assheton presided. As a result of its inquiries the select committee proposed that such a committee of the House of Commons should be appointed by standing order, and that its task should be to examine the nationalized industries.[3]

---

[1] H.C. 189–1 of 1945–6, p. 244.   [2] Ibid., p. 356.

[3] The Committee submitted two reports. The first (H.C. 332–1 of 1951–2) was concerned with the facilities available to members of the House of Commons to ask questions about the working of the nationalized industries; the second (H.C. 235 of 1952–3) dealt with proposals for a select committee of scrutiny. To both reports were appended minutes of evidence which are full of interest to the student of committees to scrutinize and control.

At first sight it would seem obvious that the model for a committee on the working of the nationalized industries would be the Public Accounts Committee, and indeed that that Committee itself might well undertake the work. The accounts of the public corporations which administer the nationalized industries—the National Coal Board, the British Transport Commission, the British Electricity Authority and its Electricity Area Boards, the Gas Council and its Gas Area Boards, the B.B.C., the North of Scotland Hydro-Electric Board—to name some of the most important bodies—are submitted annually to Parliament. It lies within the terms of reference of the Public Accounts Committee to examine them, and on occasion it has done so. It examined the accounts of the British Transport Commission in the session 1951–2, of the National Coal Board in the sessions of 1948–9 and 1950, and of the B.B.C. in 1947–8 and 1950–1, not to mention a number of less important corporations.[1] But there are at least two difficulties in the way of handing over entirely to the Public Accounts Committee the scrutiny of the nationalized industries. In the first place the Committee has its hands full already dealing with the accounts of the government departments. In the second place the Committee's expert adviser, the Comptroller and Auditor-General, has no authority to examine the accounts of the nationalized industries. Their accounts are audited by private firms of professional auditors appointed for the purpose by a minister. It is true that the Committee can call the auditors before it. When it examined the accounts of the British Transport Commission in 1951–2 it called the professional auditors of the Commission before it, a course it had adopted also in 1950, when it examined the accounts of the Overseas Food Corporation.[2] But it is clear that in examining the accounts by this procedure, the Committee is in a weaker position than when it is assisted by its own officer and that officer has himself conducted the audit.

It has naturally been suggested that, to meet the difficulties outlined above, a separate select committee should be set up to consider the accounts of the nationalized industries, since the Public Accounts Committee is already fully employed, and that the examination of the industries' accounts should be handed over to the Comptroller and Auditor-General. So far as the

[1] H.C. 235 of 1952–3, p. 2. [2] Ibid., p. 10, q. 84.

latter suggestion is concerned it seems clear that it could be carried out, but that it would involve not only a large increase in the Auditor-General's staff but also some dislocation in the accounting profession.[1] These difficulties are not insuperable. Behind them lies, however, the fundamental assumption upon which the nationalized industries have been organized, namely, that they should be run not like government departments but like businesses. The corporations are given a considerable degree of independence of ministers and of Parliament, and one example of this is that their accounts are audited not like the accounts of a government department but like the accounts of a business. So long as this attitude is adopted towards the public corporations, the methods of the Comptroller and Auditor-General seem inappropriate to the examination of their transactions.

The select committee accepted this position,[2] but it clearly hoped that, in some way, it could devise a system by which it could obtain for Parliament many of the advantages of having the Comptroller and Auditor-General, while admitting that the accounts of the corporations could not be treated just like the accounts of a government department. Consequently it recommended that the committee of scrutiny, which it proposed, should have the assistance of a permanent official, of a status roughly equivalent to that of the Comptroller and Auditor-General or Mr. Speaker's Counsel, who should be an officer of the House of Commons with high administrative experience. He would work with the assistance of at least one professional accountant and would examine the reports and accounts of the nationalized industries in order to direct the Committee's attention to matters requiring examination.[3]

The influence upon the select committee's recommendations of the experience of the Public Accounts Committee and of the Statutory Instruments Committee is apparent. It is not surprising, for a major part of the material upon which such a committee to scrutinize would work is the accounts of the corporations. At the same time it is interesting that the select committee should not have been attracted by the technique now adopted

[1] Ibid., qq. 88, 136, 144.
[2] Ibid., pp. x and xi, paras. 29 and 32.
[3] Ibid., para. 34.

R

by the Estimates Committee since 1945 and inherited from the National Expenditure Committee. In one respect, indeed, it did prefer the methods of the Estimates Committee over those of the Public Accounts Committee. It recommended that the proposed committee of scrutiny should be empowered to set up sub-committees, and thus be enabled to cover a larger field than if it acted as one body throughout.[1] But apparently the select committee was not attracted by the method of using a secretariat of House-trained clerks, as does the Estimates Committee, to organize and undertake its inquiries into the working of the industries. It realized, of course, that it must have clerks and the usual secretarial assistance just as the Public Accounts Committee and the Statutory Instruments Committee have, but it relied for the conduct of the scrutiny upon the activities of its proposed high official comparable in status to the Comptroller and Auditor-General. On one further point, it was influenced by the experience of the Estimates Committee, for it rejected the suggestion that the proposed permanent officer should be an officer from a central department of state, perhaps the Treasury. 'After consideration', it said, 'we feel that the permanent officer of the Committee, once appointed, should be a servant of the House of Commons, and not of the Government or of any of the corporations, and not removable except by an address from each House of Parliament.'[2] In rejecting what had once been the method of the Estimates Committee, the Select Committee turned not to the new methods of the Estimates Committee but to the old methods of the Public Accounts Committee.

It would be foolish to be dogmatic about the prospects of success which attend the working of a committee of scrutiny on the nationalized industries. Its subject-matter is different in important respects from that of the Public Accounts Committee or the Estimates Committee. The government, however in indicating its first reactions to the proposals of the Select Committee, showed that, while willing to acquiesce in setting up a committee of scrutiny, it was not prepared to accept some very important parts of the recommendations. There was to be no permanent official comparable to the Comptroller and Auditor-General, and there was to be no breaking up into sub-committees. The

---

[1] Ibid., paras. 25 and 35 (a).
[2] Ibid., para. 33.

committee would have the assistance of its 'House-trained' clerk
and of liaison officers from the Treasury and from each of the
departments whose ministers are responsible for the affairs of
nationalized industries.[1] In the light of this attitude the model
and methods of the Estimates Committee seem even more relevant to a consideration of the way in which a scrutiny committee
on nationalized industries might work effectively.

[1] 523 H.C. Deb., 5th ser., cols. 841–4 and 530 H.C. Deb., cols. 281–3.

CHAPTER IX

Postscript

I

IT would be foolhardy to attempt to generalize at large about government by committee in Britain on the basis of the limited and superficial survey undertaken in the previous chapters. But it is permissible surely to offer a few observations by way of postscript, if not of conclusions. And first of all a word about the role upon committees of some of our seven characters. So far as actual membership of committees is concerned, it seems proper to say that the place for the expert is upon committees to advise; the place for the interested party is upon committees to negotiate; the place for the party man and for the layman is upon committees to legislate, to administer, and to scrutinize and control. The inadequacy of these generalizations becomes apparent as soon as they are offered. There is a place for laymen upon committees to advise, and for experts—independent experts that is—upon committees to negotiate. The difficulty of being precise is made even more apparent when we consider committees to inquire, and discover that laymen, experts, party men, and interested parties might all properly find a place upon them. But while it is undeniable that no one character can rightfully be said to have an exclusive monopoly of one type of committee, it is clear also that in some cases a particular character ought as a rule to find a place upon a committee. The expert on the committee to advise, the interested party on the committee to negotiate, and the party man and the layman on the committees to legislate, administer, and scrutinize are fairly clear cases of this kind.

What about the official? His position is more difficult to describe. So far as the official of central or local government is concerned, his place is usually conceived of as around or behind or beside a committee rather than upon it. There are exceptions, but usually they tend to prove the rule. Government officials are found at times upon committees to advise and occasionally even in the chair of such committees; and their presence may be justified by saying that they are in a position to know what it is that their department wants from the committee, and it can best be obtained if officials are able to take a full part in the committee's proceedings. Yet it is well to ask on all such occasions whether the officials would not be more effective as assessors or observers or as secretaries, rather than as full members. In most cases, I suggest, they would not be less effective. Sometimes officials are placed upon committees to advise or to inquire because the subject-matter of the committee's work concerns departmental organization or a department's work. In certain of these cases it may well be true that the committee could not work effectively without this close connexion with the departments. And similarly the choice of retired officials may be justified on the ground that some people who know the ropes or are familiar with the technique of administration are often necessary if the work of a committee to inquire or to advise is to be effectively carried out. And, finally, it is apparent that officials of central and local government must play a part upon committees to negotiate where the subject of negotiation is the conditions of service in government employment. Outside these exceptional cases, however, it would seem proper to conclude that the place of the government official is not upon committees of the types we have been studying. His influence must be exerted in other ways. After all he has the chance of expressing his view when a committee to advise or to inquire has made its recommendations.

The position of the official not in government service is rather different. It is to be noted, however, that when he appears as a member of a committee to advise or to inquire or to negotiate, it is usually because he enjoys also the character of an expert or of an interested party or both. On committees to negotiate, particularly when we leave the local level, proceedings on behalf of the interested parties are usually directed predominantly by officials of their organizations. This is justified because these officials are thought to have specialized knowledge of the subject under discussion and, in particular, specialized skill in the technique of negotiation. To this extent they are experts. They are thought also to possess sufficient authority to commit their organizations. They can speak for the interested parties. As a general rule, then, the presence of the official not in government service upon committees will be justifiable upon the same grounds as those upon which an expert or an interested party would find a place upon a committee.

It is apparent, however, that the influence of the official in committee work is by no means confined to those occasions when he is made a member of a committee. All committee work is carried on under official auspices of one kind or another. The official appears as secretary, as administrator, as adviser, and as servant of committees. He is not, of course, one man with uniform views, but many men, representing many points of view and interests. The local government official, the central civil servant, the trade union organizer, and the business manager may well be in conflict with each other and fail to understand each other. But they all share the official character and may be distinguished in outlook and status and methods from certain other characters in committee work, and in particular from the layman and the party man. It is proper to say a word about this latter relationship.

2

From time to time in the course of this essay it has been suggested that the use of committees has weakened the House of Commons, the great house of laity for the nation. In particular it has been pointed out that the officials, fortified by the advice of committees upon which experts and interested parties have sat, are enabled to present to Parliament, through their ministers, proposals which are so formidably supported that the lay member of the House is unable to criticize them effectively. In the field of industrial relations, where committees to negotiate are in operation, it is usual for their agreed conclusions to come into effect without the necessity for parliamentary approval at all. The most that may be needed is the assent of a minister. Here surely is a situation where a large and important part of the nation's business is settled without reference to Parliament at all. Officials—both inside and outside the government service—and interested parties arrange these things and keep the layman out of it. Moreover, in those cases where he is allowed to express his views, party discipline comes in to keep the layman in order. A minister's assurance in the House of Commons that he is satisfied with what is proposed, and that the experts and interested parties support his view, is usually enough to ensure that what is proposed or what has been done will secure the support of the government's majority in the House. The member of Parliament in his capacity as party man represses himself in his capacity as layman. Is not the layman, in the House of Commons, on the way to becoming a lay figure?

It would be wrong to assert that there is nothing in this view. Committees to advise, to inquire, and to negotiate have undoubtedly strengthened the official in Whitehall, and there has been no comparable strengthening of Westminster. And inasmuch as officials outside the government play an important part in the work of these committees, as the preceding chapters have illustrated, one consequence of the use of these committees has been the strengthening in national life and in the social structure of the country of the official element, as against the lay element. The point is illustrated also in the working of the standing committees to legislate, where party discipline has been more strictly enforced since 1945 and where the Minister, supported by his officials, usually gets his way. When it is remembered that, by the time a bill reaches standing committee, its principles are already accepted by the House and that the only work a committee can do is to amend details, it is difficult to avoid the conclusion that party discipline in the committees to legislate is stricter than it need be. Yet the prevailing atmosphere is that ministers will seldom give way, relying upon their officials' arguments, supported by the advice of committees, perhaps, and overcoming the expressions of lay opinion.

Yet it is important not to let this view of the situation run away with us. It is too often stated in an exaggerated form. Let us remember that there is an Opposition party in the House of Commons, and that it has its say, in standing committees. Criticisms of the official view will be put forward, and although the government will almost invariably win, it will be obliged to give an answer to the criticisms put forward by the Opposition. Moreover ministers themselves are usually spokesmen of the laity. Their task is to bring common sense to bear upon expert and official sense; they must be satisfied that what they are to propose or defend is likely to make sense to their supporters, and preferably also to the public. They are not invari-

ably and incurably the mere mouthpieces of officials. Nor is
their attitude as rigid in standing committee as is often supposed, though it may be more rigid than it need be.

Let it be remembered also that while the use of committees
to advise, to inquire, and to negotiate may have strengthened
Whitehall, the use of committees to scrutinize has strengthened
Westminster. Officials meet these committees face to face, un-
protected by ministers and the party whip. And here indeed the
member of Parliament as party man gives way to the member of
Parliament as layman, for, as we saw, party plays little part in
the working of the committees to scrutinize and control. Here
lay sense confronts official sense. The Public Accounts Committee has not grown weaker in the many years of its existence;
if anything it has grown stronger and is now firmly established.
What is more, there have been added to it the Estimates Committee and the Statutory Instruments Committee, both of
which have gained steadily in strength since 1945. Now to them
is to be added a select committee to examine the nationalized
industries, and a further strengthening of the House of Commons may be achieved. These committees to scrutinize are able,
through their staffs, whether experts, like the Comptroller and
Auditor-General, or general practitioners, like the clerks of the
Estimates Committee, to stand up to the officials of Whitehall
whose work they examine. It is in these committees that the
House of Commons, as a house of laity, exercises some of its
greatest influence. Their development must be remembered
when we come to make some judgement upon the influence
which the use of committees has had upon the relative position
of the House of Commons and of the layman in the machinery
of government. The true picture is not one of all gain by Whitehall and all loss by Westminster.

The matter may be considered also upon wider grounds.
Committees to advise, to inquire, and to negotiate do something
which not only ought to be done but which the House of Commons itself cannot do. They bring to the processes of government, in the formulation and application of policy, the opinions
of experts, of interested parties, and of laymen, too, who do not
find a place in the House of Commons, and in most cases should
not. The structure of committees provides other ways of representing opinion in the country than that of territorial consti-

tuencies where representatives are chosen by party vote. The use of committees is the answer in Britain to those who advocate that people should be represented not, or not only, in terms of where they live, but in terms of how they earn their living or of what they know. Proposals for a corporative state or for functional representation or for economic or vocational houses of parliament are attempts to provide wider or more realistic representation. In Britain committees to advise, to inquire, and to negotiate go far to ensure this wider representation, while leaving the ultimate controlling power with a House of Commons recruited upon a territorial, not a functional, basis.

It is difficult to see how anyone could argue that this use of committees in modern Britain should be dispensed with in order that the House of Commons should have no rival. If the use of committees has strengthened Whitehall, the remedy lies not in weakening Whitehall but in strengthening Westminster. Ministers have a most important part to play in this sphere. They are the chief laymen, with the duty of interpreting Whitehall to Westminster and vice versa. Members of Parliament, by vigilance and criticism and liveliness, can see to it that official or expert sense is subjected to the sceptical scrutiny of the lay mind. In this sphere the qualities of the good layman, outlined at the outset, of being interested, educable, knowledgeable, and sensible but at times irrational, are almost all that are needed to ensure that the nation's house of laity plays its proper part in relation to the official. After all, so far as the law is concerned, it is the layman, whether as minister or member of Parliament, upon whom is placed the final sovereign power to decide what is to be done. Whitehall should not be blamed if Westminster does not make the most of its opportunities.

3

If committees to advise, to inquire, and to negotiate do something important which the House of Commons alone cannot do, the same is true also of the committees to administer in the town and county halls of the country. It is true that members of Parliament, by questions and debates, and through the working of their committees to scrutinize, perform an indispensable service in the control of central administration by officials. But there is a limit upon what they can be expected to do. The local houses of laity, the councils of the local government authorities, must perform the detailed work of ensuring good administration of many important services. Does the layman here tend also to become a lay figure? Is the official too strong? Our examination of committees to administer has shown that there is a danger here, too, that the layman may prove ineffective, but it is important to be clear where the responsibility for this situation rests. So far as the influence of local officials is concerned, it is rare indeed to find a case where it can be said that the fault, when it occurs, lies with them, and not with the councillors whose servants they are. Where local officials are exercising powers which properly belong to councillors, the remedy usually lies in better councillors, not in weaker officials. If councils are furnished with good laymen, exhibiting the qualities which are here suggested, officials would not be obliged to go beyond their own proper sphere or be justified in doing so.

A different set of considerations arises when we consider the relations between committees to administer in local government and the officials of Whitehall. Here there is strong ground for saying that the increase of official control over local government has weakened the responsibility and authority of the local layman. Too often committees are screens behind which official decisions are taken in the capital. It is from official control of this kind, rather than from the activities of local officials, that the decline in the position of the local houses of laity has come. There is adequate ground for saying that, in some degree and in certain spheres of local government administration, laymen on councils have been relegated to the status of lay figures by the powers of control and supervision conferred upon central government departments and exercised in practice for the most part by officials. The reduction of this control to the very minimum is essential if committees to administer are to fulfil the criteria of a good committee, namely, that they shall themselves be and seem to be responsible for what they do.

With this qualification in respect of the controlling influence of central government officials—and it is an important qualification—it is broadly speaking true to say that the position of the layman in local government depends upon the quality of those who are chosen to sit on local councils. In spite of the vague and sweeping criticisms that are made of the personnel of local councils, it seems justifiable to maintain that their quality is good. Absurd as it may appear to generalize upon such a subject, I am prepared to assert that two-thirds of those who sit upon local councils are good laymen; the rest are not so good and a small proportion are very bad indeed.

One development which has made a very great difference to the supply of good laymen—and it is probably the most influential factor—is the participation of women in public life. Indeed, Mrs. Pardiggle, of whom Dickens wrote in *Bleak House*, has thousands of descendants. The wife of O. A. Pardiggle, F.R.S., and mother of five boys, she said of herself: 'I am a School lady, I am a Visiting lady, I am a Reading lady, I am a Distributing lady; I am on the local Linen Box Committee, and many general Committees. . . . I am a woman of business. . . . You cannot tire me if you try.' Women can often enter public life at an earlier age than men, who often must wait until they retire; they can be drawn from all grades of society; and they bring distinctive qualities of judgement and criticism which are part of the make-up of a good layman. Their work on committees to administer in local government has probably done more than anything else to maintain and indeed to raise its standard. Though it would be foolhardy to say that they come nearer to being a leisured class than men, more of them can organize their time so as to include work on committees than men employed as wage-earners or professional men such as doctors and lawyers. One of the most encouraging signs that the supply of good laymen may meet the demand is the increasing and successful participation of women in committee work.

It must be emphasized also that if the supply of laymen is to be maintained, those who serve upon committees must be protected against financial loss, to put it at the very least. Good laymen are found in all walks of life; they are not confined to the leisured or retired or salaried classes. Although there is a great deal to be said for unpaid service upon committees, it is true also nowadays that some of those who perform the layman's function—members of Parliament and many councillors, especially the chairman of important committees—must devote

all their time to it if it is to be executed effectively. Public service of this kind is just as important as service in government
departments. It should be appropriately rewarded. Mr. Lloyd
George expressed the point well in the House of Commons in
1911 when, speaking as Chancellor of the Exchequer in favour
of paying a salary to members of the House, he said: 'Gratuitous
work necessarily means bureaucracy.'[1] The layman is, by definition, an amateur, but there are cases in committee work where,
if he is to be an effective amateur, he must lose his amateur
status. He must become a professional layman.

4

Though the British use committees profusely and naturally,
there are signs at times that they feel a little ashamed of their
habits. They sympathize with those who define a committee
as a collection of people who individually believe that something
must be done and who collectively decide that nothing can be
done. In this, as in so many greater matters, Mr. Churchill's
words command wide assent when he spoke of the ineffectiveness of committee work on 'those broad, happy uplands where
everything is settled for the greatest good of the greatest number
by the common sense of most after the consultation of all'.[2]
A war could not be conducted by 'a copious flow of polite
conversation'. We can sympathize, too, with the feelings that
led him on 24 May 1940, in a desperate moment of the fighting
in Europe, to write to the Secretary of the Cabinet, Sir Edward
Bridges, as follows: 'I am sure there are far too many Committees
of one kind and another which Ministers have to attend, and
which do not yield a sufficient result. These should be reduced
by suppression or amalgamation.'[3] And six months later he
wrote again to Sir Edward Bridges:

Let me have a list of all committees of a Ministerial character forming part of the Central Government, with any offshoots there may be.

2. Ask each department to furnish a list of all the committees of
a departmental nature which exist at the present time.

3. This information is the prelude to a New Year's effort to cut
down the number of such committees.[4]

[1] 29 H.C. Deb., 5th ser., col., 1366, 10 Aug. 1911.
[2] *The Second World War*, i. 464.   [3] Ibid. ii. 560.
[4] 4 Jan. 1941. Ibid. iii. 637.

It may have been from feelings of shame, too, that official circles began to speak of committees as 'working parties'. This term had long been applied to bodies of soldiers or of convicts and even to groups of ladies engaged in sewing garments for charitable bazaars, but, save possibly in the last case, it had not been employed to describe bodies of persons chiefly occupied in talk. Yet it had a more businesslike sound about it than 'committee'. The definition of 'working party' given over a hundred years ago in a military manual is not inappropriate to the working parties of today. 'Small detachments of men . . . who are employed on fatigues which are not purely of a military nature.'[1] And when the Working Party on Midwives incorporated in their organization a steering committee also, it seemed impossible that anyone thereafter could labour in vain. Whatever the reasons, the use of the term 'working party' became common, if not popular, after the war, and we have discussed some examples of it in operation.

It cannot be denied that the weaknesses of government by committee are well recognized, and not least by those who sit upon committees. The tendencies to delay, to postpone, to avoid, and to compromise are apparent in almost all the types of committee we have studied. Responsibility is difficult to discern in a many-headed institution; too easily a committee becomes a screen or a shield. And, like the rabbits, to which Mr. Churchill compared them in 1940,[2] they tend to multiply rapidly. Yet government cannot be carried on without them, and in the British system of representative, parliamentary, and consultative government they are essential. The question is not how to do without them but how to make the best of them.

If one lesson stands out more than another from the study of committees in the preceding chapters, it is that in the last resort the best can be made out of them only if they are wisely led and wisely fed. We come back again to this point that was made earlier. Save in the case of committees to legislate in the House of Commons, where the Minister provides leadership, the responsibility for leadership rests primarily upon chairmen. Everyone can recall cases where chairmen have been duffers

---

[1] Stocqueler, *Military Encyclopaedia* (1853).
[2] See p. 1.

or buffers. Generally speaking, however, the standard of leadership provided by chairmen in committees associated with British government is good. Their success must always depend in some degree upon the quality of the officials who serve the committee, whether as secretary or adviser or servant, and upon whom the primary responsibility for the wise feeding of the committee rests. The good official in committee work must display a special technique, but he must possess also a belief or faith in government by discussion, and in the value of the association of 'special' and 'non-special' minds, as Bagehot called them. In co-operation chairman and officials can bring unity out of plurality, direction out of confusion, decision out of discussion. Government by committee, where chairmen and officials perform their vital and difficult roles with skill and success, will go far in Britain to ensure not only that we make the best of democracy, but that we make the best of bureaucracy also.

Index of Committees

Accountancy Committee, of Board of Trade, 51.

Agricultural Advisory Panels, 54.

Agricultural Produce, Committee on Distribution and Prices of, 88.

Agricultural Research Council, 19.

Agricultural Statistics Advisory Committee, 49.

Agricultural Wages Board, 113.

Air Training Corps Educational Advisory Committee, 49.

Animal Feeding Stuffs Advisory Committee, 55.

Arms, Royal Commission on Private Manufacture and Trading in, 90.

Army and Air Force Act, Select Committee on, 1953, 70.

Awards to Inventors, Royal Commission, 86.

Bacon Industry Consultative Committee, 55.

Bakery Advisory Panel, 55.

Bank Amalgamations, Committee on, 88.

Brick, National Brick Advisory Council, 54.

British Broadcasting Corporation, Committees on, 71, 87.

Broadcasting, Committee on, 1925, 87.

Building and Civil Engineering Joint Committee, 54.

Building Construction Contracts, Committee on, 88.

Building Training Advisory Committee, 54.

Buildings of Special Architectural and Historical Interest, Advisory Committee on, 51.

Canteen Equipment Committee, 52.

Capital Punishment, Royal Commission on, 76, 90–91, 95.

Capital Punishment, Select Committee on, 70.

Caribbean Public Services Unification, Commission on, 76.

Catering Wages Board, 101.

Catholic Education Council, 109.

Cattle Semen, Export and Import of, Committee on, 86.

Cereals, Home Grown, Advisory Panel on, 55.

Channel Tunnel, Committee on, 91.

Child Care for England and Wales, Advisory Council on, 47.

Children and the Cinema, Committee on, 73, 78.

Church Training Colleges, Council for, 109.

Cinematograph Films Act, 1927, Committee on, 87.

Cinematograph Films Council, 57–58.

Circuit System, Committee on, 52.

Civil Servants, Political Activities of, Committee on, 25–28, 76.

Civil Service, Royal Commission on, 86, 113.

Closing Hours of Shops, Committee on, 76.

Coal Industry, Samuel Commission, 77–78, 80–81, 93.

Coal Industry, Sankey Commission on, 44, 77–78, 80–81, 85, 93.

Colonial Development, Advisory Council on, 47.

Colonial Economic Research Committee, 47.

Colonial Labour Advisory Committee, 47.

Colonial Medical Research Council, 47.

Colonial Research Council, 47.

Colonial Social Science Research Council, 47.

Colonial University Grants Advisory Committee, 47.

Colonies, Education in, Advisory Committee on, 47, 64.

Commercial and Industrial Policy, Committee on, 88.

Commercial Education Committee, 52.

Common Law, Despatch of Business at, Royal Commission on, 52.

Commons, House of:
Standing Committees of, Chapter VI passim.
Committee of Ways and Means, 8.
Committee of Supply, 8.
Committee of the Whole House, 7–9.
Select committees, use of by, 70.
Scottish Grand Committee, 120–1, 131–2, 148, 159–62.
Scrutiny committees of, Chapter VIII passim.

Companies Act Consultative Committee, 51.

General Index

Adam, Sir Ronald, 59.
Admiralty, 102, 104, 163; place of experts in, 19.
Agriculture, Ministry of: place of experts in, 17, 18; and advisory committees, 49, 53.
Air Ministry, 104, 163; place of experts in, 19; and advisory committees, 49.
Allotments Act, 1922, 167, 175.
Allotments Act, 1925, 167.
Alness, Lord, 85–86.
Amalgamated Engineering Union, 31.
Amalgamated Felt Hat Trimmers' and Wool Farmers' Association, 31.
Amalgamated Society of Cane, Wicker, and Perambulator Operatives, 31.
Anderson, Sir John (later Viscount Waverley), 73, 86.
Asphalt Roads Association Ltd., 34.
Assheton, Mr. Ralph, 239.
Association of Animal Gut Cleaners, Ltd., 31.
Association of Borough Officials of Scotland, 35.
Association of British Market Authorities, 33.
Association of Education Committees, 33, 107, 108, 115.
Association of Education Officers, 34, 107.
Association of H.M. Inspectors of Taxes, 32.
Association of Inspectors and Organizers, 109.
Association of Local Government Financial Officers, 34, 107.
Association of Municipal Corporations, 33, 105, 107, 108, 110.
Association of Municipal Corporations of Northern Ireland, 33.
Association of Organizers of Physical Education, 109.
Association of Post Office Controlling Officers, 102.
Association of Principals in Technical Institutions, 108.
Association of Teachers in Colleges and Departments of Education, 109.
Association of Teachers in Technical Institutions, 108.
Astor, Lord, 88.
Atomic Energy Research Establishment, 19.

Attlee, Mr. C. R., 45–46, 49, 71.

Bagehot, Walter, *The English Constitution*, 15, 20, 177.
Balfour, Mr. A. J. (later 1st Earl), 164.
Balfour of Burleigh, Lord, 88.
Balfour, Sir A. M. (later Lord Riverdale), 88.
Balfour, 3rd Earl, 90.
Ballast, Sand, and Allied Trades Association, 34.
Banbury, Sir F., 211, 212.
Bankes, Sir E., 90.
Bennett, Sir T., 58.
Bentham, Jeremy, 15, 20, 191–2; *On Packing Juries*, 15; *Letters to Lord Grenville*, 192.
Beveridge, Sir W. (later Lord), 71, 74–75, 77, 87; *Power and Influence*, 74, 75.
Bledisloe, Lord, 88.
Board of Customs and Excise, 102.
Board of Inland Revenue, 102, 104.
Board of Trade, 102; and advisory committees, 51, 62; and working parties, 44–45, 54–55, 56–57, 58–60.
Book Edge Gilders' Trade Society, 31.
Bookmakers Employees' Association, 31.
Bowles, Mr. Gibson, 236.
Bradford, Leeds, Halifax, Keighley, and District Textile Comb, Hackle, Gill, and Faller Makers' Association, 31–32.
Bridges, Sir E., 252.
British and Foreign School Society, 109.
British Broadcasting Corporation, 240.
British Button Manufacturers' Association, 31.
British Cast Concrete Federation, 34.
British Dental Association, 35.
British Electricity Authority, 240.
British Employers' Confederation, 31.
British Funeral Workers' Association, 31.
British Legion, 34.
British Medical Association, 35.
British Psychological Society, 109.
British Transport Commission, 240.
British Trawlers' Federation Ltd., 31.
Bryce, Lord, 98.
Buffalo Picker Manufacturers' Association, 32.
Burnham, 1st Lord, 71, 112.